TEACHING
ADVANCED
COMPOSITION

D1301078

TEACHING
ADVANCED
COMPOSITION
Why and How

Edited by
Katherine H. Adams
Loyola University / New Orleans
and
John L. Adams
Loyola University / New Orleans

BOYNTON / COOK PUBLISHERS
HEINEMANN
Portsmouth, NH

Boynton/Cook Publishers, Inc.
A Subsidiary of
Heinemann Educational Books, Inc.
361 Hanover Street, Portsmouth, NH 03801
Offices and agents throughout the world

The following have generously given permission to use quotations from copyrighted
works:
Page 108: From *The Immense Journey* by Loren Eiseley. Copyright © 1957 by Loren
Eiseley. Reprinted by permission of Random House, Inc.

Every effort has been made to contact the copyright holders and students for permission
to reprint borrowed material. We regret any oversights that may have occurred and
would be happy to rectify them in future printing of this work.

Library of Congress Cataloging-in-Publication Data
Teaching advanced composition: Why and how / edited by Katherine H. Adams and
 John L. Adams.
     p. cm.
   Includes bibliographical references.
   ISBN 0−86709−260−2
   1. English language—Rhetoric—Study and teaching. I. Adams, Katherine H.,
   1954−   . II. Adams, John L., 1950−
PE1404. T37   1990
808′. 042′0711—dc20   90-35967
                                                                                      CIP

Designed by Hunter Graphics.
Printed in the United States of America.
91 92 93 94 95   9 8 7 6 5 4 3 2 1

for Mike Keene

Contents

Preface

When I took my first teaching job at the University of Tennessee in 1981, I was hired as a specialist in rhetoric and composition with a primary teaching responsibility of courses in advanced composition. In my too many years of graduate school, I had studied literature and rhetorical theory and I had taught freshman composition. I was to step into the advanced program as an expert and lead the planning for new approaches and new courses.

In that first year, I found myself unprepared for advanced composition. The students were not freshmen in terms of their skill levels, needs, attitudes toward writing, or expectations. And my experience with rhetorical and literary theory didn't easily shape itself into the right approach for them. Ironically, when I was finally beyond a designated syllabus and text, the current/traditional requirements of my freshman teaching experience, I wasn't sure what to do. I found little help from articles, since so few concerned the advanced course, or from my first trips to MLA and CCCC. From that beginning came the impetus for this book, to gather together opinions on advanced composition from some of our best theorists and teachers. I realized at meetings that many of us were enjoying the freedom of these courses and felt that we were helping students with their writing, but that we could profit from such a dialogue.

In structuring our advanced composition classes, as Michael Keene and Ray Wallace's survey of writing programs indicates, we must begin by considering who these students are and what needs they have. Freshman composition appears in many forms, but it is now as it was in 1885, a course primarily meant to prepare students for the writing they will do in college. Advanced composition looks beyond, to the writing that the student will do in the world. In one of the theoretical pieces that begin this collection, Elizabeth Penfield points out that a small group actually chooses training at this second level, and they differ from freshmen in "interest, fluency, and experience in writing." Many write correctly, appreciate the power of language, and want to express their own ideas, but they may rely on formulas, write too abstractly, and "lack focus, details, and a sense of audience." Richard Coe, similarly, classifies his advanced students as ones who can avoid grammar errors, write reasonably clear sentences and paragraphs, and follow the most important norms of academic discourse, but who need help with responding effectively to various rhetorical situations.

For Richard Young, the students' progression to an advanced level should occur in three stages: an initial immersion in writing, a rule-based stage of precision, and experience with writing on various issues in the world beyond the classroom. For Michael Carter, the distinction has to do with levels of expertise: the writer, like the doctor, must know the rules involved and then be able to modify or even ignore them in individual situations.

In advanced composition, these definitions assert, students should move beyond set rules and formats to a more complex theoretical perspective and to real rhetorical situations, commitment, and adaptability. To succeed beyond college, writers will need to know about the essentials of real writing, not necessarily the grammar, outline, five-paragraph-theme, or term-paper basics taught in freshman courses to prepare students for college writing. They will need a higher level of basics that includes knowledge of invention and revision, style and voice, audience analysis, argumentation, and the rhetoric of various discourse communities.

Many teachers approach these goals by concentrating on the students' development as writers. In defining advanced composition, Elizabeth Penfield recommends that we help the student move "from proficiency to effectiveness" by giving "the student and the student's writing center stage." Thus her workshops, discussions, and editing groups focus on the student's writing process and research skills, and, most importantly, on the student's own vision of reality.

Similarly, in the section on course structures, Toby Fulwiler describes how students can probe the concept of personal voice by studying professional writers and themselves and how they can develop their own voices by working on various assignments. In style notebooks, papers, and peer groups, Mary Fuller has her students explore stylistic options, to move beyond the overly abstract, although grammatically correct, prose that often restricts the advanced student. To foster individual development, Sam Watson enters into a semester-long correspondence with each of his students, leading them toward awareness of their own processes, strengths, and goals for writing. In classes for peer tutors and advanced writers, Tori Haring–Smith stresses rhetorical theory to broaden the students' understanding of their own processes and those of others.

Many teachers help students do "real writing" by focusing on their ability to analyze and understand new ideas. As William Covino defines the course, advanced composition should foster dialectical thinking that allows for "contradiction, ambiguity and uncertainty": "Thus, we identify our most *advanced* writers as those who can sustain the most open discourse, widening what Kenneth Burke calls 'scope' and 'circumference' by playing multiple theses upon one another." John Gage also encourages analysis by using the enthymeme as "a practical construct for focusing students' thinking."

As Gage describes his approach, he is "presuming a classroom in which the open discussion of problematic ideas takes place." In Gage's course and in Richard Young's definition article, we see another tool for preparing students for their writing beyond college classes: advanced instruction, Young asserts, should concern "informed and appropriate action in the world." His course, Argument and Controversy, reflects that emphasis. Similarly, Jeanne Fahnestock teaches students to use the stases and Toulmin logic as they research and write on one current controversy throughout the term.

Classes that concern audience and situation may also focus on the requirements of specific discourse communities. Michael Carter asserts that development of expertise involves "a movement from the application of general process skills to the application of specialized knowledge based upon experience within a specific domain." In composition, he says, advanced training should enable students to learn about the role writing plays in constructing knowledge in a particular discipline, to analyze the special features of that writing, and to practice discourse-specific skills. Gary Olson and Evelyn Ashton-Jones consider advanced critical thinking skills as related to social-epistemic rhetoric, as involved with probing text and context, observer and community. To foster such analysis of discourse and community, Richard Coe gives his students a heuristic by which they can explore unfamiliar rhetorical contexts, processes, and genres. Timothy Donovan and Janet Carr stress research experience to enable students to enter the discourse of their own major or career.

To introduce students to specific languages and communities, Charles Anderson has students analyze the nonfiction writer's possible relationships to the group about which she writes, and then has students try out those various roles. Lynn Bloom acquaints students with the reader/writer transactions and literary techniques of nonfiction, and says of her students, "Even though they write in different voices, with different personae, they truly speak the same language, the language of creative nonfiction." In their paper on a psychology class, Olivia Frey and Mary Ellen Ross describe a group learning a specific discourse, that of psychology and psychologists.

In advanced classes, students can develop their own thinking and revision skills, voice, and style. They can also enter into current rhetorical situations—and thus into the interaction of writer, audience, language, and the world. And their instruction can lead them into the language of specific discourse communities. Thus, in James Berlin's terms from *Rhetoric and Reality,* teachers can ready students for writing beyond college by drawing on the strengths of expressionistic, classical, and epistemic rhetoric. At any university, students would profit from one course using one approach, one course with elements of more than one approach, or a sequence of all three types, moving from the writer to her role in the continuing conversation that is discourse.

Katherine H. Adams

Acknowledgments

We would like to acknowledge the encouragement given us by Mike Keene and Ted Hipple when we initiated this project. We have also been very fortunate to work with Peter Stillman from Boynton/Cook.

We owe particular gratitude to Avia Morgan of Loyola University who handled the correspondence and to Ted Cotton who helped us with our chapter. We also wish to thank Linda Petroline and other students working in the Writing Across the Curriculum Center at Loyola for their help with the final editing and compiling.

We would especially like to thank the fine researchers and teachers who contributed work to this volume.

Theoretical Perspectives on Advanced Composition: Distinguishing Advanced Courses from the Freshman Sequence

1

Advanced Composition: Where Did It Come From? Where Is It Going?

Katherine H. Adams
John L. Adams

Advanced composition is certainly a problematic term. It can be an umbrella label for any college writing course above the basic or freshman level. But it also has a narrower meaning: courses in argumentation or style taught within English departments. Even the two words can cause confusion. *Advanced* may designate course numbers above the freshman level, but the label does not insure that students with advanced skills will take these courses; in fact many students enter advanced classes because they did poorly in freshman English. And *composition* may also be a misnomer since this nineteenth-century term may not indicate the theoretical slant of many advanced courses.

Whatever the problems of definition, almost all universities do offer composition courses above the freshman level. Usually, journalistic or feature-story writing is taught in a journalism or communications department or school. Then, in the English department, there might be two or three courses in technical writing, as many in argumentation, style, or genres of nonfiction, and a couple in writing poetry and fiction. These courses might be combined to create a major or emphasis in writing. This pattern, of course, isn't universal: journalism is often taught within English departments at small colleges; many schools have more extensive creative writing offerings; and technical writing may be offered through a business or a rhetoric department. Also, many universities have recently initiated discipline-specific writing courses taught in the English department or in departments across the campus.[1]

3

Such advanced writing courses are often considered to be fairly new additions to the freshman requirement. But in early American education, students completed four years of rhetorical study and practice, a type of advanced composition. Today's advanced writing classes, which were mostly created from 1880–1910, are part of that early tradition as it was modified to suit the needs of a new type of curriculum and student in the late nineteenth century. A discussion of their history will also explain the confusions inherent in the term *advanced composition* and the distinctions among different courses. It will also help us to understand the oldest of advanced composition electives — the one still generally called advanced composition, and the one that for the last hundred years has most doggedly evaded definition.

Advanced Rhetoric Study to 1750: Learning an Abstract Discipline

At its beginnings in the mid-seventeenth century, American higher education was based on the medieval and Renaissance model of the trivium and quadrivium: logic, grammar, and rhetoric; and the lesser arts, arithmetic, geometry, astronomy, and music. Students were also expected to continue their religious training. They might find their mornings given over to large lectures and group recitations and afternoons to disputations or debates, perhaps with philosophy on Monday and Tuesday, Greek on Wednesday, Hebrew on Thursday, rhetoric on Friday, and catechism on Saturday, as was true in Harvard's 1642 curriculum (Rudolph 32).

In rhetoric and logic, study proceeded by abstract principles; students heard lectures and then memorized and recited formal rules. This system allowed for a high student/teacher ratio. It also had the backing of the current educational theory derived from faculty psychology, which maintained that students needed to develop their memories thoroughly before improving their judgment powers. At most schools, the precepts to memorize were taken from Peter Ramus. From the *Rami Logica*, students studied argument types such as definition, the more and less, comparison, and division. For their work on style, they studied tropes and figures of speech from textbooks by Ramus's disciples, Omer Talon and William Dugard (Guthrie 49–50).

To supplement this theory and drill, teachers gave some attention to the individual student's ability to write and speak. For monthly and quarterly exercises, senior examinations, and other special academic occasions, such as commencement, students performed orations in Latin, Greek, Hebrew, and sometimes in English. Seniors were most often allowed to speak publicly and to recite their own writing (Bohman 61). All students, but most frequently seniors, could also participate in syllogistic disputations conducted at monthly meetings and on special occasions. Using syllogistic logic learned from Ramus and other sources, students might defend or attack a given statement of universal truth, considering, for example, whether animals can think or whether one can sin while sleeping (Rudolph 45).

In the colonial period, then, students had few chances for practicing composition skills. Certainly, they did not complete the daily or weekly assignments that are standard today. But they did build skills in rhetoric and logic and were expected to do more sophisticated work as upper-classmen. In the principles memorized, the orations, and the disputations, there was a sense of *advanced* work that might prepare the clergyman or statesman and provide all students with solid classical training.

Building a More Practical Four-Year Curriculum: 1750−1850

By 1750, the traditional university curriculum had begun to seem impractical and irrelevant to an expanding America, especially to its growing business community. Knowledge of inductive scientific method, crucial to the new sciences that were being introduced to American colleges, as well as the desire for practice with realistic public discourse, would soon spell the end of syllogistic disputations in Latin. By 1782, Yale began instead to hold inductive forensic disputations in English every Tuesday and three Mondays per month (Rudolph 47). In these exercises, students — two to four on each side — debated current issues instead of abstract moral questions. In 1767 at King's College, students considered whether a man ought to engage in war if he were not persuaded of the justice of his cause. In 1773 at Harvard, a key issue was the legal and moral ramifications of slavery. In 1779, Yale seniors centered their commencement debates on the justice of various sorts of imposed taxations. For all these topics, students would bring forth facts and examples to back up their positions (Rudolph 45−47).

The emphasis on a more practical form of argumentation was reflected in the most commonly used texts. After the American Revolution, Ramus's popularity waned quickly. Instead of learning figures and tropes, students read Richard Whately's *Elements of Rhetoric* (1828) to study forensic argumentation, George Campbell's *Philosophy of Rhetoric* (1776) to examine induction and appeals to audiences, and Hugh Blair's *Lectures on Rhetoric and Belles Lettres* (1783) to consider the role of rhetoric in literary criticism, poetry, history writing, and the other popular belles lettres (Kitzhaber, "Rhetoric" 81−89).

In syllabi from this period, one notes a continuing and growing discrimination of the ability levels and instructional needs of students in the different college years. At Yale, Harvard, and Chicago, the students' reading and their written and oral work became more challenging in their junior and senior years: freshmen and sophomores recited famous orations, juniors did extemporaneous speaking, and seniors wrote and recited original orations. At Hamilton in 1864, freshmen worked on elocution and declamation, sophomores studied Blair, juniors read Whately and created forensic disputations, and seniors wrote themes on mental and moral philosophy, engaged in forensic disputations, and presented essays on law and history (Wozniak 35–36). Generally, then, students were moving from declamations and translations to more original thinking and writing about literature and other subject areas. Although theory was still taught in large lecture sections and practice was still infrequent, teachers were forging increasingly challenging work for each year and giving students chances to speak and write using the rhetoric appropriate to the current political, legal, and religious debates that they would enter.

A Movement Toward Requiring Only Freshman Composition: 1850–1900

This generally accepted curriculum—four years' work in speaking, writing, and theory—began to disappear after 1850 as new forces altered the college curriculum and English studies: the formation of departments, the elective system, the increasing interest in English language and literature. By 1900, speech—and thus oration, declamation, and argumentation—was being taught to fewer students, usually as an elective offered by departments or divisions of speech. As English departments began forming, their focus was on literature. At Brown in 1870, juniors still did declamations, but seniors could study English and American history through the English department. At Hobart in 1879, juniors studied the English language, Anglo-Saxon grammar, Chaucer, and Spenser, while also writing essays and orations and participating in debates; seniors studied rhetoric as well as Shakespeare and Milton (Wozniak 72–74). Soon, rhetoric courses would no longer be required of all students: in 1900 or 1910, when students could choose a major subject to study, they might be required to take three or four literature classes and no rhetoric at all.

In this time of new disciplines and new class choices, much larger numbers of students were also choosing college. In the 1870s and 1880s, this more diverse group created another change, a back-to-the-basics crisis, with parents and business people asking why Johnny couldn't write. In 1874, Harvard introduced an new entrance exam, involving "a short composition, correct in expression, spelling, grammar and punctuation" (*Forty-Eighth Annual Report* 48). As usual, many schools followed their lead. Soon, influential teachers formed a centralized testing agency, the College Entrance Exam Board. To help students reach the crucial "college level," teachers at Harvard, such as Barrett Wendell and A. S. Hill, began to urge that a required freshman course be instituted to drill into freshmen "the habitual use of correct and intelligent English" (Copeland and Rideout 2). Such a course, with emphasis on sentence style and grammar, paragraphing, and the four forms of discourse but especially exposition, was instituted in 1885 (Morison 75). By 1890, many schools had a required two- or three-course freshman sequence in which students studied grammar, the rhetorical modes, and writing about literature.

The extreme changes from 1850–1900 proved to be the death knell for a gradated curriculum in writing and speaking. For these students, beginning to major in many subjects and take a variety of electives, freshman English would be the only required writing course, training in rhetorical theory would be missing altogether, and the amount of writing practice encountered after the first year would be determined by individual choices of courses and instructors.

Development of Advanced Elective Offerings: 1880–1910

By 1880, as freshman English was becoming codified as basic or remedial work for everyone, many professors felt that such a composition course could not completely meet the needs of all students, that as students entered professional disciplines they would need more than two semesters of grammar, paragraphing, and basic forms of discourse: they would need work on theory and practice with specific rhetorical situations, as did students in earlier generations. But what type of rhetorical training would be appropriate to this practical and diversified education? How would these classes relate to students preparing for many types of careers? What would a teacher do if given just one semester in a busy curriculum? The decades from 1880–1910 would provide the answers with the establishment of a variety of new advanced composition courses as electives.

Advanced Exposition

One proper role for advanced courses seemed to be to give students, a select few, added training in audience analysis, organization, and style, in small sections and with time allotted to each student's own prose. This format seemed especially helpful for English and education majors and for students in the liberal arts who wanted more writing practice, a general preparation for advanced college work and for a career. A. S. Hill, who helped establish the freshman course at Harvard, taught the first elective advanced course there in 1877 with 20 seniors and 11 juniors (Wozniak 76). In 1887, he analyzed his students and course structure for *Scribner's Magazine.* He designed his class, he wrote, to meet the needs of his students, whose primary goal should be to learn to "put forth naturally and with the force of their individuality." He especially wanted advanced writers to get away from "theme-language."

> I know no language — ancient or modern, civilized or savage — so insufficient for the purposes of language, so dreary and inexpressive, as theme-language in the mass. How two or three hundred young men, who seem to be really alive as they appear in the flesh, can have kept themselves entirely out of their writing, it is impossible to understand. (511)

He structured his advanced composition course to evoke a more natural prose, by allowing students to develop their own topics in daily 10-minute, in-class writing sessions, an experiment that for Hill was "unexpectedly successful." His advocacy of fluency over correctness strikes a surprisingly modern tone.

> Having no time to be affected, they are simple and natural. Theme-language, which still haunts too many of their longer essays, rarely creeps into the ten-minute papers. Free from faults of one kind or another these papers are not; but the faults are such as would be committed in conversation or in familiar correspondence. The great point has been gained that the writers, as a rule, forget themselves in what they are saying; and the time will come, it is to be hoped, when they will be correct as well as fluent, and will unite clearness in thought with compactness in expression, and vigor with well-bred ease. (512)

Besides these short papers, students did longer essays in which they created arguments involving their reading from other classes.

At many colleges, English departments began to offer similar advanced classes, with frequent theme writing, individual attention, and further work on the essay and paragraph structures stressed in freshman courses but perhaps without their emphasis on correctness and set formats. Bucknell, Amherst, Columbia, and the University of Pennsylvania followed this "daily themes" model. At other schools, as at Yale, students also studied theoretical principles of rhetoric. From 1880 to 1890, only seven eastern colleges offered advanced electives, entitled Advanced Composition or Advanced Rhetoric. By 1920, however, 28 of 37 eastern colleges offered such advanced courses and they had become popular throughout the country (Wozniak 77, 129–31).

Journalism

After 1830, Americans began to see a need for higher journalistic standards—to combat the growing popularity of the penny presses, sex and crime news sheets that were the *National Enquirers* of the nineteenth century (O'Dell 1). Robert E. Lee instituted courses in journalism at Washington College (later Washington and Lee) in 1869 in hopes that a higher sort of journalism could be a rehabilitating force in the South. Not writing, though, but printing was the focus: students apprenticed at Lafferty and Company, printers in Lexington (O'Dell 13–15). The Kansas State College of Agriculture and Applied Science, Cornell, the University of Missouri, and Denver University soon offered this professional training (O'Dell 21–38).

By 1900, some schools also began to institute courses in journalistic writing, often under the course title Advanced Composition. At the University of Pennsylvania, Joseph French Johnson led students through "Exercises in Reporting, Editing of Copy, Conversations, etc." (O'Dell 48). In 1894, at the University of Kansas, E. M. Hopkins, head of the Department of Rhetoric and English Language, offered a highly experimental course in newspaper writing. In 1904, Hopkins introduced another journalistic writing course, which he later described for the campus paper: "In the fall of 1904 a volunteer section of freshman rhetoric was organized into a group of reporters, and the newspaper class proper into a corps of editors; beats were assigned, and edited. Matter was sent to the local papers including the *University Daily Kansan*" (qtd. in O'Dell 49). In the 1890s, journalistic writing was also offered in the English departments at Iowa, Indiana, and Nebraska. At Michigan, the course was taught by Fred Newton Scott, author with Joseph Villiers Denney of *Paragraph-Writing* and *Elementary English Composition*, two current-traditional texts then widely used in freshman composition courses. He structured his classes to focus on the rhetorical issues of audience and purpose, which he also stressed in graduate courses on rhetoric.

Creative Writing

As influential writing teachers like Fred Newton Scott and E. M. Hopkins began forging a curriculum in journalism, another type of advanced writing instruction was also emerging. In the 1890s, Barrett Wendell, who was instrumental in establishing the daily themes course for freshmen at Harvard and whose *English Composition* (1891) was a popular freshman text, introduced an advanced composition course for creative writers in which they could explore a variety of genres, read their efforts to the class, and submit their work to their demanding teacher/critic. According to Walter Eaton, once a drama critic for the *New York Tribune* and later a Princeton professor of playwrighting, "What Wendell did for Harvard was actually to make a place there... in which the artist could find encouragement and council." W. E. B. DuBois also enrolled, believing "perhaps foolishly, but sincerely, that I have something to say to the world...I have taken English 12 in order to say it well." Robert Herrick, later a novelist and University of Chicago professor, recorded his impression of Wendell's emphasis on individual creativity: "He has had a greater influence upon the craftsmanship of the writer than any other American man of letters" (Self 143–44). In the early 1990s, Charles Townsend Copeland continued this course at Harvard (Morison 76). Indiana started creative writing courses in 1915; Fisk University in 1920.

Technical Writing

The early 1900s also witnessed the beginnings of another type of advanced composition for another specialized audience: technical writing.

After the Civil War, engineering colleges formed quickly in response to the growing technical needs of an industrializing America, offering technical training with few courses in the humanities. But, as was true for journalism, this growing field had to listen to criticisms of its standards. By 1900, engineering journals were condemning the illiteracy of recent graduates. Almost immediately, a number of these schools began to establish English departments. The instruction at Tufts, Cincinnati, and MIT centered around the modes of discourse and correct usage as in current/traditional freshman courses then taught around the country. But by 1920, two thirds of all engineering schools had begun to require some sort of technical writing course focusing on reports and letters. After World War II, as new, more complex technologies became entrenched in the business and scientific community, it no longer seemed cost effective to have engineers both design and write: hence the birth of technical writing as a separate profession (Connors 330–42).

Defining the Course in the Middle: 1930–1970

From 1900 through the 1930s, courses in journalism, creative writing, and technical writing gained their own identities and moved away from their original label — advanced composition — and often from the English department. The label remained, however, with the A. S. Hill type of advanced exposition course. That it lacked a clear identity continually bothered the teachers involved with it.

From 1954—1971, the CCCC held invitational workshops to define advanced composition and its "aims, texts, and methods," as their report was subtitled in 1958. That year, for example, the group considered the variations within "the advanced course in expository writing": fairly large, required courses with a heterogenous group as well as small classes of dedicated writers; lectures, group work, and conferences; texts ranging from rhetorics to readers to current magazines to the teacher's notes; open-ended assignments as well as lock-step reviews of the expository modes ("The Advanced Course" 165). The group could only agree that the course was "gaining ground": "It is now being required of more and more students. Schools that have not offered it are planning to do so soon" (167). While this workshop simply recorded the diversity, the 1963 group reacted to it vociferously.

> We don't agree as to what Advanced Composition should be, or is. We all do different things, which are all good, but none of it seems to make any difference. Most students can't write when they enter college, and write worse when they leave, having inflated their vocabularies merely. We do not agree about the objectives of the course, the content, the order of topics, the number or length of essays, the emphasis various factors in composition should get, or what related materials to bring in. ("The Undergraduate Advanced Composition Course" 190)

After declaring that they all planned to go on teaching and discussing advanced composition, "whatever that is," they adjourned to the Statler-Hilton bar.

The CCCC decided in 1966—1967 to get serious about a definition for advanced exposition by designating an invitational workshop whose job it would be to decide on guidelines for this course. Designated by Richard Braddock, chaired by Richard Lloyd-Jones, and with Francis Christensen among its members, the group asserted that the course should be concerned with the student's own text, but they were unable, or didn't try, to develop more specific "guidelines": the course should cover, they concluded, "the range of the freshman course but in greater depth" ("Guidelines and Directions" 266).

Throughout this period, the courses continued their emphasis on style, fluency, and new formats. One of the few texts clearly designated for advanced college students was Harry Robbins and Roscoe Parker's *Advanced Exposition*, published in 1933, reprinted in 1935, and released in a second edition in 1940. The authors began by recognizing the difficulty of finding a text designed for the advanced course, which, they said, was offered in every college. This text is especially interesting in its omissions: it does not cover usage, sentence styles, or paragraph forms. Instead, through definitions, theoretical sections, and readings, the text covers the modes of exposition found in freshman courses. But it also deals with other more practical and difficult forms: abstracts, precis, translation, technical exposition, criticism, and the scientific, didactic, and aphoristic essays. Although the book clearly follows the paradigm that dominated the freshman world, it did try to meet the needs of an advanced group through its statement of the principles behind the modes, its sophisticated readings, and its inclusion of formats used by professional writers. If teachers did not adopt Robbins and Parker, they might rely on the freshman classics or their own materials to provide advanced work on argument, style, and essay forms.

A New Approach: Writing Across the Curriculum

During the 1970s, advanced composition was redefined by an increased emphasis on writing across the curriculum. As early as 1963, Albert Kitzhaber had called for writing courses to be offered throughout the four years of college, so that students would see writing as a basic skill of all disciplines (*Themes, Theories, and Therapy* 150–56). His recommendation for increased attention to writing echoed the first CCCC report on advanced composition in 1954: the participants wanted English teachers to "apprise the faculty of their institution of the need for writing in all courses."

Although some schools like Colgate, Grinnell, and Chicago had experimented with split courses in which English teachers graded the writing done in content courses, writing across the curriculum did not achieve real acceptance until it gained the backing of cognitive theory, of research by Langer and Vygotsky that revealed the importance of inner speech — for understanding and connecting new ideas. James Britton and other researchers labeled this language *expressive* and advocated its use across the curriculum to aid learning.

Writing across the curriculum, of course, is not simply a model of advanced composition. It has led to new freshman writing classes and caused biology and math teachers to add journals or lab notebooks to their existing classes. But the movement has extended the tradition of career-specific advanced writing instruction: juniors and seniors in many majors now study the writing specific to their own disciplines as does the creative writer, technical writer, and journalist. After faculty workshops, as at Vermont, Beaver College, and other schools, a history teacher might offer historiography or an art teacher might institute a writing-about-art class. At some schools, such as Randolph-Macon, English department faculty teach writing courses stipulated for science, social science, and business majors (Haring-Smith et al. 271).

Advanced Composition Today

In the 1980s, technical writing, journalism, and creative writing have fairly set sequences and majors, and writing-across-the-curriculum programs are encouraging us to teach the strategies and formats of particular discourse communities. And in advanced composition courses, we are still considering the skills involved in inventing many types of ideas and addressing many types of audiences: these courses are still providing theoretical grounding and practice to students with diverse reasons for writing and still trying to condense that complicated subject, "real writing," into one semester or two.

One fruitful method for classifying the many resultant approaches and courses was given by Richard Fulkerson in the first issue of *Journal of Advanced Composition.* Advanced instruction, he said, can focus on one of the four elements of the artistic transaction as discussed by M. H. Abrams: the artist, audience, work, or universe. Often the workshop and conference focus on the artist or writer—on extending her voice and confidence. Other classes focus on the audience, on persuasion, because many teachers recognize that students have done too much audience-less writing, writing without a purpose except getting a grade. The third approach—toward the work—produces many types of courses. Some concentrate on style, on new options that can improve the student's text. Focusing on the text can also mean attending to formats of writing. Thus, students can learn not just school forms like the five-paragraph theme but also real ones like the review and interview, the law brief, or the letters and reports appropriate to scientific disciplines. Another possibility is for the course to focus on the larger external world. Students might learn primary research methods, to interact with the community as they write interviews or profiles. These four emphases—on the artist, audience, work, and universe—can be combined in different ways: when students keep journals to record their own writing processes and then work with different audiences and formats; when personal writing is combined with persuasion; when style-work reinforces other assignments.

This categorization does provide a method of understanding advanced composition's diverse ways of involving students in the writer's work. But it also demonstrates the continuing lack of definition and consensus concerning an advanced curriculum. Because of this unclear sense of purpose, many teachers think that such general courses should be eliminated altogether and that advanced courses should focus on only the discourse of one community or profession, to give students specific, useful training.

Instead of either/or, perhaps a better answer would be a combination of the two approaches. In early American education, theoretical readings and recitations gave students solid grounding in various types of discourses; the orations were especially helpful to the clergyman, and readings in Whately and forensic disputations gave the lawyer experience with legal argumentation. Advanced composition courses can still provide valuable general training—a theoretical perspective, experience with many types of discourse, an appreciation of reading and writing—that can enrich students and encourage them to succeed in many genres. Then they can also pursue writing as specialists, learning about their own field and about methods of explaining it to others.

Certainly we need more discussion of the proper theories and methods for different varieties of advanced writing, for one class or a series of classes. This book should help foster a discussion of courses focusing on the writer's development, on argumentation in various rhetorical situations, and on discourse-specific writing. Such well-wrought courses will be crucial since they should form the writing minor or major and should be part of the curriculum of any student with a serious interest in writing.

Note

1. This composite picture has been created from data in Hammer-Sarody, Haring-Smith, Hogan, Kelley, and Witte.

Works Cited

"The Advanced Course in Expository Writing: Aims, Texts, Methods." *College Composition and Communication* 9 (1958): 165–67.

Bohman, George V. "Rhetorical Practice in Colonial America." *A History of Speech Education in America*. Ed. Karl R. Wallace. New York: Appleton, 1954. 60–79.

Connors, Robert J. "The Rise of Technical Writing Instruction in America." *Journal of Technical Writing and Communication*. 12 (1982): 329–52.

Copeland, Charles Townsend, and H. M. Rideout. *Freshman English and Theme–Correcting in Harvard College*. New York: Silver, 1901.

Forty-Eighth Annual Report of the President of Harvard College, 1872–1873. Cambridge: Harvard College, 1874.

Fulkerson, Richard. "Some Theoretical Speculations on the Advanced Composition Curriculum." *Journal of Advanced Composition* 1 (1980): 9–12.

Golden, James L., Goodwin F. Berquist, and William E. Coleman. *The Rhetoric of Western Thought*. 3rd ed. Dubuque, IA: Kendall, 1983.

"Guidelines and Directions for College Courses in Advanced Composition." *College Composition and Communication* 18 (1967): 266–68.

Guthrie, Warren. "Rhetorical Theory in Colonial America." *A History of Speech Education in America*. Ed. Karl R. Wallace. New York: Appleton, 1954. 48–59.

Hammer-Sarody, Kathy, ed. *AWP Catalogue of Writing Programs*. Norfolk, VA: Associated Writing Programs, 1984.

Haring-Smith, Tori, et al. *A Guide to Writing Programs: Writing Centers, Peer Tutoring Programs, and Writing-Across-the-Curriculum.* Glenview, IL: Scott, 1985.

Hill, A. S. "English in Our Colleges." *Scribner's Magazine.* 1 (Jan–June 1887): 507–12.

Hogan, Michael P. "Advanced Composition: A Survey." *Journal of Advanced Composition* 1 (1980): 21–29.

Kelley, Patrick M., et al. *Academic Programs in Technical Communication.* Washington, DC: Society for Technical Communication, 1985.

Kitzhaber, Albert R. "Rhetoric in American Colleges, 1850–1900." Diss. U of Washington, 1953.

——. *Themes, Theories, and Therapy: The Teaching of Writing in College.* New York: McGraw, 1963.

Morison, Samuel Eliot. *The Development of Harvard University Since the Inauguration of President Eliot, 1869–1929.* Cambridge: Harvard UP, 1930.

O'Dell, De Forest. *The History of Journalism Education in the United States.* New York: Columbia University Teachers College Bureau of Publications, 1935.

Robbins, Harry W., and Roscoe Parker. *Advanced Exposition.* New York: Prentice, 1935.

Rudolph, Frederick. *Curriculum: A History of the American Undergraduate Course of Study Since 1636.* San Francisco: Jossey, 1977.

Self, Robert T. *Barrett Wendell.* Boston: Twayne, 1975.

"The Undergraduate Advanced Composition Course." *College Composition and Communication* 14 (1963): 190.

Witte, Stephen P., Paul R. Meyer, Thomas P. Miller, and Lester Faigley. *National Survey of College and University Writing Program Directors.* Austin: Writing Programs Assessment Project, University of Texas, 1981. ERIC ED 210 709.

Wozniak, John Michael. *English Composition in Eastern Colleges, 1850–1940.* Washington, DC: UP of America, 1978.

2

Freshman English/ Advanced Writing: How Do We Distinguish the Two?

Elizabeth Penfield

While in a sense any writing course beyond the archetypal ENGL 101 is an advanced composition course, my definition is narrower, and in this essay I will attempt to stake out the boundaries of the course that follows freshman composition (be it one, two, or three semesters' worth) and yet may precede even more specialized writing courses taught at the upper level, those open to juniors, seniors, and in many cases, graduate students. For two-year institutions and many four-year ones, this course I am describing usually carries the generic name Advanced Composition, while those at the entry level get grouped as freshman composition, and those at the upper end (offered at a few universities with highly developed writing programs) may be distinguished by individualized names such as Nonfiction Writing, Professional Writing, and the like. Distinguishing by level and by name helps define the course, but still an exact definition remains problematic. Imagine dubbing all literature courses offered at the sophomore level *literature* and you have some idea of the different courses that can exist under a common label. Yet commonalities do exist, and though the advanced composition courses described in this chapter may differ from each other in details, they are roughly representative of those taught at most institutions.

To analyze those commonalities, it helps to start with an aerial view of higher education. Viewed from afar, the landscape varies significantly from the perspective formed at an MLA meeting. There, Ph.D.-granting departments dominate and two-year institutions are relatively invisible. But in the real world of English programs, the opposite is true: Ph.D.-granting departments represent only 5.5 percent of those institutions with programs in English, while 41.8 percent are housed in two-year colleges. Occupying a large middle ground are the BA/MA programs, some 52.6 percent of the total (Huber and Young 60). Most of the students within all these English programs are taking writing courses, but beyond that statement the figures get interesting. While 69 percent of all students signed up for English are enrolled in writing courses, 63 percent are in lower-level courses and only 6 percent are in upper-level courses (Huber and Young 44), a proportion reversed for literature courses. There, of the 31 percent of all students taking English who are enrolled in literature classes, most are taking upper-level courses (27 percent) and only a small number are in lower-level courses (4 percent). These figures highlight an important fact: most of the students taking English are enrolled in "service" courses at the lower level, primarily in freshman- and sophomore-level writing courses.

What sort of students are these anyway? From the perspective of *type* of institution, it is possible to make a few inferences. In an article published in 1987, for instance, Jasper Neel categorizes all colleges and universities into

- two year institutions (33 percent)
- non-elite private colleges (33 percent)
- regional public colleges and universities (25 percent)
- research institutions (7 percent)
- unable to classify (2 percent)

His category for research institutions is broader than that of other studies, such as Bettina Huber's survey, for Neel includes Ivy League and elite private institutions as well as flagship state and "flagship pretender" universities (37). Thus, Neel includes as research institutions colleges such as Bryn Mawr and Williams although they do not offer the Ph.D. Even with this broad definition of research institutions, two-year colleges, non-elite private colleges, and regional public colleges and universities make up 91 percent of all institutions of higher education.

Put all these figures together and a pattern begins to emerge: most students who are enrolled in English are taking freshman and sophomore courses at non-research institutions that have minimal to average admissions standards. That being the case, a look at what's going in writing classes at those four-year regional and two-year institutions may well reveal what's going on in most English departments.

There, freshman and advanced composition classes differ in kind, not just number, a difference exemplified by a comparison of external constraints, the students, and the courses themselves.

External Constraints

Department chairs initially determine who teaches what, when it is taught, and how many students can take it, but they are always at the mercy of higher-level administrators. That mercy is often absent, and freshman composition is where its absence is most obvious.

More often than not, freshman composition is a required course. No law of supply and demand applies as it does with upper-level elective classes, where a strong teaching faculty can fill courses that languish at other institutions. Sections of freshman composition fill because students must take them, and although fine teachers of composition exist, the conditions under which they work more closely resemble indentured service than academic life. A sinister correlation is embedded here: the higher the course number, the higher the status of the person teaching it. And just as teaching graduate students is the apex, teaching freshmen is the nadir. Those who teach freshman composition are often graduate students, part-time teachers, or non-tenured faculty members.

In 1978 Jasper Neel, in his *Options for the Teaching of English*, surveyed ten freshman writing programs, eight of which typify those at graduate degree-granting institutions. Over half of those eight programs staff 90 percent or more of their freshman writing courses with graduate students (1, 25, 46, 52, 57). A later study by Stephen Witte and his colleagues found that 40 percent of freshman English courses are staffed by part-time faculty (94).[1] Educational cost, not quality of teaching, controls the staffing of freshman composition.

Graduate students receive stipends not salaries; they are teaching assistants, not faculty members. While most have taken a mandatory course in the teaching of writing and may take a course in composition/rhetoric, no survey indicates *when* these courses must be taken.[2] Ideally, the courses would precede the teaching of a freshman composition class, but the reality may contradict the ideal. Although the bad old days of little or no preparation for the classroom may be over, few universities will voluntarily train teaching assistants before placing them in classrooms. In some instances, regional accrediting agencies have forced such training by requiring 18 hours of graduate courses prior to teaching,[3] but I suspect many colleges and universities subscribe to the simultaneous train and teach approach. It's cheaper.

Cheaper still are the part–time instructors whose salaries often carry no fringe benefits and typically range from $1,000 to $2,000 per section,[4] the equivalent of $8,000 to $16,000 a year for a 12-hour load. Nontenure track, limited-term contracts are only a full-time variation on the part-time problem. No matter what the name — instructor, adjunct, lecturer, visiting fill-in-the-blank — the course load is predominantly and often exclusively freshman composition and the rewards nil: no merit pay, no possibility of promotion, no course load reduction for research, no sabbatical.

More often than not, those who teach freshman composition are regarded as temporary, as amateurs, sort of Kelly-person teachers, snapped up from a seemingly bottomless pit, used, and thrown back again. What course they teach and when are givens not options, and they have little if any say, much less control, over larger matters such as the goals of the course, how those goals are carried out, and what texts are used.

These teachers are often cogs in a multisection machine. Institutions such as mine with a head count of around 16,000 students offer some 175 sections of freshman composition, a number that, without common goals and direction, could mean 175 different syllabi. To prevent that, most departments have a freshman coordinator who attempts to bring some coherence and relative uniformity to the program. Often this direction takes the form of a common syllabus, and in fact Witte's survey reports that 39 percent of all first-semester courses require that the syllabus be followed (41).

By contrast, the teacher of advanced composition seems an anarchist and a loner. Restricted only by the catalogue description of the course — one usually so general as to permit almost anything — the teacher of advanced composition is often solely responsible for developing and stating the course's goals, the means by which they will be achieved, the standards by which the students' writing will be judged, and the syllabus, if any. Implicit in this freedom is the status of the teacher. Michael Hogan's survey indicates that most teachers of advanced composition come from the professorial ranks: 26.7 percent are professors; 28 percent, associate professors; 33.9 percent, assistant professors. Only 8.8 percent are instructors, a group Hogan lumps together with graduate assistants (27). Drawn from the full-time professional ranks or occasionally from a cadre of formally or informally tenured instructors, the teacher of advanced composition enjoys options unheard of in freshman composition, often including where and when the course will be taught. And the course is regarded with a more kindly eye by administrators. Often the number of sections can be counted on one hand, thus according the course an individuality denied to the generic lump of freshman English sections. This differentiated status is also reflected in the size of the sections. Like courses in creative writing, those in advanced composition are often limited to 15 students. Hogan's survey reveals an average class size of 17 (27); in contrast, the mean class size in nondevelopmental freshman writing courses is 24 (Huber and Young 45), four students over the NCTE and ADE recommended maximum.

Taken together, the inequities that exist between freshman and advanced writing courses in matters of class size, staffing, scheduling, and control over the syllabus imply strikingly different views of what Witte and Faigley call the "institutional context" (40). Add to that institutional context crucial factors such as the tenured faculty's attitude toward the teaching of writing, the departmental and institutional policies on tenure and promotion, the merit-raise structure, and salary levels, and the inequities become egregious. More often than not, these attitudes and policies denigrate the teacher of freshman composition and reward the teacher of advanced writing.

Students

Given that Neel pinpoints 91 percent of all institutions of higher education as "non-elite," it is safe to infer that most admissions standards fall in the range of nonexistent to middling. After all, most two-year institutions and many four-year state colleges and universities have an open admissions policy, requiring only a high school diploma or a GED from within the state. Many of these entering students place into developmental English courses and work their way up through the last required course in the freshman sequence, a course that is a prerequisite for enrolling in advanced composition. Many don't get there. As students progress from freshman to sophomore year at urban institutions such as mine, retention rates of 48 percent are closer to the norm than the exception. The missing 52 percent may drop out permanently or return after a semester or two, with the result that those who do reach the level of advanced composition have undergone a difficult apprenticeship.

In 1977, Mina Shaughnessy stated that the typical student entering the CUNY system more than likely had written a total of 350 words a semester, and some had written nothing at all (14). A poll of freshman students at my own open admissions institution reveals similar figures, even 11 years later. Figures like these carry with them obvious implications: these are students unused to writing, unfamiliar with the conventions of academic discourse, afraid of error, hesitant to commit words to paper. They do not enjoy writing and may actually fear it. Many, given a choice, would not take the course; many of those who admit its necessity see it as an evil one.

Consciously or unconsciously torn between trying to improve their writing and trying to demonstrate that improvement (the student's version of the teacher's often equally paradoxical aims of teaching and testing), freshman students frequently live under the axe of proficiency testing. As recently as seven years ago, 34 percent of the institutions in a random sample (Purnell 408) required students to demonstrate their proficiency in writing by passing an exit test. Given the increased emphasis on accountability in the years since that time, that figure has now probably grown to more than 50 percent. Under the pressure of testing, students — particularly those with skills recently enough acquired that they are not yet natural — will rarely take the risks required for growth in writing. Knowing they will be penalized for mistakes, they avoid the opportunity for error. Under these circumstances, experimenting with style and exploring ideas are luxuries most students are not willing to afford. Their sentences, therefore, plod from subject to verb, forms of *to be* riddle their prose, and truisms are elevated to profound philosophical statements. Getting the paper done is more important than making it effective, and too often form substitutes for thought. If it's 500 words, it has got to be an essay.

Compared to the students in freshman composition, those in advanced composition classes appear to be from a different galaxy. Although an occasional student is dragooned into the course by an advisor who has spotted a weakness in writing skills, most take it as an elective or because they are enrolled in a curriculum that requires it. For the student who takes advanced composition as a required course — and close to a third of all English majors do (Huber 35) — advanced composition offers a perspective on a subject the student already has an affinity for. Requiring advanced composition for an English or English education major is in no way comparable to requiring freshman composition for an engineering student.

Most students elect to take advanced composition and, while they may not like to write, they enjoy having written. They have a built-in appreciation of language that at least balances if not outweighs the anxiety they feel when putting pen to paper or finger tips to keyboard. Their writing has evolved so that they no longer worry about error and instead are ready to move toward effectiveness. Yet, as Maxine Hairston points out, their writing falls short of that goal. Students who enroll in advanced writing courses write with proficiency yet often rely on formulas; their prose is stuffed with too many words and weighed down with nominalizations, passives, prepositional phrases. Their writing lacks focus, details, and a sense of audience (196–98). The goal of an advanced writing course, therefore, is to move students from proficiency to effectiveness.

To attain that goal, the advanced composition student is able to call upon a greater range of experience, both academic and non-academic, than the freshman student. Though some students may sign up straight out of freshman composition, others may come to the course semesters or years later; it's not unusual to have students enrolled who have already earned undergraduate degrees in fields other than English. This experience provides the advanced composition student with rich material to draw upon and, together with an interest in language, a willingness to take risks, and proficiency in writing, it sets the student apart from those in freshman composition.

Courses

The distinction between freshman and advanced composition becomes even clearer when one focuses on the courses themselves — their aims, the means by which they achieve those aims, and the kinds of assignments the students are called upon to undertake.

According to the survey of freshman composition courses conducted by Witte et al., the top five "real goals" identified by directors of composition programs are ranked as follows (10):

Aim	Ranking
write mechanically correct prose	1
write coherent prose	2
explore topic adequately	3
write in various modes	4
syntactically fluent prose	5 (tie)
understand one's composing process	5

Hogan's review of advanced composition reveals far different results (25–26):

Aim	Ranking
develop mature writing style	1
develop awareness of audience	2
teach expository forms	3
teach modes	4
improve skills in punctuation, grammar, mechanics	5

Note that style isn't even considered among the primary goals of freshman composition programs, yet it ranks first in the advanced course; and while "correctness" is ranked first for freshman composition, the advanced version of it is indeed advanced ("improve[d] skill") and is listed fifth.[5]

Another way of examining the difference in aims is to look at the role rhetoric plays in the two courses. At the freshman level, rhetorical principles exist and may even undergird the whole composition program, but they are covert, buried beneath concerns over fluency, correctness, clarity, development, and organization. The freshman program at the University of New Orleans is a case in point. Here, the three levels of freshman writing courses have different goals and levels of proficiency. To pass the developmental course, a student must be able to write a developed, coherent, fluent essay that demonstrates a set degree of control over errors and sentence variety. The second course, roughly everybody's ENGL 101, emphasizes modes of exposition as ways of organizing thought and moves the student away from writing about personal experiences and toward academic discourse — exposition. In contrast to essays written in the developmental course, these papers have "more assertive thesis statements, are more coherent, have more and tighter transitions, show greater sentence variety, contain more complex sentences that show appropriate relationships between ideas, and reflect a wider range of vocabulary" (*Handbook* 16). Analysis and argument are the focus of the last freshman course, and its exit examination serves as the university's test of proficiency (to graduate, transfer students must pass the equivalent of the final examination). Here the emphasis is on being able to read a text critically and then to write a paper that adequately supports or refutes the thesis of that text.

Driving these courses is a comprehensive rationale that represents a consensus of the department, and it is a rhetorically informed consensus:

1. Writing is an act of communication in which the writer addresses a particular audience in order to achieve a specific purpose.
   - Students develop skill in writing by writing and revising.
   - To write well, students need to practice writing for a variety of purposes.
   - Students can best acquire facility in using the elements of discourse, as well as the appropriate grammar and mechanics of edited American English within the context of the whole theme.
2. Reading and writing are integrally related skills.
   - Students should be able to recognize the techniques they practice both in their own writing and in the writing of others.
   - To write well, students need to understand the vocabulary, infer the thesis, and recognize structure, tone, and style in a variety of nonfiction reading selections.

Clearly this rationale is grounded in sound rhetorical principles, yet practice can overwhelm principle. The students come to these courses with such poorly developed writing skills that in spite of noble claims about audience and purpose, most teachers will settle for relatively readable prose. Witte's study also points out that "mechanically correct prose" and "coherent prose" are cited as composition teachers' "real goals" by more than 50 percent of those responding, a percentage more than twice that listed for the goal ranked third, "explore topic adequately" (11).

In advanced composition classes, however, practice follows principle: rhetorical principles are often overt. In some courses, Weaver's *Language is Sermonic,* Plato's *Phaedrus,* Emig's *The Composing Processes of Twelfth Graders,* and Daiker, Kerek, and Morenberg's *Writer's Options* expand the students' understanding of the composing process while informing their writing (Adams). In others, the ideas of Britton and Kinneavy provide a framework that invites students to explore the relationships among the writer, the reader, the world, and the message, thereby developing insights into their own writing and the writing of others (Palumbo). Jean W. Halpern sees audience, purpose, voice, organization, and polish as the five goals of an advanced composition class and then shows how these principles can be turned into practice in a variety of advanced writing classes: technical writing, business writing, journalism, and academic writing.

In my own advanced composition classes, I have tried both overt and covert ways of including rhetoric. In the past, I had often made writing and language the subjects of the advanced course, using, for example, Winterowd's *Contemporary Writer* and Mackillop and Cross's *Speaking of Words.* But that emphasis can have its drawbacks. Discussion may be too textbook-centered, assignments too constraining, the writing too "academic." In open admission institutions, the connections between the theory the students read, what they know, and what they want to know — connections that may be almost impossible to make in a freshman class — may still be at best difficult at the sophomore level, where they may require too large a leap or too much "teacher talk." In short, advanced composition students may have relatively little freedom to explore their own worlds.

These problems do not exist, however, if the student and the student's writing take center stage and rhetorical theory and information about writing become background. The student and the student's writing may be at the center of the freshman course too, but there the focus is blurred by the students' relative lack of interest, fluency, and experience in writing. In an advanced writing course, however, students are not students but writers. The syllabus I hand out the first day of class makes just that point and goes on to describe who should and should not be in the course.

> *Aim:* The course is designed to make writers aware of the process and techniques of writing nonfiction. By emphasizing how the writer observes, explains, evaluates, and persuades, the assignments will draw upon and sharpen the fundamental skills that nonfiction writers rely upon. The goal: original, readable, interesting prose.
>
> Who should be in this course? Anyone who can write competent-

ly and wants to write better, who has ideas and wants to explore different ways of expressing them, who enjoys reading good prose and is willing to help others achieve it, and who knows good writing is hard work and is willing to sweat. Who should not be in this course? Anyone who is looking for a quick fix, who wants merely to tidy up prose (or iron it out), who is looking for a course on syntax and usage. The Learning Center is the better (and free) place to find help on matters of punctuation and usage. English 2151 assumes you know most of that and are concerned with larger matters such as audience, purpose, voice, tone, and style.

From the beginning, I try to form the class into a community of writers, a goal far more attainable in an advanced than a freshman writing course.

It follows that most of the class time is spent in discussion and in editing groups, a luxury often not possible in freshman classes where the number and types of assignments are mandated by department policies. At the University of New Orleans, for instance, most of the freshman papers must be written in class. The opposite is true in my advanced composition course. All assignments are written out of class and are open–ended, although most of their forms are not. Short papers take the class through the writer's various roles of observer, explainer, evaluator, persuader, and speaker, roles that call for varied forms beyond the reach of most freshman students, such as the journal, autobiography, and personal essay as well as exposition, analysis, argumentation, lecture, and the like. To emphasize the skills and techniques called for in evaluation, for instance, the class reads reviews — of books, films, restaurants — as well as analyses — of products, poems, and political situations. When the time comes for an assignment, in this case the choice of reviewing any book, film, or restaurant, we play with ideas: How can you make yourself aware of your own biases? How do you deal with them in your writing? How do you take into account what you think your audience does and doesn't know? Questions such as these arise from thinking about how to handle a particular assignment and lead naturally to discussions of major rhetorical issues—ethos, audience, tone. And they reveal writing as the making of meaning through the choosing among options. What's *right* gives way to what's *better;* freshmen classes frequently must settle merely for what's *right.*

Mixed in with these short assignment are three major papers that, other than being longer and prose, have no constraints, an existential freedom that would paralyze many freshmen. In my advanced writing class any topic is possible, and the three papers can relate to each other or stand alone. The I-don't-have-anything-to-write-about syndrome never raises its empty head, because for the first paper I ask the class to come in with subjects and then use the editing groups to raise the kinds of questions that whittle a subject into a topic. Like Maxine Hairston, I found that "advanced students' writing is often unrealistically ambitious.... They seem unaware of the responsibilities such topics impose on them" (198). Editing groups can head off that problem at the start so that by the time the second and third paper rolls around, the responsibilities implicit in a topic become clear and hence the papers are more focused. The editing groups also have a whack at the rough drafts of these three longer papers, copies of the drafts being due the class meeting before they are to be discussed. And what these writers learn as they respond to their own writing and the writing of others they carry with them beyond the classroom walls. Husbands, wives, lovers, friends, children, and parents are enlisted as editors; at the freshman level they would more likely be ghostwriters.

The effect of having drafts read in this fashion turns up directly and indirectly in a third kind of assignment: keeping a writer's journal. These journals are a pleasure to read, containing as they do snatches of conversations, distillations of scenes, images that triggered memories, reactions to the writing read and the writing written, comments from readers. The journals themselves, I suspect, are as good a measure of the writer's progress as the finished papers; perceptions become more subtle, images more detailed, the ear for dialogue sharper.

The class's concept of style sharpens as well. At first bogged down by words that took up space but carried little meaning, accustomed to nominalizations and passive voice, attracted to a multisyllabic vocabulary, and unaffected by shapeless sentences, these writers rediscover the power of words, phrases, clauses, sentences. We play with some of the exercises in William's *Style: Ten Lessons in Clarity and Grace* and delight in shaping up prose. And because the class is motivated and cares more about their writing than they would have as freshmen, what they learn from Williams is incorporated into their writing. They readily identify the spots in their essays where they want to stress and reword the prose so that form and content together create emphasis.

By the end of the course, each person in class has written over fifty pages of journal entries, five short essays, and three extended papers. That's almost four times as much as each student would have written in my freshman composition course, and such volume and variety raise questions about evaluation. I doubt that anyone who writes that much over such a relatively short period can write consistently good prose. Knowing that to be the case and knowing too that one is apt to learn as much if not more from one's failures as from one's successes, I use this body of writing as the basis for the required final examination, an option that department policy disallows in freshman composition. In my advanced writing course, each writer comes to the final with portfolio in hand and uses it to respond to one of two assignments that make up the major part of the test:

1. Select the paper you find the most satisfying and analyze your writing of it from start to finish. Illustrate your points by quoting from the paper and remember to analyze not just recount.
2. Look through your folder, jotting down what you have learned from writing each paper; then use your notes to compose an essay on how your writing and perception of writing have changed over the semester.

The final grade is based on what each writer identifies as the three best papers written during the semester, and I am gratified when some include their final exam essays, writing which is yet to be graded. That would not happen, I suspect, in freshman English, where D's and F's lie in wait and where the students' shaky skills and the pressure of grades all too often determine the department's policies on assignments, grading, and final examinations.

I enjoy advanced composition; so do the students. I also enjoy freshman English, although I'm not so sure about the students. Advanced composition is a course that belongs to the class—to me and to those who enroll, all of us writers writing. Freshman composition belongs not to the students, not to the teacher, and not even to the department: it belongs to the university. Both those who teach it and those who take it merely fulfill a requirement that they neither designed nor chose. Most of the students write not because they want to but because they have to; both students and teachers are writers surviving, or trying to. They have no investment in the course and no ownership of it. *That* is the major difference that distinguishes freshman from advanced writing courses.

Notes

1. The page numbers given for all citations from the Witte et al. report refer to the pagination by ERIC, not the report's original page numbers.

2. Witte and Faigley's 1983 study indicates that 71 percent of all graduate programs require a course in the teaching of writing, a figure supported by Werner et al. in 1988 (207). Werner, however, does not distinguish between courses offered and courses required. Werner et al. also report a positive correlation between size of institution and the offering of a graduate level course in composition/rhetoric. Of those institutions with enrollments below 10,000, 32.6 percent offer such a course; this figure contrasts with 33.4 percent for middle-size universities and 76.3 percent for those enrolling over 20,000.

3. Such a constraint is now in place in institutions under the aegis of the Southern Association of Schools and Colleges.

4. Although I know of lower and higher figures, the typical ones are those reported in an informal survey conducted for the Association of Departments of English by Franklin, Laurence, and Denham and reported in the May–June issue of *Academe* (15).

5. Rita Sturm's later survey shows even less concern over improvement in punctuation, grammar, and mechanics in advanced composition (42).

Works Cited

Adams, Katherine H. "Bringing Rhetorical Theory into the Advanced Composition Class." *Rhetoric Review* 3 (1985): 184–89.

Britton, James. *Prospect and Retrospect: Selected Essays of James Britton.* Ed. Gordon M. Pradl. Portsmouth, NH: Boynton/Cook, 1982.

Daiker, Donald, Andrew Kerek, and Max Morenberg. *The Writer's Options: College Sentence Combining.* New York: Harper, 1979.

Emig, Janet. *The Composing Processes of Twelfth Graders.* Urbana, IL: NCTE, 1971.

Franklin, Phyllis, David Laurence, and Robert D. Denham. "When Solutions Become Problems: Taking a Stand on Part-Time Employment." *Academe* 74.3 (1988): 15–19.

Hairston, Maxine. "Working with Advanced Writers." *College Composition and Communication* 35 (1984): 196–208.

Halpern, Jeanne W. "The Structure of Advanced Composition." *Journal of Advanced Composition* 1 (1980): 45–52.

Handbook for the Freshman English Program. New Orleans: U of New Orleans, Department of English, 1987–88.

Hogan, Michael P. "Advanced Composition: A Survey." *Journal of Advanced Composition* 1 (1980): 21–29.

Huber, Bettina J., and David Laurence. "Report on the 1984–85 Survey of the English Sample: General Education Requirements in English and the English Major." *ADE Bulletin* 93 (1989) 30–43.

Huber, Bettina J., and Art Young. "Report on the 1983–84 Survey of the English Sample." *ADE Bulletin* 84 (1986): 40–61.

Kinneavy, James. *A Theory of Discourse.* Englewood Cliffs, NJ: Prentice, 1971.

MacKillop, James, and Donna Woolfolk Cross, eds. *Speaking of Words.* New York: Holt, 1978.

Neel, Jasper. "On Job Seeking in 1987." *ADE Bulletin* 87 (1987): 36–39.

Neel, Jasper, ed. *Options for the Teaching of Written Composition.* New York: MLA, 1978.

Palumbo, Roberta M. "Advanced Composition: A Course for Students in All Disciplines." ERIC, 1977. ED 147 843.

Plato. *Phaedrus and the Seventh and Eighth Letters*. Trans. Walter Hamilton. New York: Penguin, 1988.

Purnell, Rosenteen B. "A Survey of the Testing of Writing Proficiency in College: A Progress Report." *College Composition and Communication* 38 (1982): 407–10.

Shaughnessy, Mina. *Errors and Expectations*. New York: Oxford UP, 1977.

Sturm, Rita. "Advanced Composition, 1980: The State of the Art." *Journal of Advanced Composition* 1 (1980): 37–43.

Weaver, Richard M. *Language Is Sermonic*. Baton Rouge: Louisiana State UP, 1970.

Werner, Warren W., Isabelle K. Thompson, and Joyce Rothschild. "A Survey of Specialized Writing Courses for English Majors: 1975–76 to 1985–86." *Rhetoric Review* 6 (1988): 204–17.

Williams, Joseph. *Style: Ten Lessons in Clarity and Grace*. Glenview, IL: Scott, 1985.

Winterowd, W. Ross. *The Contemporary Writer*. New York: Harcourt, 1975.

Witte, Stephen P., and Lester Faigley. *Evaluating College Writing Programs*. Carbondale: Southern Illinois UP, 1983.

Witte, Stephen P., et al. *A National Survey of College and University Writing Program Directors*. Austin: Writing Programs Assessment Project, University of Texas, 1981. ERIC ED 219 779. ED 216 395.

3

The Grammar of Advanced Writing

William A. Covino

The history of philosophical rhetoric contains a strain of theorists (some as prominent as Aristotle, others as forgotten as DeQuincey) who insist that the mastery of rhetoric and writing requires a speculative habit of mind, with which the rhetor continually surveys and invents and alters relationships among the elements of knowledge, taking stock of "the origin, the influence, the changes of all things in the world, all virtues, duties, and all nature, so far as [eloquence] affects the manners, minds, and lives of mankind" (Cicero qtd. in Covino, *Art of Wondering* 36). Evading this world of changing relationships means insisting on the stability, objectivity, and neutrality of knowledge and language, insistence that occurs at the conjunction of pedantry and youthful narrowmindedness: the dogmatic teacher meets the naive student. The evasion of open, speculative discourse informs mainstream conceptions of literacy that are essentially conservative: passive students and authoritarian teachers would conserve and reiterate knowledge-as-information, in order to preserve a closed system of thought (see Covino, "Defining Advanced Composition").

One popular spokesperson for literacy as a conserving activity is E. D. Hirsch, whose *Cultural Literacy* proposes a lexicon of facts and definitions that constitute "what every American needs to know." Professor Hirsch maintains that *knowing* is a formative rather than a transformative phenomenon; that is, knowledge is something you possess rather than something you make, and its chief characteristic is stability (*Cultural Literacy* xiii, 28). Hirsch represents the "banking" concept of education, which Paulo Freire challenges in *Pedagogy of the Oppressed*: "Education thus becomes an act of depositing, in which the students are the depositories and the teacher is the depositor" (58).

31

Ann E. Berthoff has argued forcefully that forming/thinking/writing is transformation, "in which the writer continually circles back, reviewing and rewriting," synthesizing "parts and wholes, form and function, order and accident, beginnings and ends" (3, 105). Hirsch's student writes efficient sentences (see *Philosophy of Composition*) and memorizes canonized facts; Berthoff's student immerses herself in an intellectual chaos of relationships, with a view to making and remaking meaning.

The contrast between conserving and transforming views of language development finds its popular emblem in the "product versus process" debate that has informed discussions of curriculum, methodology, and evaluation for 20 years. Hirsch's student demonstrates mastery of knowledge and language as a *product:* a good mind is a bank of facts and good writing is a parcel of transparent sentences designed for "communicative efficiency." Berthoff's student demonstrates mastery of knowledge and language through the incessant redesign of words and ideas; her *product* is more *process.*

In other words, Hirsch's student writes a *formalist-objective* description of the world, and Berthoff's student writes a *dialectical* description of the world. For the formalist, knowledge and knowledge-in-language are neutral expressions of "the way it is," protected from ideological biases:

> Ideology always holds greatest sway where knowledge is least.
> ... Our ideological disagreements tend to diminish when the linguistic and historical facts are accurately described. (*Philosophy of Composition* 3)

> We have no choice in the matter [of which "forms and conventions of word order and grammar" are *standard*]. The decision was made by those who fixed our grammar at a certain stage of its evolution, and their decision will probably stand forever. (*Cultural Literacy* 79−80)

For the dialectician, knowledge-in-language is an ongoing critique, in which conclusions lead to further questions, oppositions, and relationships; she is interested in how meaning can change in light of new connections and contradictions. The practice of the writer continually circling back, reviewing and revising, exhibits critical inquiry that is necessarily ideological, because it embodies a belief in the value of change. Herbert Marcuse reminds us that dialectical thought can be the weapon of revolution against a formalist establishment:

> Its function is to break down the self-assurance and self–contentment of common sense, to undermine the sinister confidence in the power and language of facts, to demonstrate that unfreedom is so much at the core of things that the development of their internal contradictions leads necessarily to qualitative change: the explosion and catastrophe of the established state of affairs. (qtd. in Giroux 19)

Stepping back from explosion and catastrophe, I want to associate *intellectual development and maturity*—so often identified with the formalist-objective management of language in tests, in textbooks, and in the techno-bureaucracy that tells us what students need (Shor)—with a dialectical habit of mind and propose that if we wish to define and evaluate academic writing in terms of maturing intellection, we must emphasize dialectical thinking/writing that represents the mind in motion rather than the mind foreclosed. With this, I am not simply calling for more prewriting and revising in the classroom. Most often, these are merely the means to what really makes the grade: writing that eliminates contradiction, ambiguity, uncertainty (all "allowed" while the writer is composing preliminary drafts), writing in which singular focus and a clear intention and hobgoblin consistency are the marks of excellence.

However, by presenting contradiction, ambiguity, and uncertainty as the *ends* of "good writing," we encourage the irreversible disruption of formalist-objective positions and teach our students that growing up means conversance with quite different ways of seeing. Thus, we identify our most *advanced* writers as those who can sustain the most open discourse, widening what Kenneth Burke calls "scope" and "circumference" (*Grammar* 59–85) by playing multiple theses one upon another.

Michael Basseches, whose presuppositions about learning in the 1980s recall Vygotsky's emphasis on the dialectical interaction of mind and society, investigates what may be called the society of ideas in the mind, that is, the dialectical interaction of contradictory propositions and perspectives that he associates with adult development. Basseches's conclusions about the relationship of intellectual maturity to dialectical ability, and the schemata he proposes to represent dialectical thought-in-language, deserve interpretive summary here insofar as he validates and gives shape to the idea that advanced writing is the deliberate disruption and transformation of formalist-objective positions.

Basseches defines dialectic as "developmental transformation (i.e., developmental movement through forms) which occurs via constitutive and interactive relationships" (22; I am excluding Basseches's occasional italicizing, here and elsewhere). Before describing the schemata that may represent such relationships, Basseches emphasizes the "dangers" of dialectical thought:

> I do not want to present dialectical thinking as either an intellectual or psychological panacea. Dialectical analyses are not without costs. The willingness to question the permanence and intransigence of the boundary conditions of a problem, and to ask about situations which lie beyond those boundaries [means]...We may be questioning precisely those points of reference which provide us with a sense of intellectual stability and coherence about our world. (29)

Dialectical thinking does not necessarily lead to greater individual comfort, to a greater sense of well-being. The types of thinking that are conducive to comfort and security are, on the one hand, "universalistic formal thinking," which asserts universal truths and universal order; and on the other hand, "relativistic thinking," of the sort that Christopher Lasch criticizes in *The Culture of Narcissism:* the relativist will defend his viewpoint as just as valid as any other, acknowledge that the world is diverse, and defer altogether questions of value (every statement of value is, for the relativist, just another opinion).

Basseches would extend Piagetian cognitive theory to account for post-adolescent development. He concludes that "Piaget has never described particular methods of transcending the stability provided by the closed-system structure of formal operational thought so that continuing dialectical progress in the construction of knowledge can occur" (54). Dialectical thinking is both more inclusive and more flexible than its alternatives, hence the dialectician's appeal as a more capable "problem solver": "Dialectical approaches are more permeable than formalistic approaches by the perspectives of other people who may define a problem in fundamentally different ways" (55). While the political consequences of dialectical thought (summarized by Marcuse above and central to Marxist theory) are recast and sometimes disguised by Basseches in the language of developmental psychology, the schemata he presents are indicators of both quantifiable intellectual complexity and a speculative, potentially radical attitude toward power and authority.

Basseches interviewed 36 students and faculty members (nine freshmen, nine seniors, nine professors) at Swarthmore College about "the nature of education." From transcriptions of these interviews, he abstracted "moves-in-thought...which seemed clearly related to dialectical outlooks and analyses" (68) drawn from "the work of many writers within the dialectical tradition" (72; e. g., Hegel, Marx, Engels, Ollman, Unger, Kosok, Gould, Von Bertalanffy, Piaget). These moves-in-thought are represented as 24 dialectical schemata.

Motion-oriented schemata are moves in thought that represent both fluidity and the processes of change:

1. *Thesis-antithesis-synthesis* movement in thought is "recognized in the sequence of people's thoughts [form] rather than in the words they use [content]" (80). One thought (A) leads to an alternative (not-A), then to a synthesis that transforms A and not-A.

2. *Affirmation of the primacy of motion* expresses the idea that "motion or change is basic to human existence, and thus to human knowledge" (81). Basseches's respondents declare in various ways that "the world is always changing."

3. *The recognition and description of thesis-antithesis-synthesis movement.* Here the user of Schema 1 is conscious that she is using it, stating, for instance, "you have to take your opinion and jive it with other people's and that is the only way you are going to ever find out what reality is—a kind of comparative thing" (86).

4. *Recognition of correlativity of a thing and its other.* Thus, "x is relative to y and...y is relative to x" (89), or in other words, thesis is only knowable in terms of antithesis: "you wouldn't be aware that you had that view unless there was something opposing it or a different view to contrast with it" (91).

5. *Recognition of ongoing interaction as a source of movement.* The subject recognizes that *movement* results from two things in relationship: "Society works on the individual who works on society" (Basseches interview 94).

6. *Affirmation of the practical or active character of knowledge.* A reflection on the nature of knowledge, the expression of what Berthoff would call "knowing your knowledge" or "interpretating interpretations"; recognition that knowledge is something that "works in the world":

> Well, I guess I would have to see "true" as a relative thing, just like Aristotle's physics was probably true for Aristotle and Newton's physics is probably more true for us...Even though Einstein's physics, we know, is probably more true, we still...Newton's is true and when we react on the basis of that schema we...It works in the world and so it's...I guess that is all I mean by true— working when you react to it. (Basseches interview 96)

7. *Avoidance or exposure of objectification, hypostatization, and reification:* One resists "viewing an abstraction or a mental [or cultural] construct as real, substantive, [stable,] and concrete (e.g., a person's I.Q.)" (98). One respondent states, "Just to say the word 'objective' is to be self-deceptive" (100).

8. *Understanding or describing events or situations as moments (of development) of a process:* "Whereas causal explanation can be viewed as understanding events as necessary 'effects' of specific 'causes' against a background of fixed laws, historical explanation can be viewed as understanding events as 'moments' against a background of basic ongoing motion and change" (101). As one respondent says, "If you want to know what the honors program at Swarthmore is today, you have to look at the history of the honors program...in the context of the history of the college" (104).

The recognition of change and process is basic to all of Basseches's schemata, and separating the schemata into groups seems mainly a matter of emphasis. While the first group (#1—8) emphasizes knowledge-as-motion, remaining groups emphasize knowledge-as-form and knowledge-as-relationships. Since motion, form, and relationships are each constitutive of each other, the remaining schemata can be understood as extensions or variations of #1—8, and thus allow for briefer explanation.

Form-oriented schemata (#9, 10, 11) generally express the awareness or view that any form or system does not exist in isolation, apart from a constitutive or transformative context:

> I have been trained, I mean, in a kind of tradition that believes that reason can be...can solve all problems and if one...and I think that view was so much a part of the intellectual tradition that I am a part of, that is a part of me. (Basseches interview 108)

> You can't talk about adequacy unless you have a frame of reference to talk about it in, right? (Basseches interview 112)

For the first speaker, tradition can constitute identity. For the second speaker, words are "all very diffuse," without "reference points"; he recognizes that meaning is not inherent or stable in language, but is formed and transformed as the frame of reference changes.

Relationship-oriented schemata (#12, 13, 14, 15) emphasize "attending to and conceptualizing the nature of relationships":

> Education can't be independent of society and education can't be a separate institution which trains children in a way different from society, because it is society, and it is a part of society, and it will never be able to function independently of society. (Basseches interview 115)

> It goes both ways. Something that you learn out of your classes and you can then apply to your experiences, and you can also have your experiences stimulate you perhaps in your specific studies. (Basseches interview 120)

Metaformal schemata (#16—24) refer to the recognition of forms *as* forms, systems *as* systems, in order to "find the way...[that] networks hook into [or contradict] each other" (137). Metaformalist thought comprehends larger organizational structures; such comprehension is stated most broadly by the respondent who says, "I take in the physical world and I apply a schema to it...I test my schema all the time because it tells me how to react to the world" (139). Metaformalist thought conceives the world, and the ideas and institutions that populate it, as transforming and transformative systems.

With special emphasis on disequilibrium and contradictions that occur within and across systems and forms, Basseches emphasizes the importance of recognizing contradiction as a positive force, quoting Hegel:

> But it is one of the basic prejudices of traditional logic and of common-sense conception that contradiction is not such an essential and immanent determination as identity; indeed, if we were to consider a rank order and if both determinations were to be kept separated, contradiction would have to be accepted as deeper and more essential. For identity, in contrast to it, is only the recognition of the single immediate, the dead being; but contradiction is the source of all motion and vitality; only in so far as something contains contradiction does it move, has it drive and activity. (123)

Significantly, faculty members displayed a broader range of dialectical schemata in the interviews than did seniors, who employed more dialectical "moves" than freshmen. (Basseches associates these differences less with the respective ages of the respondents than with the practice in dialectical thinking that a liberal arts college can provide.) While Basseches is careful to question his own findings and their implications, his research does allow us to isolate a lexicon of dialectical expression and associate this lexicon with adult development. Thus, we find ourselves at the nexus of psychology, philosophy, pedagogy, and genre, inclined to define mature thinking-through-writing with the elements of "motion and vitality," "drive and activity," perhaps inclined further to set aside formal unity and single-mindedness as the criteria for mature writing and instead to encourage dialectical discourse from our students. Basseches's schemata would seem adaptable to student writing; that is, one might describe and evaluate the grammar of advanced composition in terms of demonstrated facility with dialectical moves-in-thought. With some practice, students and evaluators could become more adept and efficient at producing and recognizing schemata in their writing: the formal academic theme would be replaced by the 24-schemata essay as the measure of higher-level literacy.

Recognizing along with Ann Berthoff that "English teachers, it seems, will accept almost anything if it is packaged" (96), we will want to question whether a package of dialectical strategies (Basseches calls his schemata "24 distinct tactics which thinkers may learn to employ") comprises another formalism, robbed of "motion and vitality" at the moment its elements are stabilized. This problem with schemata does not indict Basseches or others compelled to array their research data thus; the persuasive point remains that, if we want advanced thinking through writing to reflect a broad and supple intellect, we will admire the text that is deliberately tentative, disruptive, and dialogical rather than logical. The "A" student is one whose mind-on-the-page is always changing, calling into question his latest conclusion (see Paul Feyerabend on the importance of such "counterinduction" for advanced students).

This student emerges from a pedagogy of conflict, in which, "rather than celebrating objectivity and consensus, teachers must place the notions of critique and conflict at the center of their pedagogical models" (Giroux 62). The fact that "standardized evaluation and modern management methods [have come to] dominate educational decision making" (De Castell, Luke, and Egan 5) makes such pedagogy unwelcome and unlikely (Giroux 66), especially when college is seen as preparation for a technocracy that relies upon smooth organizational functioning. When a dialectical thinker goes to work, disequilibrium and change can result, which threaten the maintenance of stable data and systems (Basseches 359).

Then again, the work world has changed, and is changing, in ways that invite workers capable of multiple data interpretations to join the team and "interface." Identifying advanced writing with tolerance for ambiguity, suspended judgment, and the disclosure of incompatible perspectives may "empower" the future employees of a postmodern American workplace that depends on software and software-critics. While some have argued that there is an American aversion to ambiguity that is especially strong in the technocracy of financial and service industries (Basseches suggests this in his chapter on adult development in the workplace, 338ff.; see also Levine, especially 31–39), others propose that only by embracing ambiguity can workers thrive in the postindustrial information age. Two different but strangely complementary proposals for a postmodern workplace that valorizes the ongoing critique and revision of data—from J. F. Lyotard, Professor of Philosophy at the University of Paris, and Shoshana Zuboff, Professor at the Harvard Business School—lead us to consider further what sort of advanced writing instruction may lead to advancement in the world of work.

In *The Postmodern Condition: A Report on Knowledge,* Lyotard insists that the value of knowledge, in postmodern institutions and businesses that see the world as a colloquy of language games with no transcendent meaning, consists of "performativity":

> The question (overt or implied) now asked by the professionalist student, the State, or institutions of higher education is no longer "Is it true?" but "What use is it?" In the context of the mercantilization of knowledge, more often than not this question is equivalent to: "Is it saleable?" And in the context of power-growth: "Is it efficient?" ...What no longer makes the grade is competence as defined by other criteria — true/false, just/unjust, etc. — and, of course, low performativity in general.

> This creates the prospect for a vast market for competence in operational skills. Those who possess this kind of knowledge will be the object of offers or even seduction policies. Seen in this light, what we are approaching is not the end of knowledge — quite the contrary. Data banks are the Encyclopedia of tomorrow. They transcend the capacity of each of their users. They are "nature" for postmodern man. (51)

The successful player in this scenario is one with "imagination," which Lyotard identifies as the capacity to think metaphorically, "connecting together series of data that were previously held to be independent." Thus the responsibility of postmodern education is "training in all of the procedures that can increase one's ability to connect the fields jealously guarded from one another by the traditional organization of knowledge" (52). This is the ability that Lyotard associates with "interdisciplinary studies." It is the ability that Cicero accords the perfect orator (above), and that has been associated throughout the history of rhetorical theory with topical invention, an ability devalued under the aegis of a formalist-objective epistemology.[1] It is the ability that requires a dialogic classroom exploiting the ambiguity of information (via, for instance, Burke's dramatistic ratios, Freire's generative themes, Lyotard's "interdisciplinary teams...imagining new moves or new games"). *Transmitting* established knowledge is the job of the data bank, not the teacher.

Shoshana Zuboff's *In The Age of the Smart Machine: The Future of Work and Power* argues that computer technology has made the traditional industrial workplace and the hierarchical division of labor obsolete and inefficient. The accessibility and transparency of computer information "increases the visibility of a firm's productive and administrative activities" so that "organization members can 'see' and understand the business in new ways" (158). With workers trained in the "application of intellective skills to data," the workplace is a location for communal critique of information and procedures, and the most valuable workers are those whose capability with information is most comprehensive and flexible, who understand that "work is, in large measure, the creation of meaning" (394).

In a workplace where knowledge-as-information is accessible to all via electronic technology, and authority and power are distributed among those able to manipulate language patterns (Pattison 186) and continually create "new moves" that innovate and improve company business, the potential for tyranny remains, as we learn from one of the workers Zuboff interviewed:

> They say that in a new flexible system the criteria for advancement are fitness and ability instead of seniority. But who gets to say you are fit? Who decides what is fit? It will turn out to be that if you are nice

to your supervisor, if you do what your supervisor wants you to do,
that is what makes you fit. (406).

The invitation to an open discourse—from teachers who encourage
multiple perspectives and irresolution in student writing (see, for
example, Zeiger's "The Exploratory Essay" and Covino's dialogue
assignment in "Defining Advanced Composition") and from employers
who encourage the critique of company data—may defer the question
of final authority and judgment, but cannot ignore it. Someone decides
what discourse is "fit."

So we arrive at the problem of evaluation. Imagine a writing
classroom in which students are being prepared to enter a postmodern
workplace that scorns the formalist-objective valorization of permanent
facts, a workplace that rewards players who can rearrange and re-
formulate discourse to make new connections, new emphases, and new
knowledge. In this classroom, the best students are those who can
ambiguate facts and conclusions, by introducing new and contradictory
information ("research") via moves-in-thought that are recombinative
and critical (Basseches's schemata are such moves). Who or what is the
supervisor here? Who or what decides which discourse is most fit,
which writer is most advanced? There are perhaps three possibilities:[2]

1. *Consensus.* The writer/worker is supervised by the group-in-
   dialogue. The possibility for determinant consensus is argued by
   Habermas, who supports "the universality of an uncoerced consensus arrived at among free and equal persons," consensus that
   comprises "normative content" (40, 341). Lyotard refutes Habermas, arguing that social pragmatics is "a monster formed by the
   interweaving of various networks of heteromorphous classes of
   utterances (denotative, prescriptive, performative, technical,
   evaluative, etc.)" that makes "metaprescriptives common to all of
   these language games" impossible and unjust, except when consensus is a "temporary contract": "any consensus on the rules
   defining a game and the 'moves' playable within it must be local, in
   other words, agreed on by its present players and subject to eventual cancellation" (65–66). If we activate Lyotard's proposal, the
   players themselves—writers/students/workers—may decide that
   everybody "advances," for different reasons at different times.

2. *Performativity.* The writer/worker is supervised by the utility of
   her discourse. Writing that is operational, allowing for action that
   is more productive or efficient or effective or profitable than
   before—writing associated with material progress—counts most.
   Such writing may be dialectical, but *must* be practical. Performativity
   "brings the pragmatic functions of knowledge clearly to light, to
   the extent that they seem to relate to the criterion of efficiency: the

pragmatics of argumentation, of the production of proof, of the transmission of learning, and of the apprenticeship of the imagination [to the requirements of a system administration]" (Lyotard 62).

3. *Paradox.*[3] The writer/worker is supervised by "the desire for justice and the desire for the unknown" (Lyotard 67), and therefore continually exploits the incommensurable. One exemplar of such writing is Montaigne (Lyotard 81; Covino, *Art* 47–57), whose "allusions to the conceivable" (Lyotard 81) through the juxtaposition of dissimilars offers a syntax of the unknown while continually upsetting the dogma that feeds intellectual oppression and injustice. In this practice, the writer is artist, the writer is poet, broadly associative and outside the rules of logic or utility or consensus; the writing is "not a statement about the world; it is an attempt to create, out of hieroglyphs imprinted by the world upon the ego of the writer, another world" (Updike 25).

It may be that emphasizing writing as a postmodern *art,* supervised by paradox, more than a postmodern *skill,* supervised by consensus and performativity, will give us more workers alert to the tyranny that can attend "fit" discourse. It may be that our most advanced writers will always be misfits.

Notes

1. Vico's lifelong argument against Descartes represents the opposition of topical philosophy to positivism. See especially "On the Ancient Wisdom of the Italians" and "On Contemporary Methods of Study" in Pompa.

2. I am indebted to Lyotard for the lexicon that follows, but I have recontextualized, applied, and elaborated his text rather audaciously.

3. Lyotard features the term *paralogy,* which is, simply put, the generation of new ideas that violate prevailing presuppositions. I find paradox a similar but more accessible term in the context of this discussion.

Works Cited

Basseches, Michael. *Dialectical Thinking and Adult Development.* Norwood, NJ: Ablex, 1984.

Berthoff, Ann E. *The Making of Meaning: Metaphors, Models, and Maxims for Writing Teachers.* Portsmouth, NH: Boynton/Cook, 1981.

Burke, Kenneth. *A Grammar of Motives.* 1945. Berkeley: U of California P, 1969.

Covino, William A. *The Art of Wondering: A Revisionist Return to the History of Rhetoric.* Portsmouth, NH: Boynton/Cook, 1988.

———. "Defining Advanced Composition." *Journal of Advanced Composition* 8 (1988): 113–22.

De Castell, Suzanne, Allan Luke, and Kieran Egan, eds. *Literacy, Society, and Schooling: A Reader.* Cambridge: Cambridge UP, 1986.

Feyerabend, Paul. *Against Method.* New York: Schocken, 1978.

Freire, Paulo. *Pedagogy of the Oppressed.* New York: Continuum, 1986.

Giroux, Henry A. *Theory and Resistance in Education.* South Hadley, MA: Bergin, 1983.

Habermas, Jurgen. *The Philosophical Discourse of Modernity.* Cambridge: MIT Press, 1987.

Hirsch, E. D. *Cultural Literacy.* Boston: Houghton, 1987.

———. *The Philosophy of Composition.* Chicago: U of Chicago P, 1977.

Lasch, Christopher. *The Culture of Narcissism.* New York: Warner, 1979.

Levine, Donald N. *The Flight from Ambiguity.* Chicago: U of Chicago P, 1985.

Lyotard, Jean-Francois. *The Postmodern Condition: A Report on Knowledge.* Trans. Geoff Bennington and Brian Massumi. Minneapolis: U of Minnesota P, 1984.

Pattison, Robert. *On Literacy.* New York: Oxford UP, 1982.

Pompa, Leon, ed. *Vico: Selected Writings.* Cambridge: Cambridge UP, 1982.

Shor, Ira. *Culture Wars.* Boston: Routledge, 1986.

Updike, John. "The Writer Lectures." *The New York Review of Books* 35.10 (1988): 23–26.

Zeiger, William. "The Exploratory Essay." *College English* 47 (1985): 454–67.

Zuboff, Shoshana. *In the Age of the Smart Machine: The Future of Work and Power.* New York: Basic, 1988.

4

The Rhythm of Education and the Teaching of Writing

Richard E. Young

> After all, the whole affair is merely a preparation for battling
> with the immediate experiences of life, a preparation by which
> to qualify each immediate moment with relevant ideas and
> appropriate actions.
>
> Alfred North Whitehead, *The*
> *Aims of Education*

What do we mean by *advanced composition?* As the articles in this
collection demonstrate, it has come to mean many things. It is not a
technical term in rhetorical studies, or has not quite become one yet,
in part because there has been no widely shared referent. In practice,
it can refer to almost any writing course beyond freshman composition:
to various courses different from freshman composition, which is in
itself highly diverse; to what is in effect a reiteration of freshman
composition designed to give students more practice in writing; to
courses that are in time, energy, knowledge, or skill more demanding;
even to upper-level courses with a remedial function, designed for
poor writers who somehow passed the freshman course. What is considered advanced in one curriculum, in that it follows other writing
courses, may not be considered advanced in another curriculum. At
my own school, Carnegie Mellon University, argument is formally
introduced in the freshman course, whereas in many other schools it is
an advanced course that may be elected after a freshman course in
exposition. Definitions of *advanced* at the present time, then, are ad
hoc and stipulative, rather than conventional and generally applicable.[1]

Doubtless this indeterminancy of meaning is due to the absence of any generally shared conception of a disciplinary sequence, of a curriculum in which one writing course or sequence of courses provides the necessary basis for subsequent course work. Though proposals for more sophisticated curriculums have been made (e.g., Kitzhaber 100ff.; Moffett), in practice there has been nothing comparable to, say, the complex and integrated language curriculums of ancient Rome or Renaissance England, in which a term like *advanced* would have had some generally shared meaning.[2] The rudimentary sequence of freshman composition, which usually emphasizes basic issues of linguistic hygiene, followed by courses in literature that cultivate by example and critical analysis an understanding of the higher reaches of linguistic art is shared by nearly every program in English studies in the country. However, it offers no basis for sequencing courses whose primary objective is the development of rhetorical abilities.[3] Writing courses at the college level tend to follow one another like beads on a string, any one of which might well take the place of the other in a particular curriculum. But in a structured curriculum *where or when something is* has to do with *what it is*. If it does not, the notion of advanced has little significance.

One possible rationale for an ordered sequence of writing courses (if not a curriculum in rhetoric and composition at least a significant contribution to one) was provided by Alfred North Whitehead in *The Aims of Education*. Whitehead argued that the acquisition of any intellectual discipline is a dialectical process that moves from freedom to discipline and back again to a freedom transformed by the powers conferred by discipline. To borrow Whitehead's terms, the acquisition of any discipline moves, broadly speaking, from a "romantic stage," through a "stage of precision," to a "stage of generalization" that embodies features of both the prior stages. Whitehead calls this process of intellectual growth the "rhythm of education" (15–41).

The romantic stage is the stage of initial involvement with the subject. Here, for the student, "the subject-matter has the vividness of novelty; it holds within itself unexplored connexions with possibilities half-disclosed by glimpses and half concealed by the wealth of material" (17). It also provides the motive for learning in the subsequent stage, for the initial excitement of involvement leads naturally to a desire for greater precision and control. "The stage of precision also represents an addition to knowledge. In this stage, width of relationship is subordinated to exactness of formulation" (18). It is the stage of precise analysis, of detail, of technique and the technology of the subject, of what we in the academic community usually think of as intellectual discipline, a narrower conception of discipline than Whitehead has in mind (32). The stage of generalization emphasizes the application of disciplinary knowledge to action in the world beyond the classroom. It constitutes a transition from the activities distinctive to the classroom to activities in a larger community in which the student aspires to effective participation.

Lest the scheme look too tidy, Whitehead notes that these stages of mental growth are neither sharp-cut nor mutually exclusive. Students do not leave behind the excitement of the romantic stage when they enter the next stage, nor can the teacher ignore the need for motivation. And when they enter the final stage, ready to turn their attention to problems of the world, they bring with them detailed technical knowledge and, if they have been well taught, a vision of new possibilities. Each of the stages is the result more of a growth of ability accompanied by a natural change of emphasis or focus of attention than of a leap to concerns that are wholly new. As Whitehead remarks, "The final stage of generalisation is Hegel's synthesis. It is a return to romanticism with added advantage of classified ideas and relevant technique. It is the fruition which has been the goal of the precise training. It is the final success" (19).

With a basis for sequencing courses comes the possibility of a general, nonarbitrary definition of *advanced composition*. We could, I suppose, define it as either of the two stages beyond the romantic, which would be defined in this scheme as the beginning stage. However, perhaps *advanced composition* refers most appropriately to the last stage, that is, to the stage in which students focus their attention on informed and appropriate action in the world. This conception of *advanced* requires us to reexamine what we mean by courses we label as *introductory* and *intermediate* in a way that more common definitions seldom do. For it presupposes that there is a specifiable discipline to be acquired, that the acquisition proceeds by a coherent and cohesive sequence of stages, and that in working through the stages the student is being prepared to engage the immediate experiences of living.

We can easily think of several sequences of writing courses that embody Whitehead's rhythmic pattern. For example, suppose that the general goal of a writing program for undergraduate students was a knowledge of the principal modern rhetorics and the development of rhetorical abilities emphasized in each. (I am here, and throughout, treating composition as the pedagogical branch of rhetorical studies.) We can imagine a curriculum in which the course or courses in the initial romantic stage would be driven by some variant of what has been called "neo-romantic rhetoric" (D'Angelo 159), for example, Macrorie's rhetoric or Elbow's. That is, the kind of rhetoric studied would coincide in its major emphasis with the emphasis in Whitehead's first stage. Courses in the second stage would make use of rhetorics that have elaborated methodologies, that is, rhetorics that lend themselves naturally to a technical approach (e.g., classical rhetoric, tagmemic rhetoric). Courses in the third stage would directly address rhetorical action beyond the classroom (e.g., writing in specific professional communities, the writing associated with active citizenship). The sequence I have suggested embodies quite different arts of rhetoric on the grounds that the thrust in each seems to mirror Whitehead's stages. I am assuming that the various rhetorics do not, or need not, exclude one another on the grounds of theoretical incompatibility, as some would have it, but that each contains its own truth and that they can be brought into complementary relationships if seen as related to stages of growth in rhetorical ability.[4]

Other sequences are possible. The rhythmic pattern Whitehead describes applies to the teaching of any subject matter or skill, no matter how broad or narrow. This being the case, his argument applies equally to teaching and learning only romantic rhetoric or only classical rhetoric, whether in a single course or in a sequence of courses. That is, either could be the basis for an entire writing program and still be taught in a way consistent with Whitehead's pattern. For romantic rhetoric is not without a concern for precision and utility. Capturing accurately the personal vision of the writer requires mastery of a substantial craft; and self-knowledge and personal growth have long been regarded as ending ends of that rhetoric. And it does not stretch the imagination too far to consider the romance of classical rhetoric, to see it as being taught in such a way as to open up new and engaging possibilities for the novice writer that provide the motivation for further study. Furthermore, much of its history has been an effort to make explicit and precise the distinctive features of expert performance; and application in the world was there from the beginning. The same pedagogical possibilities are there for other rhetorics as well. A sequence of courses that is informed by a single rhetorical theory, however, would have narrower goals than the sequence I described earlier, and it might be harder to staff since it presupposes a group of faculty who all control the same rhetorical theory, which is, with the exception of current-traditional rhetoric, a rarity in most English departments.

However, if Whitehead's very general principle allows for several possible sequences, it is not so general that it provides an umbrella for all conceptions of advanced composition. It would exclude certain familiar kinds of courses and, by implication, sequences of courses, for example, the introductory creative writing course that conventionally follows freshman composition, any course that is in its content and focus essentially a repetition of freshman composition, and any course that focuses on the theory and technical niceties of rhetorical art while deemphasizing action in the world. This is not to say that all other sequences and ordering principles are necessarily wrong; alternative definitions of *advanced* may have special value in particular situations. But the cogency of Whitehead's argument does put pressure on us to reexamine our writing programs and their underlying principles. Given the present unsettled state of English studies, perhaps the best we can hope for at the moment are reasonable definitions of *advanced composition* that can be implemented in particular programs. Adoption of a single, widely shared definition appears to depend upon broader and deeper changes in English studies as a whole, which are likely to be slow in coming.[5]

If advanced composition, as I am defining it here, is concerned principally with informed and appropriate action in the world, what specific sorts of action can such a course be concerned with? Obviously there are many possibilities. The course I want to discuss, Argument and Controversy, is as the title suggests devoted to argument in the context of social controversy. More particularly, it is devoted to developing the student's ability to enter real-world controversies in a way that is both original and useful. The situation students learn to enter is the one Burke calls "the unending conversation":

> Imagine that you enter a parlor. You come late. When you arrive, others have long preceded you, and they are engaged in a heated discussion, a discussion too heated for them to pause and tell you exactly what it is about. In fact, the discussion had already begun long before any of them got there, so that no one present is qualified to retrace for you all the steps that had gone before. You listen for a while, until you decide that you have caught the tenor of the argument; then you put in your oar. Someone answers; you answer him; another comes to your defense; another aligns himself against you, to either the embarrassment or gratification of your opponent, depending upon the quality of your ally's assistance. However, the discussion is interminable. The hour grows late, you must depart. And you do depart, with the discussion still vigorously in progress. (110–11)

Students

The course, an elective for junior and senior English majors concentrating in writing, is designed with the assumption that the students control the conventions of Standard Edited English and have been introduced to the conventions of argument.[6] Argument and Controversy is very much easier to teach if students have some technical knowledge of classical rhetoric and Toulmin's logic; otherwise one has to introduce technical issues on a need-to-know basis. This is, of course, possible to do, but a stage-three course is obviously easier to teach if students coming into it control certain technical concepts and methods. Even though the assumptions the course makes about student preparation are reasonable given its place in the curriculum, the world is imperfect and some students enter who are less qualified than they ought to be. But they all have had freshman composition or been exempted from the requirement (i.e., they meet the prerequisites), they all have some interest in the course as it is not a program requirement, and they all have more competence as writers than most of their peers since the course was designed primarily for students who are majoring or minoring in writing.

Course Objectives

The objectives of Argument and Controversy elaborate the goal of enabling students to enter controversies originally and constructively:

1. Ability to analyze and summarize the essential ideas and structure in another's argument.
2. Ability to evaluate an argument, which includes the ability to isolate and analyze problems that arise as one reads the arguments of others.
3. Ability to identify and analyze the relationships among arguments in complex controversies.
4. Ability to identify points at which one can enter a controversy usefully and with originality, i.e., where one disagrees with a position in the controversy, where others have not already responded to it adequately, and where one is capable of making an informed and reasoned argument.
   a. Ability to use the classical method for isolating the stasis in opposing positions.
   b. Ability to analyze the rhetorical situation when such disagreements emerge.
5. Ability to develop one's argument in a way that is appropriate to distinctive features of the rhetorical situation.

The first three objectives focus on the structure and meaning of existing arguments and the relation of one argument to another; the remaining two address directly the process of creating new arguments in response to points of opposition discovered in the controversy. All are essential to the ability to enter a controversy effectively: that is, one must be able to understand the arguments that make up the controversy, how one's position differs from the positions of others and what the defects of opposing positions are, and how one can create an argument that is appropriate to that particular context. All, in one way or another, are also concerned with problems, which function both as motives for arguing and as parts of arguments. *Problems* here can refer to defects we perceive in the world around us, including defects in the arguments of others, which may, if sufficiently intrusive in our thinking, provide motives for arguing (Bitzer 6−7). *Problems* can also refer to structural units in argumentative discourse, since it is a common rhetorical strategy to point to such defects in explaining why we are entering a controversy with an argument of our own. I am assuming, then, that arguments are essentially efforts to address problems and, hence, that developing skill in problem analysis and formulation must be a significant goal of the course.

Course Structure

The organization of academic instruction tends to be strongly linear (first A is studied, then B, then C, etc.), a reflection of the fact that courses extend over time and of the scholar's tendency to approach a subject analytically. This linear structure is clearly appropriate for the presentation of ordered bodies of information, a survey course in history, for example, but it is hardly the optimal way of structuring a course in writing arguments, where students must know a good deal about rhetoric and rhetorical processes before they can carry out the first assignment. As Kitzhaber has remarked, "When someone teaches composition, he is trying to cultivate in the student a bafflingly complex intellectual skill. Instruction in it does not proceed in a systematic and sequential way, where one thing must be learned before the next can be understood; instead, a student needs all things at once whenever he composes anything as long as a paragraph" (89−90). It would seem inappropriate to treat words this week, sentences next week, paragraphs next, and so on, each to the exclusion of the other, and to make writing assignments based on that classwork, even though that is the organizational principle of many composition texts. The same can be said about teaching to each of the course objectives in isolation from the others, since all are parts of a single process; to borrow Burke's words, all are part of the process of putting your oar in a heated discussion. Such an item-by-item approach would atomize the process when the student needs an integrated understanding of the whole activity. One important problem the teacher must address in the design of a writing course, then, is how the immediate need for knowledge of the entire composing process can be reconciled with the necessarily sequential nature of the course.

When a baby is born, it does not learn first about logic, then about itself, then about feeding, then about mother, somewhat belatedly about father, and so on. It learns, no matter how imperfectly, about a number of things in context and concurrently. Gradually, through repeated exposures, the components of the infant's mental world become clearer, better defined, and more controllable. To a great extent, we continue to learn that way throughout our lives.[7] The same sort of gradual accretion through repeated exposure is even more apparent in the development of complex skills, since learning a skill requires practice in context. One way around the difficulty of needing to know everything at once when things can only be taught one at a time is to build into the course structure a functional redundancy.

Argument and Controversy is organized in a series of cycles during each of which, in a sense, the entire course is taught. The organization of the course might be seen as an application of Bruner's concept of the "spiral curriculum" (13, 52−55): the course, as it develops, revisits the basic ideas and objectives of the course repeatedly, building on them and extending their implications. Instead of teaching to each of the course objectives in turn, the instructor treats them as aspects of a single activity, though from cycle to cycle the emphasis shifts from one objective to another. In the current version of Argument and Controversy there are five cycles of varying lengths, though the number of cycles has varied in the past and may well vary in future versions of the course. (For the course syllabus, see Appendix 1.) Each cycle culminates in an argument of one sort or another. In the most recent version of the course, the five required arguments are a critique of an argument, an argument that a problem exists, a refutation, and two extended arguments that enter complex controversies. (For an illustration of a paper assignment, see Appendix 2.) The course objectives allow for some variation in the kinds of arguments assigned.

Peer Evaluation

The course makes extensive use of peer evaluation, sometimes in the class as a whole, more often in groups of three or four students, since I want them to get comfortable about making and taking criticism, and that seems to happen most readily in smaller groups. The student evaluations of each other's drafts are guided by primary-trait scales, a response to research suggesting the usefulness of scales in developing critical knowledge and writing abilities and the importance of providing guidance for students doing peer evaluations (Hillocks 156−60, 166−68). The same scales are used subsequently by the teacher in evaluating the finished paper. All the scales are developed in discussions by the students and teacher and focus on the aspects of argument stressed in one or another of the cycles (e.g., the essential characteristics of responsible refutation, the use of evidence, or the clear presentation of the stasis); that is, the scales are ad hoc rather than generic. (For an example of such a scale, see Appendix 3.)

Peer evaluation guided by scales serves at least three purposes in the course:

1. It provides another especially useful kind of feedback to students about their work.
2. It helps to develop critical judgment about effective argument in context; criticism is brought to bear first on the work of others, where it is easier to cultivate, and then on one's own work, which is harder but for their development as writers, more important.
3. It provides the members of the group with an audience that is reasonably knowledgeable about the controversial issue.

This last point is worth stressing: the student group does more than simulate a real audience; it *is* a real audience, one that contains different positions on the issue, like the populace at large, but that is considerably more knowledgeable about it than the general populace. The students become a real audience by extensive reading, critical analysis, and writing on problems in a single controversy. By the middle of the semester, many are arguing about the issues addressed in the controversy not only during the class but before class starts, and they are often still arguing as they walk out the door. Somewhere along the way they stop being students of the controversy and become participants in it. I suspect that for many of them it is the first time in their lives that they have been sufficiently well informed about a major social controversy to feel capable of making a serious contribution. There is a certain pleasure in that and a sense of power. When they reach that stage they stop grumbling about more reading on the same issue.

Texts

The text or texts for the course must (1) address the issues in rhetorical theory that bear on the objectives of the course and (2) offer collections of readings on social controversies that give the student a good grasp of their complexity. Experience with such collections suggests that if they are to be effective, they must provide more than numerous selections on the general issue, although that is important; they must present at least the primary positions taken in the controversy, and they also must present one writer responding to another. Various readings on an issue do not necessarily add up to a controversy (though students might be asked to construct an imaginary controversy out of such readings).[8] I ask students to supplement the collection with arguments they find in their reading outside the classroom, the intention being to help them see more of the complexity of the controversy and at the same time break down the barrier between the classroom and the world outside, thus giving them a stronger awareness of the reality of the controversy and its immediate presence. With this knowledge and awareness come, finally, genuine occasions for entering the controversy.

As the students read, contemplate, argue with each other, and write and rewrite about the controversy during the semester, their own positions become clearer and better defined. Differences appear that seem to surprise them; when we come right down to it, most of us, I suppose, have some difficulty believing that positions other than our own can be as reasonable as our own and held with the same conviction (Abercrombe). The students are even more surprised when they find themselves moving away from the often unconsidered positions they held early in the semester to more thoughtful ones. And some are more willing to articulate their positions when they begin to realize that the positions of others are corrigible and feel that they are developing the ability to defend their own. Though they sometimes complain about focusing on only one or two controversies during the semester ("Not another argument on abortion!"), a complaint that at times seems to me like those ritualistic complaints about dorm food, they also display a sense of pride in their new-found authority on a controversial issue and in their growing ability to participate constructively in the dialogue.

Appendix 1
Calendar/Syllabus for
76−323: Argument and Controversy
Spring Semester, 1989
Richard E. Young   Department of English

N.B. — The dates for units of the course and due dates for papers are only approximations intended to provide a sense of the pace of the course; the particular needs of the class will modify the calendar somewhat. Actual due dates will be given at the time assignments are made.

Cycle 1: The structure of argument   1/17/89−2/6/89
Analyzing arguments
  Analyzing for form and meaning
    Form as pattern
    Identifying the motive for arguing
    Identifying the thesis and support for the thesis
      Varieties of claims—fact, value, policy
Summarizing and outlining individual arguments
  Functions of summary in argument and controversy
Criteria for evaluating arguments

Exercises: Outlining and summarizing arguments, developing a scale for evaluation

Paper 1: Critique of an argument. Due: 2/6

Cyce 2: Context and interpretation 2/6−2/20
Context of situation
  Analyzing rhetorical situations for significant features
    Rhetorical situations
      Problems, constraints, and appropriate audiences
        The motive for argument
          Analyzing for the problem
Analysis as interpretation − "spinning" a situation
  Problems and warrants
Criteria for evaluating interpretations

Exercises: Analyzing rhetorical situations for problem, appropriate audience(s), and constraints; developing a scale for evaluation

Paper 2: "Spinning" a rhetorical situation: articulation and explanation of a problem. Due: 2/20

Cycle 3: Argument in context − adaptive responses 2/20−3/6
Kairos
Analyzing for the crucial issue and stasis
Adapting argument to situation
  Kinds of argumentative situations and implications − triadic, dyadic
    Conditioned variations in patterns of argument
Criteria for judgments of cogency

Exercises: Adapting simple arguments to contexts, writing dialogue as a means of understanding alternative positions, analyzing crucial issues in controversies; developing a scale for evaluation

Paper 3: Entering a controversy − refutation. Due: 3/6

Cycle 4: Analyzing and entering controversies 3/6−4/10
Analyzing controversies
  Grouping arguments
    Treeing the controversy to discover and reveal relationships
    Identifying the crucial issues
Developing generalizations and modes of appeal
  Supporting claims: using the work of others

Exercises: "Treeing" a controversy; developing a scale for evaluation

Paper 4: Entering a controversy constructively and originally − an argument of fact, value, or policy. Due: 4/10

Cycle 5: Analyzing and entering controversies 4/10−5/3
Form as expectation

Exercises: Treeing a controversy; developing a scale for evaluation

Paper 5: Entering a controversy constructively and originally—an argument of fact, value, or policy. Due: 5/3

Appendix 2
The Refutation

The assignment calls for a refutation of an argument, sometimes called a *confutation.* Although this form of argument can stand alone, as, for example, in a letter to the editor in which you attack a point made in an earlier argument by an opponent, it is probably more commonly found embedded in longer, more complex arguments.

The object of a refutation is to eliminate an opposing position from serious consideration if not by the opponent himself, which is usually too much to hope for, then at least by others who are following the controversy. The sort of refutation we are discussing here is an instance of triadic argument, in which the reader you are trying to influence is not the opponent but a third party. (Arguments that attempt to influence the opponent directly, dyadic arguments, usually have different characteristics.) In attacking the position of another, you need not present your own, although the nature of your attack often at least implies where you stand; it is a question of where the emphasis lies—on the merits of your position or on the defects of the opponent's. In a refutation the emphasis is on the defects of the opponent's position.

Because they have some common features, the refutation is sometimes confused with the critical evaluation; both, for example, may adversely criticize someone's argument. But the critical evaluation may criticize any features of someone's argument (e.g., its style, structure, significance, the intelligence of the position); in fact, the critic need not even see himself in opposition to the argument but can praise it for its virtues. In contrast, the refutation is an attack on some significant feature of the opponent's position (e.g., the thesis, a major generalization in the argument, an implication of the argument, his handling of evidence, a specific objection brought against your position).

Whatever else belongs in a refutation, these things seem essential:

1. A brief statement of the issue addressed by the argument you are refuting.

2. A summary of the opponent's argument on the issue, or that part of the argument that you want to attack. Note that your summary should include only what is necessary to enable the reader to understand what you are attacking; your omissions should not, however, result in a distortion of the opponent's position. A good summary is accurate and fair.

3. A statement of why you are attacking the opponent's argument. Your statement will usually address either an error in the argument's handling of facts and assumptions about the world or an error in the principles of good reasoning. In either case you set up a standard against which you measure the opponent's statements. What are the facts relating to the issue and, in contrast, what does your opponent say they are? What constitutes good reasoning and, in contrast, what does your opponent do? The first is a test of whether what the opponent says corresponds with reality; the second is a test of the opponent's use of the principles of logic. At times you may want to raise the issue of flaws in presentation: clumsy choice of words, rudeness and discourtesy, offensive attempts at manipulating the audience, etc. But such "errors of accommodation" are probably best introduced to reinforce more fundamental criticisms.

When people object to the argument of another, they sometimes make the mistake of attacking everything they can find wrong with it, from invalid inferences and distortions of fact to misspelled words and bad punctuation. The effect is rather like trying to kill someone by nibbling him to death. Go after the important defect, the one crucial to the effectiveness of the argument.

Since a refutation normally is part of a longer argument, there is value in learning to be brief, going to the heart of the matter immediately.

Appendix 3
Peer Evaluation Scale

Date _____

Author's Name _____
Reader's Name _____

REFUTING AN ARGUMENT

1. Is an orienting statement provided that explains the context in which the arguments (yours and the opponent's) function?
     no 1 2 3 4 5 yes
   Comment:

2. Is the opponent's argument, or that portion of it that you want to refute, clearly, accurately, and fairly summarized?
     no 1 2 3 4 5 yes
   Comment:

3. Is your thesis (primary claim) clearly stated?
     no 1 2 3 4 5 yes
   Comment:

4. Are your thesis and other generalizations (subordinate claims) sufficiently supported?

> no   1   2   3   4   5   yes

Comment:

5. Is your prose consistent with conventional standards of grammar and usage?

> no   1   2   3   4   5   yes

Comment:

Additional comments:

Notes

1. The range of definitions of *advanced* as well as the difficulty of defining the term can be seen in the following: Kitzhaber, "The Writing of College Students after the Freshman Year," in *Themes, Theories, and Therapy;* "Guidelines and Directions"; Hogan; McCullen; and Adams.

2. We might contrast the discussions of rhetorical education in Clark and Sister Miriam Joseph with accounts of present-day writing progams. See, for example, critical comments made in 1963 about offerings for non-majors in Kitzhaber (esp. 13, 59−61). A similar view about offerings for majors can be found a decade later in Wilcox's remark that "the great variety or confusion of programs for the major in English points to one of two conclusions: either departments of English have not faced up to the task of deciding just what constitutes an essential plan of studies for undergraduates who would specialize in their discipline, or that decision cannot be made and that plan cannot be devised because their discipline cannot be defined" (133). Though the last 15 years have brought significant changes in the teaching of writing, there is little reason to believe that the profession has moved much closer to a shared conception of rhetorical education in English departments; see, for example, Hartzog (esp. 30−43, 70−71).

3. For a discussion of this sequence and the assumptions on which it is based, see Kaufer and Young.

4. For discussions of the complementarity of various rhetorical approaches, see Young and Greene. For a view that affirms one theory while excluding others from consideration, see Knoblauch and Brannon.

5. I have confined my discussion to the tertiary level of education, but since first-language education does not begin at the college level, any fully developed conception of sequence would have to recognize the role of secondary and primary education as well, as it does now, for example, in the mathematics curriculum.

6. To date, the course has been offered in three versions. It was first offered as a "designated writing course" for Carnegie Mellon students exempted from freshman composition; that course was part of the writing-across-the-curriculum program then under development. In Spring 1988, it was offered for junior and senior rhetoric students at SUNY Binghamton, most of whom

were going into law or on to graduate school. It is now being offered at Carnegie Mellon as an elective for junior and senior English majors, most of whom are concentrating in professional or technical writing. It is this last version of the course that is described in this essay.

7. Virtually everyone in this country knew that John Kennedy had been shot five and a half hours after the bullets struck him, and they learned that among a hundred other things that day. Twenty-five years later, we are still learning about what happened on that day in Dallas. For a discussion of the cumulative nature of the learning process, see Becker.

8. I have tried two texts so far, Barnet and Bedau's *Current Issues and Enduring Questions* and Rottenberg's *Elements of Arguments*. But *Current Issues* is not for my purposes sufficiently sophisticated in its rhetorical apparatus, and some of the collections of readings are not really controversies but only issues on which over the years different positions have been taken (i.e., in some collections of readings there are no confrontations, only differences on an issue). In some, however, as in the case of the abortion controversy and capital punishment, the readings do give a sense of the actual struggle now going on in the society. The rhetorical apparatus in *Elements of Argument* is more nearly what the course requires though the collections of readings are not as extensive as I would like. At the present time, the rhetorical text that seems most appropriate for the course is Kaufer, Geisler, and Neuwirth's *Arguing from Sources: Exploring Issues through Reading and Writing,* which has only recently appeared; it would have to be supplemented by readings on one or more controversies.

Works Cited

Abercrombe, M. L. J. *The Anatomy of Judgement.* 1960 New York: Penguin, 1969.

Adams, Katherine H. "Bringing Rhetorical Theory into the Advanced Composition Class." *Rhetoric Review* 3 (1985): 184–89.

Barnet, Sylvan, and Hugo Bedau. *Current Issues and Enduring Questions: Methods and Models of Argument from Plato to the Present.* New York: Bedford-St. Martin's, 1987.

Becker, Samuel L. "Rhetorical Studies for the Contemporary World." *The Prospect of Rhetoric.* Ed. Lloyd F. Bitzer and Edwin Black. Englewood Cliffs, NJ: Prentice, 1971. 21–43.

Bitzer, Lloyd F. "The Rhetorical Situation." *Philosophy and Rhetoric* 1 (1968): 1–14.

Bruner, Jerome S. *The Process of Education.* Cambridge: Harvard UP, 1961.

Burke, Kenneth. *The Philosophy of Literary Form: Studies in Symbolic Action.* 3rd ed. 1941. Berkeley: U of California P, 1973.

Clark, Donald Lemen. *Rhetoric is Greco-Roman Education.* 1957. Westport, CT: Greenwood, 1977.

D'Angelo, Frank J. *A Conceptual Theory of Rhetoric.* Cambridge: Winthrop, 1975.

Greene, Stuart. "Romance and Rhythm in the Teaching of Writing." *Freshman English News* 14.3 (1986): 20–24.

"Guidelines and Directions for College Courses in Advanced Composition." *College Composition and Communication* 18 (1967): 266–268.

Hartzog, Carol P. *Composition and the Academy: A Study of Writing Program Administration.* New York: MLA, 1986.

Hillocks, George., Jr. *Research on Written Composition.* Urbana: NCRE/ERIC, 1986.

Hogan, Michael P. "Advanced Composition: A Survey." *Journal of Advanced Composition* 1 (1980): 21–29.

Joseph, Sister Miriam. *Rhetoric in Shakespeare's Time.* New York: Harcourt, 1962.

Kaufer, David S., Cheryl Geisler, and Christine M. Neuwirth. *Arguing from Sources: Exploring Issues through Reading and Writing.* San Diego: Harcourt, 1989.

Kaufer, David S, and Richard E. Young. "Literacy, Art, and Politics in Departments of English." *Composition and Literature: Bridging the Gap.* Ed. Winifred Bryan Horner. Chicago: U of Chicago P, 1983. 148–158.

Kitzhaber, Albert. *Themes, Theories, and Therapy: The Teaching of Writing in College.* New York: McGraw, 1963.

Knoblauch, C. H., and Lil Brannon. *Rhetorical Traditions and the Teaching of Writing.* Portsmouth, NH: Boynton/Cook, 1984.

McCullen, Maurice L. "Looking Backwards: Advanced Composition to Freshman English." *Freshman English News* 4.2 (1975): 1–2.

Moffett, James. "A Structural Curriculum in English." *Harvard Educational Review* 36 (1966): 17–28.

Rottenberg, Annette T. *Elements of Argument.* 2nd ed. New York. Bedford-St. Martin's, 1988.

Whitehead, Alfred North. *The Aims of Education* 1929. New York: Free, 1968.

Wilcox, Thomas W. *The Anatomy of College English.* San Francisco: Jossey, 1973.

Young, Richard E. "Concepts of Arts and the Teaching of Writing." *The Rhetorical Tradition and Modern Writing.* Ed. James J. Murphy. New York: MLA, 1982. 130–41.

5

What Is *Advanced* About Advanced Composition?: A Theory of Expertise in Writing

Michael Carter

It was impossible for Bernice Dicks to hide her discouragement as she described the state of advanced composition in 1982. Based on an exhaustive review of the literature—telling in its brevity—and a detailed survey, Dicks somberly announced that except for the fact that it is a nonfiction writing course with freshman composition as a prerequisite, advanced composition has distressingly eluded definition (173–78). It is neither fish nor fowl. Or, as a relative of mine used to say in explanation of why he disliked casseroles, it contains no histologically identifiable matter. Dicks summed up her findings this way:

> Unfortunately, the wealth of models [offered by this survey] suggests again that advanced composition may well prove impossible to define once and for all: if, as Peter Dowell at Emory wrote to me, "the content is at the discretion (or whim) of the individual instructor," then we really are no farther along toward a statement about the course than we were when CCCC started out in 1954 to pin the creature to the wall. (186)

And we have not come much farther since 1982. The difficulty in pinning the creature to the wall is that we can't identify it, we can't say what is advanced about advanced composition. In an earlier survey, Michael Hogan found that most teachers of advanced composition consider their courses extensions of freshman composition, as indicated by the fact that most of the textbooks used in advanced composition classes were freshman texts (22–23). Dicks also found that the lack of definition for advanced composition encouraged teachers simply to incorporate the same format they use in their freshman classes, "requiring a 'harder' textbook, more writing, and increased one-on-one attention" (181). Indeed, two of the most popular textbooks for advanced composition, one by Maxine Hairston and the other by Richard M. Coe, are nearly indistinguishable from most freshman rhetorics, differing in degree rather than in kind.

I believe, however, that advanced composition should be more than just a "harder" freshman course. If advanced composition is to have any viability at all, it must be founded on a theory that (1) shows how advanced composition is different in kind from freshman composition and (2) shows how advanced composition is developmentally related to freshman composition. The "harder" approach achieves only the latter.

In this paper I propose such a theory, which I call a theory of expertise in writing. The premise is that an advanced composition course should lead a student toward expertise in writing. The question, of course, is what is expertise in writing? Is it the ability to write without grammatical errors or to write with complex syntax? Is it the possession of a large repertory of structural models or of powerful composing strategies? Indeed, I suggest that one of the problems with teaching writing in general and certainly with teaching advanced composition in particular is that we do not know what it is that comprises expertise in writing. The theory that I offer here may help to solve this problem.

This theory of expertise in writing is founded on psychologists' research in expertise. At its most basic, I define the development of expertise as the movement from behavior that is governed by general process strategies to behavior that is governed by specialized knowledge. The development of expertise *in writing* is the movement from global writing strategies to sophisticated knowledge of special rhetorical situations. Expertise, then, is the result of specialized knowledge that comes from experience in a specific writing situation. As this knowledge grows, the writer is able to write within that situation (and others that are similar) much more quickly and efficiently. This concept of expertise in writing is particularly appropriate to this discussion of advanced composition because the concept offers a way to identify what advanced writing is. In addition, it points to a broader structure on which a full writing curriculum may be built.

The Relationship Between General and Specific Knowledge

The issue of expertise is crucial to education because our concept of *what* proficiency is and *how* we become proficient—that is, how we achieve expertise — rules our educational philosophy. In our century, the notion of expertise has been characterized by a pendulum swinging back and forth between general and specific knowledge.

At the beginning of this century, education was imbued with the generalist philosophy that had dominated teaching for many centuries. Generalists conceived of education as a mental discipline and the mind as a sort of muscle that must be strengthened by rigorous exercise. The best known of these Nautilus machines for the mind was Latin, the standard of mental regimen for centuries. The idea was that the mental discipline that one would gain by studying Latin could be transferred to performance in specific domains outside of Latin. This generalist theory of transferability, intuitive at best, was undermined early in the century by the psychologist E. L. Thorndike whose research in the transfer of learning demonstrated that learning one skill, however general, has little effect on performance in another skill. Thorndike's studies laid to rest, for a while, the muscle metaphor of education and encouraged educators to develop curricula that stressed specific instruction for specific skills — the rise of practical education (Glaser 93).

The swing back toward generalism was initiated by the information-processing boom of the sixties and seventies, the main advocates of which were cognitive psychologists whose goal was to understand human cognition through the use of computers. Early computers, of course, were simply very rapid calculators, programmed to work according to certain specific algorithms. The breakthrough for information-processing theorists came when they discovered that they could program computers to "think" the way people think, not by the specific formulas of algorithms but by heuristics (Dreyfus and Dreyfus 5–6). The epitome of the early "thinking" computers was Newell and Simon's *General Problem Solver,* a computer program that could solve a variety of problems using as its primary heuristic strategy a means-ends analysis (Newell and Simon 414–38). A study by Ernst and Newell showed that by focusing on this heuristic, *General Problem Solver* had acheived broad generality without any loss of specific problem-solving power. The implications of this research were all too clear: performance is based largely on an underlying strategic process that could be isolated, studied, and taught; thus, successful performance was a result of the application of powerful heuristic strategies. This research launched the general process movement of the seventies, characterized by courses in problem-solving techniques that, like Latin of old, promised general, transferable powers that would improve performance in many areas (Glaser 95–96). Expertise was once again considered mainly a function of generality — this time, general processes.

The general process movement seems to have suffered the same fate as Latin. Mayer reports that there is little evidence of the transferability of general process skills to specific areas of performance (344–

45). The problem is that the work of the information-processing theorists was based primarily on puzzles and games—context-free, "knowledge-lean" problems that demand human subjects to perform without the use of specialized knowledge or skills. In other words, the research results have been misleading: they highlighted the use of general procedures because that is all that was necessary for solving the kinds of problems the researchers used (Glaser 96).

Recent research on the differences between experts and novices demonstrates that expertise is a function of specialization.[1] Studies of experts in many fields—from chess players to physicists—have demonstrated that experts are successful in their fields because they bring to their performance "domain-specific knowledge" attained through much experience within that domain. Indeed, it is no accident that *expert* and *experience* share the same Latin root. Novices, on the other hand, are novices specifically because they lack this knowledge and are forced to rely on general process skills and surface-level features of a problem.[2]

Psychologist Robert Glaser offers schema theory as a way of explaining the significant role of domain-specific knowledge in expert performance. He describes schemata as modifiable structures that act much like theories: schemata are internal models that form the bases for testable hypotheses and may be modified if the hypotheses prove inadequate to experience. And also like theories, schemata enable us to make predictions and act on these predictions. Experts evidently have very highly organized schematic structures *related to the specific field of their expertise*. Expert schemata are developed and refined over a long time. The process begins with naive schemata or temporary models that, "when they are interrogated, instantiated, or falsified, help organize new knowledge and offer a basis for problem solving that leads to the formation of more complete and expert schemata." Thus, Glaser describes the process of knowledge acquisition as "the successive development of structures which are tested and modified or replaced in ways that facilitate learning and thinking" (101). Schema theory, then, explains how expert knowledge differs from the knowledge of novices and how that expert knowledge is developed.

Just as Thorndike did many years ago, expert-novice researchers have forced us to reevaluate our ideas of expertise. Can one become an expert by learning general skills that can be transferred to tasks in specific domains? Expert-novice researchers suggest not. Rather, expertise is very much a product of knowledge within the specific field, which allows the expert to act much more effectively and efficiently than those who do not possess that knowledge.

Educational psychology has returned to a domain-specific concept of expertise. But the search for a theory of expertise in writing demands an accounting of the relationship between general skills and specific knowledge, especially how specific knowledge is developed—that is, how expertise is achieved. Understanding this relationship will be crucial to understanding what is advanced about advanced composition.

One of the best explanations of the relationship between general skills and specific knowledge in the development of expertise may be found in *Mind Over Machine* by Hubert and Stuart Dreyfus, the former a philosopher and the latter a computer scientist. In this book, the Dreyfuses trace five stages in the acquisition of expertise. Though the primary purpose of their book is to demonstrate why artificial intelligence cannot achieve full human intelligence, the book also helps us understand what makes an expert.

In stage one, the novice learns "context-free rules," which means that he or she performs on the basis of a set of rules that are applied regardless of the situation. For example, a third-year medical student learns the procedures for taking a patient's history and physical and uses these procedures no matter who the patient is or what the problem is. The novice becomes an advanced beginner, stage two, with some experience in applying the rules and with the acquisition of more sophisticated context-free rules. Applying the rules in specific situations allows the learner to begin to see that the rules are meaningful, not a result of arbitrary decree. Rules begin to become situational as distinguished from context-free. Continuing the example, as a first-year resident the doctor applies the procedures of taking a history and physical in more specific situations but still has trouble pulling out the relevant data for diagnosis and treatment.

Stage three, or competence, comes with more experience in real situations and is marked by less of a reliance on rules and more of an adoption of hierarchical decision-making procedures. At this level, the performer has achieved a much greater awareness of the variables in a situation and must choose a plan to organize the variables in order to improve performance. Later in her residency, the doctor still has to rely on the rules of diagnosis and treatment but manages these rules more effectively and even knows when to break them.

The next stage is proficiency. Up to this point the learner's performance has been essentially rule governed; even when the rules were broken, performance was based on a conscious decision stemming from a perceived goal. Going beyond competence is to go beyond reliance on rules. At this stage, performance relies more on "holistic similarity recognition" than on the conscious decomposition of the features of a situation, more on know-how and intuition than on rationality. In other words, performance is based on the recognition of familiar situational patterns that are formed after much experience. As a chief resident, the doctor has seen so many patients that she hardly thinks about the rules anymore, depending instead on her experience to guide her response.

Expertise, the final stage, is marked by an even more fluid performance that is seldom based on analytic, conscious deliberation. The skill is so much a part of the performer that he or she is not really aware of it: experts do what works. There is little need to analyze a situation into decision and action because the expert has built up a large repertory of situations, each of which encompasses decision and action. Experts react intuitively to most situations without having to rely on rules or plans; instead, they rely on the familiarity that comes from experience (Dreyfus and Dreyfus 16–36). After working for a while in private practice, the doctor has developed a "feel" for patients and can elicit and process information she needs for diagnosis and treatment very quickly and efficiently.

According to the Dreyfuses' scenario, the development of expertise is the movement from a dependence on rules to guide behavior to a dependence on the *intuition* founded on experience within a particular domain. Expertise itself may be characterized by domain-specific knowledge, but the route to expertise begins in the realm of general rules that guide behavior. Looked at one way, the development of expertise may be defined as sloughing off the rules and strategies. Looked at another, it is an increasing reliance on knowledge developed in a specific domain. It is important to note, however, that the interaction of rules and domain-specific knowledge is not merely coincidental but causative. It is *because* of the increase in domain-specific knowledge that the performer needs to rely less and less on operational rules. And it is *because* operational rules demand a diminishing amount of cognitive energy that the performer can develop and use more and more sophisticated knowledge schemata. Thus, the two work together to help in the development of expertise.

This model suggests two key features for a theory of expertise. The first is that expertise is a function of specialization. No one can be an expert in general. The second feature is that the development of expertise is a process of moving from general skills to domain knowledge. General skills and context-free rules are a necessary step toward expertise. There are a few cases in which the intuition of expertise is generated without beginning at the early rule-guided stages, but such cases almost by definition fall into the category of *idiot savant*. But this developmental continuum can move in the reverse direction, too. It is necessary to fall back on a solid basis of rule-guided behavior at times when one is out of the domain of one's expertise (Glaser 102; Bransford et al. 1083). Returning to the example of the doctor, even though she is an expert in her own field, when she encounters a problem that is outside her specialization, she is once again a relative novice and must fall back on the rules and/or seek advice from experts.

The relationship between general skills and domain-specific knowledge also offers a model for learning, a concept of progress. The theory of expertise presents a concept of learning as moving toward expertise. Learners begin as novices, relying on the rules that guide performance. The act of learning may be understood as the development of more sophisticated schemata accompanied by the diminishing need for rules. Learning, however, need not always end in expertise; indeed, I would speculate that learning rarely leads to expertise, given the amount of experience that expertise demands. Any movement along the continuum toward expertise may be called learning.

Expertise: The Idea of an Advanced Composition

The purpose of this paper is to offer a way to describe expertise in writing. This concept is important to composition because our notions of expertise, whether recognized or not, must guide our research and pedagogy. It is particularly important to advanced composition, because the way we define expertise must indicate what we think is advanced about writing.

The theory of expertise has two major implications for the teaching of writing. First, expertise in writing is a function of specialization. There is no such thing as an expert writer in general. Writers become experts only within rhetorical contexts in which they gain much experience and facility. Instead of being an expert in all kinds of journalism, for instance, a writer may be an expert at writing market analyses for the *Wall Street Journal* or at writing movie reviews in the *New Yorker*. Instead of being an expert in all children's literature, a writer develops expertise in producing illustrated books for three- and four-year-olds or in writing young adult fiction. Thus, the domains within which writers develop the domain-specific knowledge that leads to expertise are rhetorical contexts.

Let me hasten to add that expertise in writing does not necessarily imply that writing becomes easy. Rather, expertise within a particular rhetorical context allows the writer to perform more efficiently within that context. This streamlining of performance is made possible by the diminishing necessity, as writers gain expertise, for calling on explicit rules to guide the writing act. And because writers spend less energy on process strategies, they can spend more energy on higher-level aspects of discourse. Writers who must write outside their areas of expertise must call again on general process strategies to guide their performance.

The second implication is that the development of expertise in writing is a movement from the application of general process skills to the application of specialized knowledge based on experience within a specific domain. Learning to write, then, means starting with generalizable skills and strategies practiced in generalized writing situations. By *generalized writing situations* I do not mean the *general* topics written to *general* audiences, which invite vacuous, *general* prose. Rather, I mean a wide variety of writing contexts or (a little farther along the continuum toward expertise) writing that focuses on the broad academic community. At this point, the emphasis of writing is more on the application of the generalizable skills and strategies than on the special characteristics of the kind of discourse. These may include such strategies as exploratory heuristics (looping, cubing, tagmemics, etc.), methods for identifying and analyzing audiences, tactics for organizing ideas, and so on.

At the middle point of this developmental continuum, general skills and specific knowledge bear an approximately equal influence on writing and writing pedagogy. To get to this level, writers have gained more control over the general strategies by using them in more specific contexts. Pedagogical concerns shift from teaching generalizable strategies to helping students apply those strategies in specific contexts; thus, the strategies become more specialized. A key part of this movement toward the specific is the concentration on a particular rhetorical context and a greater concern for the specialized features of that context. In short, writers learn to apply more specialized strategies to specific writing contexts. As writers go beyond this point toward expertise, they depend less and less on explicit strategies and rely more and more on the *intuition* developed through the experience of writing within a particular rhetorical context. Such expertise, of course, takes a long time to develop and is certainly beyond the expectations of a single year of freshman composition and probably even advanced college writing. The idea is to guide students *toward* expertise.

This application of the theory of expertise to writing has specific implications for advanced composition. I began this paper with Bernice Dick's lament for advanced composition. The problem was that most advanced composition courses were nothing more than "hard" freshman composition courses. I suggested that for advanced composition to be a viable course in the college curriculum it must be founded on a theory that (1) shows how advanced composition differs *in kind* from freshman composition and (2) shows how advanced composition is developmentally related to freshman composition. I think that the theory of expertise in writing meets both of these criteria.

First, the theory of expertise in writing provides an answer to the question, what is *advanced* about advanced composition? Whereas freshman composition is mainly concerned with more generalized discourse contexts and has as its goal the development of generalizable skills, advanced composition is mainly concerned with more specialized discourse contexts and has as its goal the specialization of general skills and the development of knowledge related to writing in specific fields. Thus, expertise is *not* defined simply as achieving greater facility with general skills, whether they be grammar, style, or process strategies. Rather, the purpose of the advanced composition course is to lead students toward the expertise of specialization.

The idea of specialization in advanced composition is not new. W. Ross Winterowd, for instance, distinguished between transferable skills and local skills and pointed to local skills as the focus for advanced composition. Richard Fulkerson divided discourse into the elements of writer, reader, text, and universe and recommended that advanced courses could allow the student to specialize in one of these, for example, courses in advanced self-expression or advanced rhetoric. J. C. Mathes set up the specialized writing categories of public discourse, social systems, and organizational communication, suggesting that each one offers certain advanced skills that advanced students must master. And Faigley and Hansen describe a writing-across-the-curriculum program in which students write in specialized contexts according to their majors: fine arts and humanities, social sciences, natural sciences and technologies, and business. Though the idea of specialization in advanced composition is not new, the theory of expertise provides a theoretical foundation for advanced composition that clearly distinguishes it from freshman composition.

It is the *discipline-specific* program that provides the clearest approach to specialization in writing. According to the theory I have presented, the goal of such advanced courses should be to lead students toward expertise in their disciplines by: (1) teaching them the role that writing plays in the construction of knowledge in their disciplines; (2) helping them analyze the discourse of the discipline so they can learn the specialized features of that discourse and the role that those features play in the discourse community; and (3) providing them opportunities for writing within the discipline, to apply the general strategies they have previously learned to specialized situations.

This idea of advanced composition as a discipline-specific course may raise fears in the hearts of composition teachers. We tend to see ourselves as generalists, yet the theory of expertise suggests that the focus of advanced composition is specialization, a suggestion that may generate doubts about our role in these courses. What sort of contribution could we make? I think that no matter what the teaching arrangement for such courses — composition teacher only, team teaching with a specialist, or specialist only — the composition specialist possesses skills and knowledge that are crucial to the course. According to the theory of expertise, experts writing within their own specialization are usually not aware of what makes their performance effective. *Our* expertise as writing specialists provides a corrective for the blindness that comes with expertise in other disciplines, the blindness that may not allow experts to see the specialized features of their discourse, the role of discourse in creating knowledge within their discourse communities, or the procedures they use when they write. So we experts in writing are crucial because we can bring to discipline-specific discourse our knowledge of discourse analysis, of knowledge structures in discourse communities, and of writing process. Whether we construct a course with the help of experts and teach it ourselves (e.g., Faigley and Hansen; Moore and Peterson) or guide those experts in teaching writing themselves (e.g., Fulwiler), writing teachers must be the keystone in building advanced writing courses, a role that could have the additional benefit of letting our colleagues in other fields discover that we are more than just the drill sergeants of grammar.

In addition to showing how advanced composition differs from freshman composition, the theory of expertise also shows how the two are related. The continuum from novice to expert suggests that expertise builds on general skills; thus, both general skills and specialization are important in the development of expertise. It is the role of earlier composition courses, particularly high school and college freshman courses, to teach students explicit strategies for the writing process, general strategies that students may apply in a variety of domains. Earlier courses should also lay the groundwork for discourse analysis, perhaps focusing on the relatively broad domain of writing in college. Advanced composition courses should build on this knowledge of strategies and metadiscourse to help students both understand and write more effectively in specific rhetorical contexts.

Another way of understanding this relationship is to go back to the Dreyfuses' five steps toward expertise. I would describe high school and freshman composition as leading students through the steps of beginner and advanced beginner in the context of academic and professional discourse, learning relatively context-free rules and applying them in such a way that the rules start to become situational. Advanced composition picks up at that point and leads students through competence and proficiency. Competence represents a mastery over the rules and a much greater awareness of how they apply to specific situations. Proficiency is characterized by a dependency less on rules and more on the intuition that comes from experience in writing within a particular context. Expertise itself is perhaps beyond the abilities of college students, requiring extensive experience within a field.

I have offered this theory of expertise in writing as one way of clearing up the identity crisis that advanced composition has suffered for so long. But I think that the theory also demonstrates the importance of advanced writing courses in colleges. It encourages us to take a wider perspective of growth in writing ability, to see the teaching of writing as part of a broader development of expertise. Indeed, the concept of expertise in writing provides both the justification and the theoretical structure for a full college writing curriculum, whether it is advanced writing courses offered in the English department or writing-across-the-curriculum courses taught by specialists in the field or a combination of both. If we limit writing instruction to the generalizable skills and relatively general writing contexts of the freshman course — or even the "harder" courses offered by some as advanced composition — then we are only partially doing our jobs as writing teachers. Our job is to lead students toward expertise in writing, a journey that freshman composition only begins.

Notes

1. Two excellent reviews of this research may be found in Bransford et al. and in Glaser. These reviews are particularly helpful because they discuss the research in terms of its educational implications

2. See, for instance, Bransford et al. 1079; Chi, Glaser, and Rees; Chi, Feltovich, and Glaser; Larkin, "Teaching Problem Solving" and "The Role of"; and Schoenfeld and Herrmann.

Works Cited

Bransford, John, et al. "Teaching Thinking and Problem Solving: Research Foundations." *American Psychologist* 41 (1986): 1078–89.

Chi, Michelene T. H., Robert Glaser, and Ernest Rees. "Expertise in Problem Solving." *Advances in the Psychology of Human Intelligence.* Vol. 1. Ed. Robert J. Sternberg. Hillsdale, NJ: Erlbaum, 1982. 7–75.

Chi, Michelene T. H., Paul J.Feltovich, and Robert Glaser. "Categorization and Representation of Physics Problems by Experts and Novices." *Cognitive Science* 5 (1981): 121–52.

Coe, Richard M. *Form and Substance: An Advanced Rhetoric.* New York: Wiley, 1981.

Dicks, Bernice W. "State of the Art in Advanced Expository Writing: One Genus, Many Species." *Journal of Advanced Composition* 3 (1983): 172–91.

Dreyfus, Hubert L., and Stuart E. Dreyfus. *Mind Over Machine: The Power of Human Intuition and Expertise in the Era of the Computer.* New York: Free, 1986.

Ernst, George W., and Allen Newell. *GPS: A Case Study in Generality and Problem Solving.* New York: Academic, 1969.

Faigley, Lester, and Kristine Hansen. "Learning to Write in the Social Sciences." *College Composition and Communication* 36 (1985): 140–49.

Fulkerson, Richard. "Some Theoretical Speculations on the Advanced Composition Curriculum." *Journal of Advanced Composition* 1 (1980): 9–12.

Fulwiler, Toby. "How Well Does Writing Across the Curriculum Work?" *College English* 46 (1984): 113–25.

Glaser, Robert. "Education and Thinking: The Role of Knowledge." *American Psychologist* 39 (1984): 93–104.

Hairston, Maxine. *Successful Writing.* 2nd ed. New York: Norton, 1986.

Hogan, Michael P. "Advanced Composition: A Survey." *Journal of Advanced Composition* 1 (1980): 21–29.

Larkin, Jill H. "The Role of Problem Representation in Physics." *Mental Models.* Ed. Diedre Gentner and Albert L. Stevens. Hilldale, NJ: Erlbaum, 1983. 75–98.

——. "Teaching Problem Solving in Physics: The Psychological Lab." *Problem Solving and Education; Issues in Teaching and Research.* Ed. David T. Tuma and Frederic Reif. Hillsdale, NJ: Erlbaum, 1980. 111–25.

Mathes, J. C. "A Taxonomy of Communication Acts for the Design of Advanced Writing Courses." *Journal of Advanced Composition* 1 (1980): 53–57.

Mayer, Richard E. *Thinking, Problem Solving, Cognition.* New York: Freeman, 1983.

Moore, Leslie E., and Linda H. Peterson. "Convention as Connection: Linking the Composition Course to the English and College Curriculum." *College Composition and Communication* 37 (1986): 466–77.

Newell, Allen, and Herbert A. Simon. *Human Problem Solving.* Englewood Cliffs, NJ: Prentice, 1972.

Schoenfeld, Alan H., and Douglas J. Herrmann. "Problem Perception and Knowledge Structure in Expert and Novice Mathematical Problem Solvers." *Journal of Experimental Psychology* 8 (1982): 484–94.

Winterowd, W. Ross. "Transferable and Local Writing Skills." *Journal of Advanced Composition* 1 (1980): 1–3.

6

Advanced Composition as Fishing Pole: Principles, Processes, Practices

Richard M. Coe

Advanced Composition is an ambiguous title, affixed to a wide variety of courses—most of them useful, not all of them truly advanced. Indeed, "Advanced Composition" often serves students who, after completing two or three years at the university, have been sent back to the English department because professors in their majors judge that they did not master what "should" have been taught in freshman composition. Courses for such students are literally re-medial, for they reteach essentially the same material as regular composition, with perhaps some special emphasis on the particular tasks that face upper-level university students. One could quibble over titling such courses. Advanced Composition—I am about to do so—but the courses do meet a real need. Because they cover essentially the same material as first-year composition courses (and often use textbooks written for first-year courses), however, such courses present few special pedagogical problems.

When you take a genuinely advanced course in anything, you do not expect it to be essentially the same as the regular course; after a brief review of basic principles and standard processes, you expect to learn sophisticated principles and subtle processes that advance you beyond ordinary competence. Insofar as Advanced Composition is advanced composition, our first, somewhat tautological axiom should be that it must advance beyond ordinary composition. At least in the United States, this means beyond freshman composition, the course

71

that, in principle, brings everyone up to standard, up to minimal competence (if I may be excused the phrase), so that they can write what the university requires them to write.

If freshman composition is a preparation for writing at the university—and I think that is what it most commonly is, especially in its incarnation as a "service" course—then advanced composition should be for students already competent at such writing. What would you teach the students you gave A's in freshman composition for mastering most of what that course covers? What would you teach the students who already write well enough to get consistent A's on their term papers in their majors if they asked to learn whatever comes next in composition? Beyond traditional rules and precepts, beyond Strunk and White and the research paper, beyond "prewriting," freewriting, and journals, beyond straightforward applications of rhetorical concepts like purpose and audience, what is there to teach?

Defining advanced composition as a course for those who have mastered the standard writing curriculum does engender a few problems. For one, our discipline is far from unanimous about what should be taught in ordinary composition courses (and the majority of those who teach writing are not even part of our disciplinary community). And the law of uneven development most certainly applies to the development of writing abilities. Most advanced writers still retain a few elementary problems: one still dangles modifiers, another's "natural" voice sounds like gobbledygook, yet another punctuates by "breath pause" with idiosyncratic results—and many still suffer from overly self-critical, painfully inefficient writing processes. Still, the word *advanced* requires drawing a line somewhere somehow.

Very tentatively and minimally, let me suggest that those who have mastered regular composition

1. Avoid most errors of spelling, grammar, and usage, especially what we might call the "mortal sins," (i.e., those errors that especially upset readers of job applications, proposals, term papers, and other such documents);[1]

2. Usually write reasonably clear, correct sentences and unified paragraphs and avoid "wrong words" and "awkward" sentences (at least when in good control of the subject matter);

3. Know, at least approximately, the conventional forms of academic discourse and follow the most important norms of academic discourse, especially the one that demands opinions be backed by reasons and evidence;

4. Have some strategies for discovering material (both in the library and in their minds); and

5. Have some sense of audience and how to write purposefully for the audiences they normally address.

My university's advanced composition course developed as it did partly because the preceding describes the students who first registered for it. And our noncredit writing courses developed similarly because they were aimed not at secretaries, entry-level professionals, and lower management, but at upper and middle management and professional writers, people who were already succeeding as writers. What should one teach such students?

The most common answer to this question brings us to specialized writing courses. These range from writing for science and technology (sometimes taught under the guise of writing-across-the-curriculum) to business writing, technical writing, proposal writing, and other such courses. These courses generally review the principles taught in regular composition and apply those principles to special writing tasks. Like remedial courses for advanced students, specialized writing courses are important and legitimate. Though these courses may not teach any advanced principles or processes of composition—indeed, they sometimes focus on writing tasks that are intellectually and rhetorically simpler than a term paper—these courses typically do teach students to handle writing tasks they will face in their majors and after graduation.

These courses, I should add, are most consistent with traditional assumptions. Traditional composition courses, though they dabble in process, essentially teach good form and the basic modes of discourse. Thus, it makes sense within the traditional framework to define advanced composition as instruction in special forms and modes. But this definition makes less sense within process assumptions. If one believes in a process approach, the key question should become, what is advanced process?[2]

Let me make a sharp distinction. I am not objecting to specialized writing courses. Indeed, our noncredit writing program at Simon Fraser offers many, from proposal writing to cookbook writing. We also offer, within our engineering department, a credit course in Engineering Communications. The issue is not whether, but how to teach such writing courses—how to create proper advanced university courses that develop students' understanding of "how words work in discourse" (Richards 8) while applying that understanding to a particular genre of writing.

By way of what Kenneth Burke might call a heuristic tour de force, let us ask what advanced composition might be if it were neither remedial composition for "advanced" students nor composition of specialized forms. What are advanced principles of composition? What is advanced process? What do advanced writers do that intermediate writers do not? What do those who write as professionals do that those who have just mastered freshman composition still do not know how to do? What should students be able to do before we may say they no longer need writing teachers?

A Prototype

As taught in philosophy and composition courses, definition is a negative process, a division between A and *not-A,* which may lead to invidious as well as useful distinctions. As performed outside philosophy and composition classes, definition ordinarily proceeds more by prototype (cf. Gardner, ch. 12, esp. 346), and that is what I proffer here. I certainly do not mean to suggest a prescription for what advanced composition should be—our courses were created in response to particular students and a particular departmental mandate—but I hope the following description of key features of Simon Fraser University's advanced writing courses will be usefully suggestive.

The first time I taught advanced composition at SFU in 1980 I had a class of 17 students, almost all of whom were already good writers. Few had difficulty getting A's on term papers in other courses. Few made significant errors of spelling, grammar, or usage. Most already understood what can be learned form Strunk and White (and would also have been offended by Strunk and White, for the reasons articulated by Worby and Ohmann). Most had a good sense of their normal audience (i.e., of how professors read when they grade) and of conventional term paper form.

Five of the 17 (four women and a male Marxist) had some variation of this complaint/desire: "I know how to write to get A's on term papers, and I know how to write in my own voice to satisfy myself; what I want to learn is how to write in my own voice and still get A's on my papers." As I understood it, this was a statement about writing with contradictory purposes (to get A's, to learn, to feel good about what one has created) for contradictory audiences (the grader and oneself) on contradictory occasions (external evaluation and a learning experience).

Though many of my colleagues have significant doubts about Richards's literary criticism, our advanced composition course is founded on the assumption underlying his *Philosophy of Rhetoric,* that general principles of how words work in discourse can be learned and applied to particular writing tasks and problems. Our advanced composition course explicitly stresses theory—both because theory is useful (at least to those who know how to apply theory, which should include all university graduates) and because the belief that people should understand why they do what they do is a defining value of humanistic education. Only those who grasp theory, explicitly or intuitively, can adapt basic principles to new contexts.

Believing this, we go beyond regular composition by demanding more independence, which means both more theory and more self-help (including heuristics for self-help). We go beyond regular composition by covering advanced subject matter, such as paragraphs with two topics, contradictions of voice, collaborative writing, writing on non-"narrow" topics, writing for mixed audiences and "popular" audiences (hence issues of readability and techniques like appositional definition). We turn students inward to investigate their own writing processes, and we turn students outward to investigate specific discourse communities. Though pedagogy varies from course to course and instructor to instructor, we share the folllowing defining goals:

1. We want students to come to understand their own creative writing processes—and how to intervene in their own processes to improve the quality of both process and product. They should acquire techniques for dealing with process problems (e.g., procrastination).

2. We want students to understand writing as a social, communicative process that takes place in discourse communities. They should learn to deal with complex rhetorical contexts (e.g., contradictory purposes, multiple and/or hostile audiences). They should come to understand the implications of rhetorical contexts by writing for widely divergent purposes, audiences, and occasions (including nonspecialist audiences with no better than average—say, grade 10—reading abilities: the public).

3. We want students to understand the relationship between form and process, structure and strategy. Thus, they should learn how to initiate themselves into new discourse communities by analyzing discourses to reveal the functions of formal continuities. Ideally, they should also learn how to invent new forms for new purposes.

For both humanistic and practical reasons, students in their *last* writing course should learn how to help themselves thereafter. Our typical opening set of activities and assignments, therefore, helps students examine their own processes, describe their own problems, define their own goals, and monitor their own progress. Our typical closing assignment helps students learn how to teach themselves any particular type of writing they may later need to master. In between, the course confronts students with writing tasks that involve realistically complex (even contradictory) purposes, audiences, and occasions. It embodies both *generative rhetoric* and a New Rhetorical understanding of form-in-process.

Process Analysis

Our advanced composition instruction typically begins by focusing students' attention on their own motives, goals, and writing processes. This may be good pedagogy in any writing course, but it is especially important for advanced students. For one thing, many of their goals turn out to be process goals: to produce writing with less pain and/or procrastination; to manage their writing time more efficiently; to produce more per hour, day, or week. For another thing, when they run into writing blocks or other problems after they have left our course, they should know how to deal with them — and that means knowing how to intervene in their own writing processes. As Linda Flower has written, "Good writers...guide their own creative process[es]" (45).

This principle underlies not only our four-credit advanced composition course, but also our noncredit, special genre Writing Program courses. Our proposal-writing course, for instance, is a two-day intensive, which costs $275 and is taken by people who already write proposals at work, who know perfectly well what a proposal is and what proposals look like in their specialties. What they want to learn is how to write more effective proposals — without wasting time. Aside from examples (all of which have to do with proposals), the first day (the first half) of the course is indistinguishable from any of our advanced writing courses in its focus on teaching students to guide their own writing processes.

We teach students, when they have problems, to pay attention to their writing processes, to look at the relationship between process and product (cf. Della-Piana, Coe and Gutierrez, and Coe, *Process* ch. 1). We teach many standard process techniques — freewriting, heuristics, audience analysis, cut-and-paste revision, and so on — but always urge individual students to adopt particular techniques in relation to self-defined goals. We also teach new applications of standard technique (e.g., overcoming a writing problem by freewriting not on the topic, but about the problem; see Hungerford 23–27).

A first assignment might ask students to write about their own motives, strengths, weaknesses, problems, and goals as writers. Here is one such assignment:

> Describe as specifically as you can the strong and weak points of your writing. Wherever you can, give concrete examples.
>
> Be sure to list strengths as well as weaknesses. Be sure to consider not only sentence-level strengths and weaknesses, but also strengths and weaknesses in such areas as finding good material, insight, organization, and adapting to particular audiences.
>
> A good way to approach this assignment is to review 10 or 12 fairly recent writings. If you are a student, it might be particularly useful to use papers written for courses you took from several differ-

ent instructors in the past year or two. If you write at work, try to choose writing that has been edited or commented upon by several different supervisors. Then generalize any feedback you received and any insights you now have about the strong points and flaws of those writings.

Commenting on an early version of this assignment, which asked students to "describe your main writing problems," Richard Adler said his first response was, "Good gravy, I hope this assignment didn't work."

> ...I immediately scanned the next two paragraphs for the results. I was greatly relieved to find the statement, "...this assignment confused my students. In the first place, most of them did not know what their main writing problems were." My past experience was once again borne out. If the students *knew* what their problems were, the odds are high that they would have corrected them.

I do believe that defining a problem precisely improves the odds of devising a solution, but I am not quite so sanguine as Adler that knowing what a problem is leads so frequently to solving it. I therefore ask each student, after doing the assignment, to reduce it to two lists: major strengths and main problems (in rough order of priority). Each student then rephrases each problem positively as a *goal* (and also adds forward-looking goals, based on their motives for taking the course, such as mastering a new type of writing). Then, in class and in conference, I help students flesh out each goal with (1) a plan for achieving it without undermining strengths, (2) a time limit or schedule, and (3) criteria for judging to what extent the goal has been achieved. The plan must say how the new ability will be integrated in the student's writing process.

While this is going on, the students are also—perhaps more importantly—analyzing their own individual writing processes. The day they turn in their first assignment—and it could be any first assignment, not necessarily the one just explained—I ask them to freewrite at length about how they wrote it. I have them take that freewriting home and add two types of detail: (1) what they may view as "nonwriting" behavior (e.g., washing the dishes before starting to draft) and (2) what happened on paper (e.g., if the freewriting says, "And then I read the draft over and fixed a few sentences," I want to know what sort of "fixing"). Finally, I have them turn this narrative into a process analysis by adding comments about whether what they did in this case is typical (and if not, about what does usually happen). The reason for this staged assignment is that, if simply asked to write an analysis off their own writing processes, students too often write about some ideal process (e.g., how they write the one time in ten when they manage to get started well in advance of the deadline).

When students hold their lists of problems next to their process analyses, they often have Eureka responses, for a weakness in the written product is often a direct and obvious consequence of some weakness in the process. At any event, the means for dealing with virtually any writing problem should include a decision about when during the writing process that writer will pay attention to that problem. Thus a problem like

I make too many unsupported generalizations

is transformed into

From now on I will underline each generalization in my draft. I will make sure I have qualified each and explained how I know it is true. And I will give an example. By next month I will no longer receive complaints about unsupported generalizations, and by the end of the year I will no longer need to use this underlining procedure.

The solution is precisely located—during early revision, just after drafting—and turns on adding an extra procedure to the student's writing process.

While the students are doing these analyses, they are learning, both in class and in their assigned readings, about the composing process. They are learning various techniques for invention, revision, audience analysis, and so forth. But they are not learning "the right way to write." The assumption is that they already have writing processes, and the first axiom is "if it ain't broke, don't fix it." They learn about the composing process so that they can decide how best to change whatever aspects of their existing processes are contributing to their problems.

Rhetorical Contexts

Although composition specialists routinely assert that students should learn to write for a wide variety of purposes and audiences (cf., for example, NCTE, "Standards"), most university composition courses teach, at best, a rather narrow range. Sometimes without any explicit discussion off the nature of academic audiences, we teach students structures appropriate for writing with intellectual rigor to well-educated audiences, most often specialists. At least in its incarnation as a service course, freshman composition is primarily instruction in academic writing. For all our references to "the general reader," we do not ordinarily teach students how to communicate technical subject matter to general readers of average education (which in North America these days means roughly grade 10 reading ability or lower). Both these types of writing are important and difficult, and involve drastically different applications of the general principles of composition.

One way to focus students' attention is to insist that each piece of writing have a specifically defined rhetorical context, and to respond and grade accordingly. This rhetorical context may be stipulated in the assignment or, more often, stipulated by the student. In either case, I insist that it be typed on the title page. Then I respond to (and grade) each piece of writing according to my estimate of how well it would achieve the stated purpose(s) with the stipulated reader(s) on the specific occasion(s). The ultimate criterion becomes Donald Murray's question: "Does it work?" If in my estimate the piece of writing would totally fail to achieve its purpose(s) in reality, then it fails in my course—which, as in a real writing situation, means not an *F* but a rewrite.

Significantly, the primary role of the instructor becomes not judge, not critic, not even reader—but editor. That is, the instructor evaluates each student's manuscript just as an editor does, by imagining how well it would work, how well it would achieve its purpose(s) with its intended readers on the likely occasion(s)—and then by giving advice about how it might be revised to work better. (To assure a wide range of rhetorical problem solving, I also insist each student write at least once with the purpose of presenting complex, specialized material to a nonspecialized audience that reads at or below the grade 10 level.[3])

Imagining realistic rhetorical contexts usually means confronting contradictory purposes and audiences, which are quite common in real writing situations. Confronted, for instance, with this sentence from a government brochure on "conjugal violence," "Abused women can seek help from establishments in the health and social services network, namely the local community service centres and the social service centres," students should be led to see the contradiction between the writer's overt purpose (encouraging battered women to seek help) and the writer's tacit purpose (satisfying a supervisor by emphasizing a verbose description of the department's network). Can we rewrite to achieve both purposes, or must this writer make the hard choice? Our textbooks talk about writing with *a* purpose, for *the* audience; they do not give much advice about multiple and conflicting purposes, audiences, occasions. Advanced composition courses should.

Generative Rhetoric

Most of our students at SFU have had considerable instruction on the level of words and sentences. They often say that what they want is to "improve my style," and much of their revising is defined by a desire to evade two marginal comments—"wrong word" and "awk"—but where they are weakest, where they need most help is "beyond the sentence" (and especially beyond the paragraph). I often suspect this is because form has been taught in traditional terms (that is, inaccurately and dogmatically) or not taught at all (because it is supposed to arise organically from subject matter or process).

Our approach to form, organization, arrangement, *dispositio* is not traditional (though it may be classical). It is rather in keeping with New Rhetorical conceptions put forth by Richards and Burke in the 1930s, more recently espoused by Christensen, Berthoff, and D'Angelo, and elegantly argued by Phelps just a few years ago (see Coe, *Toward a Grammar* 19−22). For all the ways in which these rhetoricians do not see eye to eye, they all see writing as a forming process, all put form in relation to function and process. Traditional composition instruction treated form as textual. Consequently, form became procrustean — matter that would not fit the standard structure was chopped off; other parts of draft might be stretched absurdly to fill the form. Early process advocates objected to formalism because they remembered it was artificial, procrustean, even algorithmic (cf. Dixon). But the distinguishing feature of what one might call the new formalism is that it studies form in process, formal structures as they function in social and individual creative and communicative processes.

Burke, for instance, suggests a poem is what happens when an intuition (i.e., an inchoate insight, an unarticulated strategy for verbally encompassing a situation) is juxtaposed with an appropriate (poetic) form (*Language* 32−37). He argues that writers who deny this function are unconscious of their own process (or dishonest). If form is, as Burke asserts, "an arousing and fulfillment of desires" (*Counter-Statement* 124), it is not just textual but psychological. And if it is psychological, it is also social.

We assume that rhetorical structures are *pre-pared* ways of responding, that they embody a social memory of standard strategies for responding to types of situations the community encounters repeatedly. When writers see past the uniqueness of a particular situation and recognize it as familiar, they activate (at least provisionally) a structure they have previously decided is generally appropriate to that type of situation. New types of situations or purposes, of course, often call for new strategies, which may be embodied in new structures (cf. Coe, "Rhetoric 2001"; also Davis and other feminists).

We have various pedagogical strategies for helping students grasp this functional, contextual conception of form. One is to teach them several forms for the same general function (such as classical and Rogerian persuasion), thus confronting them with the implications of formal choices (cf. Coe, "Apology," esp. 24−26). Another is to help them analyze the functional implications of prescribed structures (e.g., the parts of a scientific report or of a proposal), to see form as heuristic. When this analysis leads to contradictions (e.g., between their communicative purposes and the standard structure of term papers in their majors), we try to help them understand and perhaps sublate those contradictions—as experienced writers often can (cf., for example, MacDougall).[4] Through the writing tasks we assign, we lead them to understand formal rhetorical structures in relation to rhetorical contexts and discourse communities.

Product Analysis

Instead of teaching paticular types of writing—there are, after all, so many, and the world is changing too quickly to allow us to predict accurately which our students will need five or ten years hence—we teach METAHEUR, a heuristic for analyzing any particular type of writing in order to learn it. This becomes something of a test: have students mastered the principles of composition well enough to use them independently to analyze new material? It is also a base: students should emerge with confidence that they can, in the future, teach themselves any new genre they need to write.

The crux of the assignment is the heuristic, which attempts to make conscious and explicit much of what freelance writers do before adapting a piece to a particular medium.[5] The assignment attempts also to concretize the concept of discourse community as both a generative and constraining context for writing. One reason this tends to be a final assignment is that the questions make more sense to students toward the end of the course, after they have met concepts like *cumulative sentence* and *level of generality*.

The students are told to choose a specific type of writing—feminist criticism of Shakespeare, storybooks for young children, feature articles for ski magazines, term papers that get *A*'s from literature professors—and then to create a mini-manual for people who might want to do that type of writing. Although they may refer to published manuals as secondary sources, this writing must be empirical, based on the students' analyses of samples of the discourse—because one object of the assignment is to create self-reliance and self-confidence. (I also encourage students to do this assignment collaboratively.)

Thus METAHEUR guides writers to a description of the parameters within which a particular type of writing should be produced. (See figure 6–1.) This heuristic helps generate a description of the constraints within which writers produce that type of writing. The assignment is based on the assumption that the nature of such constraints and their priority varies from one discourse set to another. And, paradoxically, because the immediate focus is on written products, the success of the assignment depends upon the students' prior understanding of writing as process as well as on their understanding of the practical relationship between structure and strategy, product and process.[6]

Figure 6–1
Metaheur

Subject Matter

1. What kind of material is usually treated? Does there seem to be a shared heuristic that some or all of the writers use to generate their material? Could you invent such a heuristic? Is there any sort of material that is noticeably avoided?

2. Do the writers seem to share approaches, methods, or techniques for handling the material? How are writings focused in this discourse? Are there certain key terms, root metaphors, or standard analogies that recur in this discourse? Are there "buzz words"?

Rhetorical Context

3. What basic purposes does the writing serve? Is it primarily expressive, explanatory, persuasive, or literary? Is there a "hidden agenda" beyond the overt purposes? Are distinct purposes emphasized in different parts? What specific functions does this type of writing serve within its discourse community?

4. Who reads this type of writing? Why? What do you know—and what assumptions do the writers seem to be making—about the knowledge, attitudes, beliefs, and vested interests of the readers?

5. Where is this type of writing usually published? Is it likely to be read casually or seriously, for entertainment or for use? If the writing must be accepted by one or more editors before it reaches its readers, what can you surmise about these editors' motives and criteria? How would you name and describe the discourse community that reads this type of writing?

6. Is there a common persona that the writers adopt? Can you detect shared values? Do the writers take a particular stance and, if so, what does it imply about readers' expectations? How formal are the word choice and usage?

Structure and Style

7. Is there a standard format or typical structure for the whole writing or any part of it? Which of the basic patterns of development are used regularly? Are different patterns used in different parts? How do the writings begin? How do the writings end? What sorts of transitions predominate? How long are the paragraphs and how are they typically structured? Do most paragraphs have topic sentences (and if so, where)? What is the relationship among levels of generality within typical paragraphs and for whole pieces of writing?

8. How long are most of the writings in your sample? How long and difficult

continued

Figure 6-1
Continued

are the words and sentences? What is the level of readability? Do any particular sentence patterns stand out? How many sentences are ten or more words longer than the average sentence? How many are five or more words shorter than average? Is the style nominalized or is more meaning carried by verbs and adverbs? To what extent are there overt figures of speech? Is there a standard jargon? How would you rate this writing on a scale of abstraction? Does the text have texture (i.e., many cumulative or embedded modifiers)?

9. What is missing? Are there any structures that are noticeably avoided? What unique features does this discourse have that were not elicited by the preceding questions?

10. What other significant features characterize this type of writing?

In Sum

Through this prototype course description, I have tried to suggest some genuinely advanced directions a composition course might take. Amidst the pressures of the "eighties" to be pragmatic and provide students with immediately useful "job skills," I try to remember the old adage about the virtues of giving a hungry person a fishing pole instead of a fish. This advanced composition course — especially the opening and closing assignments — empowers students to learn without teachers. Although rigorous and demanding considerable discipline, although based on recent research and recent theory, this is in one critical sense a "sixties" course: it attempts to do what really ought to be done instead of settling, in the way of the "eighties," for what is "possible." It empowers students by helping them grasp principles and develop abilities that allow them to get beyond needing teachers to help them handle whatever comes next. It works well at Simon Fraser University. I hope it also suggests directions that might be usefully explored elsewhere.

Notes

1. Some conventions of grammar, punctuation, and usage are more important than others. The following is a short list of "mortal sins," which often lead readers to judge a writer illiterate, hence unintelligent and not worthy of their attention. Though this judgment may be unfair, it is real (see Hairston).

Faulty agreement: subject-verb or pronoun-antecedent
Unclear or ambiguous pronoun reference
Ambiguous dangler

Faulty and ambiguous parallelism

Apostrophe errors

Sentence fragment or comma splice (of the sort that indicates a lack of "sentence sense")

Run-on (fused) sentence

Blatantly unidiomatic expression (especially of the sort that indicates second-language or dialectic interference)

An excessive number of errors that would otherwise be merely "venial sins."

2. I do not use the terms *form* or *traditional* lightly. As Linda Robertson emphasizes (376−78), there is a sharp dichotomy between traditionalists, defined by their formalism, and those who have raised the banner of process. So sharp is this dichotomy, so clear is it to the advocates of process that formalism is the mark of the enemy, that it sometimes seems impossible to have a dispassionate discussion about form and structure in composition (though, obviously, almost all of us teach it, one way or another, from time to time). Indeed, I have been accused of giving succor to the enemy for trying to discuss how form, structure, and the modes of discourse might be reconceived and taught within the framework of a New Rhetorical process approach. For a fuller discussion of the distinctions between traditional and various process approaches to developing writing abilities, see Berlin, Faigley, and Coe, "Apology" 13−15.

3. I started making this demand after reading a letter written to an adult basic literacy group by the Solicitor–General of Canada. His letter included sentences like these: "It seems clear to me, therefore, that if we are to address this problem, we must do much more to stimulate interest and, even more importantly, to allay the anxieties that now play a large part in deterring inmates from entering the school program. . . . The granting of privileges will not be denied to inmates not participating in Adult Basic Education, but participation would be a positive factor when the granting of such privileges is under consideration. . . . It is perfectly appropriate for literacy skills to be one of the factors considered in the granting of parole. . . . We now believe that the institutions should, wherever possible, ask for the same prerequisite skills that are demanded elsewhere, and we hope that this approach will not be seen as punitive, but rather, as an incentive to acquire the necessary education." Why, I wondered, would an intelligent, well-educated politician write such sentences to an adult basic literacy group. It occurred to me that he, and the staffer who presumably drafted the letter, may not know how to write sentences that can be understood by people who read well below university levels — that *they* are in this sense functionally illiterate (i.e., incapable of performing a literacy task required by their work). And then it occurred to me that they could have passed through my composition courses without necessarily acquiring this important ability. Since I regularly inveigh against gobbledygook and government documents addressed to the public in prose beyond the average person's reading ability, I decided I had to take more responsibility here.

4. Whenever I use the word *sublate* in a manuscript addressed to English teachers, some editor always asks me to define it. Why, I am not entirely sure, for the work appears in my *Webster's New Collegiate Dictionary*, and both

editors and English teachers presumably own dictionaries. But I am convinced there is some significance in the pattern. *Sublate* is a key word, the English equivalent of the German *aufhebung* — except that *aufhebung* is a perfectly ordinary word, understood by ordinary Germans, whereas *sublate* is a somewhat technical, philosophical term. *Sublate* is a key word because it can open the door to dialectical thinking, something that English speakers, perhaps influenced by several centuries of Anglo-American empiricism and pragmatism, tend to find particularly difficult. *Sublate* means to conserve and to transcend at the same time. Linearly logical thinkers tend to find that a contradiction (which it is, logically), but this contradictory concept can help writers (and others) avoid reducing contradictions to simplistic either/or choices. Besides, just about every major change I can think of involved both a transcendence and a conservation of what existed before. Somehow I keep thinking that if people knew the word *sublate* they might stop being surprised by this fact about the nature of change.

5. The undergraduate students on our main campus are often amazed to learn that freelance writers will prepare to write an article by researching not only their subject but also the magazine in which they intend to publish. The students who take our downtown, noncredit writing courses — for the most part, people who already write successfully in their work — are quite the contrary of amazed. I think this contrast says something about how traditional composition instruction, though it may prepare students for academic writing, fails to prepare them to write in other contexts. Though it claims to teach the principles of good writing, traditional composition instruction actually teaches one particular type of discourse. Though one may argue that such instruction is appropriate in courses which prepare students to write at the university, it is not so clearly appropriate to more advanced writing courses.

6. Just as the result of the opening process assignment was formally a proposal (encompassing both supralineal process analysis and a problem-solution structure), so the result of this assignment is formally causal explanation by analysis of contextual constraints (see Coe, *Process*, 359–70).

The theoretical assumption is that writing is a stochastic, equifinal, and multifinal process. The writing process is always purposive, hence not random, but stochastic (from the Greek, to aim, to guess) because it is more often goal-seeking or goal oriented than goal-directed (i.e., stochastic as the term is used in system theory and cybernetics). There may be more than one satisfactory process for producing any particular type of writing (hence *equifinal*). And a variety of written texts may satisfactorily fulfill the same particular purpose (hence *multifinal*). This terminology comes from that attempt to model *organized complexity* — a good title for the writing process — which goes under the name of General System Theory.

This theoretical tangent has multiple implications, a few of which I have discussed elsewhere. One key implication is that a complex stochastic process like writing is not best described by attempting to follow temporally as writers write — because the whole point is that, efficiency aside, a writer may work in *any* order as long as the final product is satisfactory. The process is best understood by describing not a writer's behavior, but the system within which that behavior makes sense (cf. Cooper), especially the parameters of the task and how various writers adapt to them. Though different writers may perform the process using various techniques in distinct sequences these parameters define and explain the limits to individual differences.

Works Cited

Adler, Richard R. "Response" to Richard M. Coe, "The Practicalities and Politics of Error." *Language, Culture and Curriculum.* Ed. Kenneth Reeder and Donald C. Wilson. Vancouver: Centre for the Study of Curriculum and Instruction Monograph (University of British Columbia), 1978. 20–22.

Berlin, James A. "Contemporary Composition: The Major Pedagogical Theories." *College English* 44 (1982): 765–77.

Berthoff, Ann E. *Forming/Thinking/Writing: The Composing Imagination.* Portsmouth, NH: Boynton/Cook, 1982.

Burke, Kenneth. *Counter–Statement.* 1931. Berkeley: U of California P, 1968.

——. *Language as Symbolic Action.* Berkeley: U of California P, 1966.

Christensen, Frances. "A Generative Rhetoric of the Paragraph." *College Composition and Communication* 16 (1965): 144–56

Coe, Richard M. "An Apology for Form; or, Who Took the Form Out of the Process." *College English* 49 (1987): 13–28.

——. *Process, Form, and Substance,* 2nd ed. Englewood Cliffs, NJ: Prentice, 1990.

——. "Rhetoric 2001." *Freshman English News* 3 (1974): 1–13.

——. *Toward a Grammar of Passages.* Carbondale, IL: Southern Illinois UP, 1988.

Coe, Richard M., and Kris Gutierrez. "Using Problem-Solving and Process Analysis to Help Students Solve Writing Problems." *College Composition and Communication* 32 (1981):262–71.

Cooper, Marilyn M. "The Ecology of Writing." *College English* 48 (1986): 364–75.

D'Angelo, Frank. *A Conceptual Theory of Rhetoric.* Cambridge, MA: Winthrop, 1975.

Davis, Fran. "A Practical Assessment of Feminist Pedagogy: Work in Progress." *Inkshed* 7.5/8.1 (November 1988); 1–3.

Della-Piana, Gabriel. "Research Strategies for the Study of Revision Processes in Writing Poetry." *Research on Composing:Points of Departure.* Ed. Charles Cooper and Lee Odell. Urbana, IL: NCTE, 1978.

Dixon, John. "The Question of Genres." *The Place of Genre in Learning: Current Debates.* Ed. Ian Reid. Victoria, Australia: Deakin University Centre for Studies in Literary Education, Typereader Publication, no. 1, n.d. 9–21.

Faigley, Lester. "Competing Theories of Process: A Critique and a Proposal." *College English* 48 (1986): 527–42.

Flower, Linda. *Problem-Solving Strategies for Writing.* New York: Harcourt, 1981.

Gardner, Howard. *The Mind's New Science,* rev. ed. New York: Basic, 1987.

Hairston, Maxine. "Not All Errors Are Created Equal: Non-Academic Readers in the Professions Respond to Errors in Usage." *College English* 43 (1981): 794–806.

Hungerford, Anne. *Advanced Study in Writing for Business and the Professions.* Vancouver, BC: Writing Program (SFU), 1989.

MacDougall, A. Kent. "Boring from within the Bourgeois Press." *Monthly Review* 40.6,7 (November, December 1988): 13–24; 20–24.

National Council of Teachers of English. "Standards for Basic Skills Writing Programs." (March 1979).

Ohmann, Richard. "Use Definite, Specific, Concrete Language." *College English* 41 (1979): 390–97.

Phelps, Louise Wetherbee. "Dialectics of Coherence." *College English* 47 (1985): 12–29.

Richards, I.A. *The Philosophy of Rhetoric.* London: Oxford, 1936.

Robertson, Linda R. "Why Dionysius II Can't Write: Plato's Confessions of a Failed Teacher." *College English* 48 (1986): 376–84.

Worby, Diana Zacharia. "In Search of a Common Language." *College English* 42 (1979): 101–5.

7

Advanced Writing Courses and Programs

Michael L. Keene
Ray Wallace

If you read the literature being published today about writing, or if you talk with people at the CCCC convention, what kind of writing do you hear about other than freshman composition? Usually technical writing, writing across the curriculum, and creative writing, and maybe a little about ESL and writing centers. What else could there be?

In our experience, a subject that *doesn't* often come up is advanced composition. Where is it, and what is it? Is there any set curriculum or sequence? Do people major in it? Minor in it? How does the generic title relate to technical writing and other specific course labels?

To posit an answer to these questions, and thus to consider the types of advanced composition being taught and its role in writing and English programs, we conducted a poll of 12 colleges and universities. The schools were selected for geographic distribution, for a mix of large and small schools, and for inclusion of both public and private institutions. We asked each school's representative the same set of questions concerning their course offerings and their successes and problems, but we also allowed ourselves the freedom to stray from our pre-arranged script whenever the situation seemed to merit it. We were especially concerned about what we called the *fourth-quadrant,* courses in exposition and persuasion or advanced workshops that might come under the advanced composition label. Our questions are given here.

Series One: The Setting
What size is the school?

What is the mix of rural and urban students?

What are the number and type of writing faculty (professional, tenure-track, or tenured)?

What percent of the whole faculty teaches freshman composition? What percent teaches any other writing courses?

Do literature majors have to take any writing course beyond the freshman level?

Is there a major or minor in writing?

Series Two: Writing Beyond the Freshman Level: About Technical Writing, Creative Writing, and Writing Across the Curriculum

How many *different* courses and sections are there?

How many faculty teach those courses?

How many students take this in one calendar year?

Series Three: The Fourth Quadrant (everyone else's "other" category)

How many different (other) writing courses do you have — and how many sections — that are not covered in the three previously mentioned areas?

How do these courses articulate (as, for example, part of a writing major or minor) with the other kinds of writing courses?

What are the *core* textbooks for these courses?

How is this course not just "more of the same" — different from freshman composition?

Do you have a writing center that advanced composition students *can* use? Do they? Is it remedial help?

Is there a writing fellows program?

What's the biggest problem with advanced composition at your school?

May we call you back if we have further questions?

Part One of this essay summarizes the results of our phone discussions. Part Two offers our thoughts on the larger significance of the results of that survey.

Part One: Results

The Northeast

College A has 5,100 students; because of national recruitment and a prestigious reputation, the students come from many locations. There are 53 professorial English faculty: 22 tenured and 31 nontenured. All the nontenured faculty and a few tenured faculty teach freshman composition. The English department only offers a literature major. There is no major or minor in writing.

College A doesn't offer technical writing courses, but it does have eight or nine creative writing courses, a total of 10 or 12 sections per year. Four or five faculty teach these classes, which enroll fewer than 18 students per section.

College A has a university-wide expository writing program, with a tutorial program for students and with writing-intensive sections in most fields. Faculty in other disciplines who teach the writing-intensive courses are assisted by subject-qualified teaching fellows who are also trained in teaching writing. Quite a few of these courses are generically titled The Writing of...(Social Science, History, or whatever). This program is run by a campus-wide Committee on Expository Writing.

The English department has three of the fourth-quadrant type of courses. Each year, it offers 10 sections of a modern prose course, usually filled with AP freshman and other students from all departments. The second course, prose traditions, is usually offered in three sections of around 15 students. It differs from the first one by considering an expanded historical range of authors. The third course is a senior-level nonfiction prose writing workshop (one section, 15 students), taught each year by a different well-known author.

According to the faculty member we interviewed, the biggest problem is that the other departments in the university don't pay enough attention to writing; only in a class specifically devoted to writing does a student receive writing instruction and practice. In other words, the biggest problem is maintaining and improving the very good skills the freshman program develops. In the English department, because it is primarily literature-oriented, convincing faculty to teach or develop advanced writing courses is difficult.

The East

College B has 30,000 students, from rural and urban areas. The English department has 55 faculty members, with 13 in creative writing and 10 in other kinds of writing. None of the other faculty teaches any writing courses beyond the freshman level, but all College B students have to take at least one advanced writing course. The literature majors usually satisfy that requirement by taking creative writing. The only writing major is in creative writing.

College B offers two technical writing courses, with 80 sections of one (1800 students) and 10 of the other (180 students) each year. These courses are taught mostly by adjunct faculty, plus a few of the professorial staff. The department also offers 12 creative writing courses each year, totalling 75 sections, involving 1500 students. There are no writing-across-the-curriculum courses in the English department, but several dozen in other departments.

College B has one advanced composition course (the text is Hairston's *Successful Writing*), plus a course in peer tutoring taken mostly by students who plan to go into teaching. There is a writing center that the advanced composition students can use, but they are much more likely to be working there, especially after taking the peer tutoring course.

The college offers 10 sections of the advanced composition course each year; of the peer tutoring course, three. There is a determined curricular effort to make the advanced composition course different from freshman composition. The advanced course focuses more on invention, arrangement, and style. It is more sophisticated analytically and stylistically. It was described as a "genuinely wired-up course," complete with detailed attention to audience analysis. The biggest problem with advanced composition at College B is finding staff to teach the courses.

The Southeast

College C has 17,000 students, a rural/urban mix. The English department has 35 faculty members, of whom seven are writing specialists. Most of the faculty teach freshman composition, but (other than the writing specialists) none teaches any other writing courses. No literature majors take expository writing beyond the freshman level, but there is a minor in creative writing. College C offers one technical writing course, taught by one faculty member and one adjunct. It enrolls 22 students per section. Many sections of the seven creative writing courses are taught by four or five faculty, with 15 students per section. This school has no writing-across-the-curriculum program, although there is a legal writing course and a social work writing course. There is one advanced composition course (the text is either Hairston or nothing), with four sections per year. The course differs from freshman composition in that the students have ample freedom to write what they want to write. No literature majors take it. Some of the advanced composition students use the school's writing center, mostly for remedial help. The biggest problem with the advanced composition course is that, because of a lack of publicity and a lack of faculty, "the good word hasn't gotten out."

The South

College D enrolls just under 10,000 students and offers degrees from the B.A. to the doctorate. The students are 60 percent rural and 40 percent urban. The English department has 60 faculty members, 40 of whom are either tenured or tenure-track. The department offers a

B.A. in English and American Literature and a minor in literature. All of the faculty teach freshman composition, and five faculty teach advanced writing courses. No advanced writing courses are required of English majors.

Technical writing is taught four times per year by two faculty members, reaching 66 students. Creative writing is taught twice a year by two faculty, reaching 30 students. Writing across the curriculum has been developed under an NEH grant, and all new instructors across the campus have to teach writing in all classes. (The program is not governed by the English department.)

The only advanced composition course is expository and narrative writing, an elective for English majors that has not been taught since 1983. There are two writing centers, but both are perceived as remedial and are not used by advanced writers.

The writing expert there said the advanced composition course had become obsolete because other courses taught the same thing: "Writing across the curriculum reaches all the students each semester. Technical, creative, and business writing courses reach smaller groups. English majors are not seen to need an advanced writing course because the major is in literature: "writing courses are perceived as unnecessary for them."

College E enrolls 25,000 students from a rural/urban mix. There are 48 professorial faculty members. Many graduate students and lecturers currently hold teaching positions. The professorial staff includes five creative writing teachers, four technical writing teachers, and four rhetoric/composition teachers. There is no writing-across-the-curriculum program, although some departments have "writing intensive" courses. Most freshman composition sections (about 90 percent) are taught by instructors or graduate students.

The English department offers either a traditional literature or a writing (technical or creative) undergraduate degree. A writing minor (on either the B.A. or M.A. level) is also available. Students are now beginning to be interested in pursuing a rhetoric Ph.D. The writing center is expanding but is still mostly remedial. Students may use eight computer labs on the campus.

Undergraduate literature majors are required to take one writing course beyond the freshman sequence, while undergraduate writing majors take four or five. The technical writing courses are the most popular (four or more sections of advanced technical writing per semester, plus three other technical writing courses once a year), both with the English majors and with students from other disciplines, producing a demand the department cannot satisfy. Creative writing (poetry, fiction, screenwriting) courses are offered in four sections a semester. Two sections of an expository writing course and one or two of a persuasive writing course, taken by English and business majors, are also offered each term.

The major problem with advanced composition at College E is that the faculty most interested in teaching it are spread too thin, having to teach other writing courses (as well as graduate-level courses) where the demand, both from English majors and students from other departments, is more pressing. In addition, they feel somewhat uncertain as to just what the advanced courses are designed to accomplish, and the students who take the courses tend to have widely differing skill levels and expectations.

The Midwest

College F enrolls between 3,000 and 3,500 students per academic year, offers degrees from the associate level to the masters, and has a student body described as 90 percent rural. In the English department, there are 20 faculty members, only five of whom are tenured or on tenure-track lines. The rest of the faculty are part-time instructors. All faculty teach freshman composition, but no writing major or minor is offered. College F does not have a writing center, and the only undergraduate degree is literature-based. However, advanced expository writing is required for all English majors, the only writing course these students must take after the freshman level. Only one section of this course is offered each semester. Additionally, one technical writing and one creative writing course are taught each year. A few experimental writing-across-the-curriculum courses have been recently created.

In terms of advanced composition, two faculty take turns teaching this course, but neither has composition or rhetoric training, and the course is described as a responding-to-literature course. Interestingly enough, the two faculty who *are* trained in rhetoric/composition are not allowed to teach the course because it is considered upper division and—as untenured faculty—they cannot teach upper division. These two faculty members cannot see much pedagogical difference between their freshman composition classes and this advanced class; to them, standing admittedly on the outside, it seems to be just more of the same.

College G enrolls 10,000 students and offers both undergraduate and graduate degrees to the specialist rank. The student body is described as 50 percent rural and 50 percent urban. The English department has 53 faculty, 34 of whom are either tenured or tenure-track. A writing expert at this school claimed 98 percent of the faculty teach freshman composition and that the department has developed a very successful writing center. At the undergraduate level, the English department offers both a B.A. (without teaching certification) and two writing minors (in either professional or creative writing). At present, the literature majors must take one writing course beyond the freshman level, but this requirement is regularly opposed at each curriculum meeting. The department offers two courses in advanced document design each semester, reaching 80 students per year. There are three creative writing courses (beginning, intermediate, and advanced) after the freshman level; six sections are taught each year, reaching 150 students. This institution is in the process of implementing a writing-across-the-curriculum project.

In advanced composition, the English department offers a junior-level writing class in six sections each semester. It is required of English, special education, and professional writing minors. In the past two years, 12 different faculty members have taught it. A writing expert there noted that Hairston's text was the usual one and that this course differs from freshman composition in that it involves more work on heuristics and discussion of rhetorical theory.

The biggest problems with the advanced composition course at College G were these: the faculty were uneven in their preparation for teaching composition (only one had any formal rhetoric/composition training); and since students only needed a *C* in freshman composition to enter the class, their abilities varied drastically.

College H enrolls 23,000 students and offers degrees from the B.A. to the doctorate level. The English department has 70 members, of whom 45 are tenure-track. The student body at this university consists of 20 percent rural, 40 percent suburban, and 40 percent urban. The English department offers both a B.A. and B.S., as well as minors in writing and ESL. Very few tenured or tenure-track faculty teach freshman composition; this "chore" is left to graduate assistants enrolled in masters and doctoral programs and to the instructors who are not tenure-track. However, about 10 percent of the faculty do teach upper-division writing classes. To graduate, English majors must take one advanced writing course after the freshman sequence.

At this institution all the writing courses are taught on computers (both IBM-compatible and Macintosh). The two undergraduate technical writing courses are taught by six faculty members, and they serve 150 students each year. The three creative writing courses are taught by five faculty members and reach 160 students. The writing-across-the-curriculum courses, which reach 500 students per year, are not taught by English faculty.

Three courses seem to fall into the category of advanced composition: an advanced grammar and usage course for writers, an advanced composition course, and a writing seminar course. The grammar course is exactly what its name implies. The advanced exposition course is designed "to add sophistication to the writer's style." In it, content is stressed over form. The writing seminar stresses writing for publication, with each student working on three projects over the semester. There is a writing center that the advanced composition students do in fact use, mostly to get reactions and opinions from a skilled reader.

The writing expert there claimed that the major problem with advanced composition in this institution was that the expectations of the faculty and the students do not match. The advanced composition teachers often feel that students are ill prepared for advanced work and, in fact, still need remediation. An associated problem is that the freshman composition course lacks a core structure; thus the students' writing backgrounds are quite varied when they arrive in the advanced exposition course.

The Southwest

College I has 50,000 students, with a mix of rural and urban backgrounds. The English department has 85 faculty members, of whom six are writing specialists. There is no major or minor in writing: the literature majors take no writing courses beyond the freshman level.

College I does not offer technical writing courses, but it does have 8 or 10 creative writing courses comprising 10 or 15 sections. These classes are taught by five or six people. A handful of writing-across-the-curriculum courses, designated as "substantial writing component" courses, are taught in other departments.

The only other course is advanced expository writing. Three sections are offered each year. The students are juniors and seniors; none are English majors. The course focuses on explanatory and persuasive writing and includes some oral presentations. The main problem with the course is that there aren't enough sections or faculty members willing to teach it.

The Northwest

College J has about 11,000 students, mostly from a rural background. There are 22 faculty members in the English department, with one writing specialist. About a third of the faculty teach freshman composition, and two or three teach other writing courses. There is no major or minor in writing, but a writing course beyond the freshman level is strongly recommended for English majors.

College J has a technical writing course (25 sections per year, with 22 students per section) that can substitute for second semester freshman composition. It is taught by three regular faculty members. There are two creative writing courses (eight sections) taught by four faculty members. The creative writing classes have 15 students per section. There is no writing-across-the-curriculum course at College J.

College J has two other writing courses, totalling four sections. Both courses are referred to as advanced composition. These two courses don't articulate with the other writing courses at all. Their core texts are various essay collections, and the courses differ from freshman composition mostly in that they involve more peer instruction. Education majors take one of the courses, and English majors take the other. While there is a writing center, the advanced composition students do not use it (it is mostly remedial). The biggest problem with advanced composition at College J is that no one knows what it is. The courses cannot be very advanced because the students who take them think they need more basic instruction, and, in fact, they do.

The West

College K enrolls 12,000 students, and the English department offers degrees at the bachelor's and master's levels. The English department has 23 professorial faculty, of whom six are writing specialists. Students at the college are mostly from an urban background. About 20 to 30 percent of the whole faculty teach freshman composition, and 50 or 60 percent of the nonwriting faculty teach the other writing courses. The college has both a major and minor in writing, as well as a cross-disciplinary major shared with the journalism department. Literature majors do not have to take any writing courses beyond the freshman level.

The department offers two technical writing courses, plus a special projects course and a co-op course. These add up to 15 sections per year. Seven faculty teach these courses, which enroll about 140 students per year. The special projects and co-op courses happen only occasionally and involve only a few students when they do. There are no writing-across-the-curriculum courses.

Creative writing offerings in College K include 9 or 10 different courses, a total or about 12 sections per year. Two regular faculty teach these courses, which serve about 200 students.

The courses that concern us most here are expository writing, advanced expository writing, persuasive writing, and advanced persuasive writing — for a total of 10 or 12 sections per year, with 15 to 20 students in each section. Students from all over the college, including writing majors and minors, often take one of these courses. These classes use many different texts, or no textbook at all. The courses differ from freshman composition in that they are not just about "how to succeed in college," but more specifically about "getting to be a writer." Students in the advanced composition courses use the department's writing center, both for help with their writing and for its computer work stations.

The biggest problem with advanced composition at College K, according to the writing specialist we interviewed, is the wide mix of students in the classes. Some students are in the classes just to "fill out their schedules," and others are there to become professional writers. Lack of staffing contributes to the problem since only a handful of these courses can be taught each year, so that the more basic and the more advanced writers get mixed in together in both the exposition and persuasion classes.

College L has 3,000 students, from a rural/urban mix, with a large percentage (20 percent) of ESL students, most of whom are recent immigrants to the area. The English faculty consists of 10 professorial staff and two lecturers. Each semester, all faculty teach at least one section (and sometimes two) of either the traditional freshman composition course or an ESL composition course. All English majors are considered to be literature majors, and they are required to take one other writing course after the freshman composition course. There is no major or minor in writing at College L.

College L has no creative writing courses, but each semester the English department offers two sections of advanced technical writing and business writing. In addition, one section of advanced composition is offered once each year. A university-wide writing proficiency exam is given to all students at the end of the junior year. The pass rate on this exam is low, about 45 percent on the first attempt. Students are advised (but not forced) to take one of the post-freshman writing courses to prepare for the exam; they cannot retake freshman composition to brush up on their skills. Despite this advice, most students rely instead on simply taking the exam again and again.

There is not an active writing-across-the-curriculum program. The writing center is not equipped to deal with advanced composition students, but there is a computer-assisted composition lab with staff to help the advanced students.

The advanced composition course is not the most popular writing option for either English majors or those other majors (business, education, and science) who must also take a writing course. Most students prefer to take the technical writing course; if it is not available, they try for the business writing course. The advanced composition course is taken mainly by English majors; faculty generally teach it as a responding-to-literature course.

The biggest problem with advanced composition at College L, according to the person we interviewed, is that no one really wants to teach it, in large part because no one is really certain what it is supposed to achieve. The course most often turns into a harder section of freshman composition.

Part Two: What Does It Mean?

Of course, a survey of 12 schools of varying size across the nation can have only limited validity when used as the basis for generalizing about nationwide phenomena. But we did note startling similarities among these randomly selected institutions, regardless of size and location.

Today, with more and more underprepared students being admitted to all types of colleges and universities across the country, a variety of methods are needed to help them improve as writers throughout college. Although advanced composition courses historically had the major role in satisfying this need, students today can choose among writing-across-the-curriculum, technical writing, business writing, creative writing, and ESL courses, among others. These writing courses—both inside and outside the English department—have been quite responsive to what students perceive to be their needs as writers in academic settings and as future professionals. Also, when institutions look at the nature and role of writing instruction campus-wide, they frequently start writing-across-the-curriculum programs, often sited outside the English department. This increases the number of students (other than English majors) who look to their own departments for advanced writing instruction. While some students take an advanced composition course followed by, say, technical writing, instances of students who are not English majors taking more than one advanced writing course seem quite rare. (For that matter, instances when English majors take more than one such writing course are also quite rare.) Thus, the population that takes advanced composition seems often to be restricted to English majors. The only way to alter that situation would involve a fundamental change in the basic philosophical nature of advanced composition itself.

Other problems lessen the popularity of advanced composition courses: they are very difficult to staff, and there is no real consensus about what they should cover or what approach(es) they should take. At some institutions, advanced composition is not very popular with the faculty—including the few writing specialists who may be stressing other kinds of writing experiences, perhaps in literature-based courses or subject-specialized writing courses. The writing faculty's energies are also taken up by designing graduate curricula.

The course's identity is perhaps a more crucial problem than is staffing. What we saw, in our limited survey, was that no one was quite sure what the course was supposed to be. There were often significant differences in expectations about the course's identity—even within the faculty at an institution, and certainly from institution to institution — and faculty expectations frequently differed from those of the students. The students themselves had such varied backgrounds that addressing their needs seemed to require an impossible variety of approaches. And while individual faculty members could often explain the pedagogical rationale for their own advanced composition course, we could neither adequately locate such specific courses on any kind of spectrum, nor begin to discover how any kind of consensus might evolve among writing faculty. For example, while a number of professionals seem to feel the course needs to teach *higher order* rhetorical skills, these skills never seem to be the same from college to college. Beyond that, an alarming number of people told us that there was not a great deal of difference, in fact, between freshman composition and advanced composition; generally, what we saw as the most common difference was that the latter requires longer papers. In a worst-case scenario, advanced composition seems to mean an ill-defined, badly organized writing experience that repeats (or covers for the first time) the elements of instruction our profession might be more likely to expect to see in freshman composition.

We are left feeling that advanced composition will follow one of three paths. Down one path, the course will simply fade away — either because it is seen as redundant in light of the existence of other advanced writing options, or because it is simply seen as unnecessary in and of itself. Down another path, the course will continue muddling along, needing more definition, occasionally spinning off discipline-specific courses. Down the third path there is what we see to be a brighter future, one that involves people who specialize in rhetoric and composition finding an identity for advanced composition and persuading our colleagues and students of its importance — that this course offers something significant the other advanced writing courses do not (perhaps the skills students need to succeed in careers regardless of discipline, perhaps advanced thinking skills, perhaps lifetime writing skills that are not directly career-related). This double task — that of finding an identity for advanced composition courses and convincing our colleagues and students of the course's usefulness — is well within our individual intellectual abilities, but may be beyond our collective will. If so, it would be ironic in the extreme: imagine a profession coming into being through teaching writing to freshmen, and then subsequently, in effect, abandoning those same students at the next level because we cannot, or will not, come to a consensus as to what that next level should contain.

A Variety of
Course Structures

8

A Personal Account
of a Course Called
Personal Voice

Toby Fulwiler

During the fall semester of 1987, at the University of Vermont, I taught for the first time a newly conceived course called Personal Voice. I had actually designed this English course (subsequently numbered 172) in 1984, a year after I arrived at Vermont from Michigan Tech, in order to develop what I call a 50/50 course, one that would bridge the gap between writing courses and literature courses, paying deliberate attention to both reading theory and writing process. I also wanted to make the study and practice of personal forms of writing a legitimate activity for professors and students alike within our department — which the addition of this course at the upper level would accomplish.

When asked to write this chapter, I looked over the journal that I had kept along with my students in 172 and found embedded therein a nearly complete history of the development of Personal Voice, warts and all. Though I always keep a journal along with my students in the courses — both composition and literature — that I teach, I seldom have so complete a record as I found this time, no doubt because the course was new and I wanted good notes from which to revise for next time. I decided to use the journal structure as the basis for my account of English 172, which necessitated both the strategic editing of original entries and the judicious fabrication of new entries to make the record intelligible to an unintended audience. In all important dimensions, the resulting chapter follows the contour of the original journal. In addition, where appropriate, I have added actual samples of student writing from the class.

11/29/84   Personal Voice was approved by the department as a new upper-division writing course (English 172) — one of only a handful of junior/senior writing courses that English majors could take. Of course, there was a heated debate about what, exactly, was "personal" voice: Did Dickens (etc.) have one, and how do you know? The proposal finally passed as part of a package introduced by the Writing Committee to add three new writing courses to our listings (also approved were The Writing Process [171] and Writing Literary Criticism [173]). We presented 172 as a 50/50 course — half writing and half reading — which seemed to increase its appeal to our literary colleagues.

11/17/86 [U.S. Air]   My sabbatical year goes well. A relief to write and travel rather than teach and meet. When I return I will teach for the first time the new writing course Personal Voice.

1/4/87 [Florida]   In St. Petersburg, at the Poynter Institute, to attend a four-day conference involving writing teachers and journalists. Yesterday, on the beach north of the Hilton, I wrote the whole first draft of "Finding Your Voice," which will be either the first or last chapter of *College Writing* [a textbook for Scott Foresman]. I planned to make "voice" my first chapter, since getting control of one's voice is what the book — and most first-year writing courses — is about. But more and more I think voice needs to be last, as everything else in the book (style, format, revision, editing, etc.) is part of developing one's voice. (Isn't 4 years of college all about "finding your voice"?)

1/5/87 [Florida]   Talked to Peter Elbow about his graduate course on voice at Stony Brook. We agreed to exchange reading lists. Already he's given me a perspective on voice I had somehow overlooked — the importance of remembering that *voice* (in writing) is metaphoric. Of course. We talk about voice on paper in order to say something about tone, pitch, rhythm, and gesture — all those elements that are concrete and identifiable parts of one's actual oral voice. However, when writing teachers talk about voice, they deliberately move this metaphor into more philosophic and aesthetic dimensions, making it stand for who we are, what we believe, what *we* stand for.

4/15/87   Book orders are due: I need to plan Personal Voice for next fall. Part of the course will focus on theory — the James Britton essays [in *Prospect and Retrospect*] — to ground our study in his developmental theory of language; Britton makes strong connections between spoken and written *expressive* language. Also Winston Weathers's *An Alternate Style*, which gives us a vocabulary for talking about the more idiosyncratic features of *personal* voices. (That's going to be a tough distinction — how "voice" is something different from "style.")

As for more literary readings, I'm thinking about Loren Eiseley—who writes with a simple and strong voice from the point of view of an anthropologist—maybe *Immense Journey,* his first book. Here I want to make the case that voice can be a matter of concern to all writers, regardless of field. I also want to do *Let Us Now Praise Famous Men* by Agee and Evans, which has the greatest variety of voices in any nonfiction work. (Do I mean voice or style when I say that?) And I'll have them each buy a subscription to *The New Yorker* (educational rate: 16 weeks for $5) to read the most current voices of good nonfiction writers (not yet sure how I'll work *New Yorker* readings into the class).

8/8/87 [Lake Superior, Michigan] Writing assignments for Personal Voice:

- One paper in which each student investigates the voice of a non-fiction writer, identifying its characteristic features (a 10-minute oral report; a draft shared with a writing group and one with me; a final draft for the portfolio).

- A second paper on a free topic (anything of the writer's own choosing) in which the writer writes in his or her most comfortable or effective or favorite voice. (I'll ask for several starts; select one to develop and include in the portfolio.)

- The third paper will be an investigation and analysis of one's own voice based on whatever voice history each writer can locate (old college papers? high school papers? earlier?). Perhaps parents can forward these from home, or students can get them when they go home for Thanksgiving.

- Journals will be used throughout as foundational to all writing assignments—a place in which to examine one's personal voice as well as comfortably practice it.

- *The New Yorker* will be handled in weekly oral reports—students taking turns recommending articles to each other? I'll not know in advance what we can use, but that's fun and will let the students in on a sense of discovery for the class—yes, this is an exploratory course, where new things can be discovered by all. No reason for exams.

- Portfolio. I don't want to mess with grades too early in this course. Will use portfolios more which are more common in writing than literature classes—like art classes—where students will work on this or that paper all term long, receiving comments but not grades. At the end of the term I'll collect portfolios, which will include each finished paper plus all prior drafts. This will allow me to see the evolution of each paper as well as the final copy. Give one grade based on the whole portfolio?

8/31   Voice class starts tomorrow: class list shows 22 students (6 seniors, 12 juniors, 4 sophomores). Half are English majors, the rest in Arts and Sciences, except one major each in business and education. What do they expect? What do I? I've made copies of the "Voice" chapter from my *College Writing* manuscript, which won't be actually published until next January. I'll hand that out and invite written responses to it for next class. I want to show how *I* define and conceive of voice....

Wrong. First, I need to find out *their* conceptions before coloring them with mine....

First thing tomorrow, I'll ask students to "define *voice*" in a 5-minute freewrite and see if we can generate a consensus list — which I'll save and refer back to later on (or give back when they begin to analyze their own voices?).

Need to explain the nature of the class, a reading/writing/theory class.

Need to explain why portfolios will be better than exams — to put grades in the background.

Remainder of first class, I'd like to do the Wallet Exercise: (1) to loosen people up, (2) to encourage close documented observation, and (3) to practice making careful inferences from mute data (silent voices?). We will build on all these as course progresses.

9/1 [1:40 p.m.]   Before I even take roll, I ask for some preliminary definitions of voice. I am able to catch the following:

Carter: Voice is really a metaphorical fingerprint.

Sarah: The writing all clearly reflects *me,* how I think and feel, but this *me* aspect varies with subject and frame of mind at the time I am writing.

Gail: My personal voice is my most vulnerable, my most open and emotional...yet because it is private, it's not very risky.

Jackie: The aspect of my voice that is really *me* is in my personal letters.

Marcia: My dominant voice is an automatic, reflexive one that hasn't time to step outside and edit itself.

Gail: Order and structure are so ingrained by now that I naturally use paragraphs, even in my journal.

[2:00 p.m.]   I've asked people to exchange their wallets with a neighbor and make a detailed list of what they find in there. The class is exactly 22, so after demonstrating with my wallet — pulling out credit cards, photos, a driver's license, a twenty dollar bill — I turned them loose.

The idea is to make an objective list first (credit and medical cards, licenses, photos, money), then make more subjective inferences, and finally to ask 3 yes/no questions of the wallet owner (and take good notes). The journal-writing assignment, due next class, is to compose an inferential personality sketch of your partner in 1 or 2 pages.

At first they were confused, then they laughed, then they really got into it. (The two people without wallets are using their book bags.)

9/3 [1:40]   Two journal writes will structure this second class meeting; after each I want some sharing and will make an OHP [overhead projector] list, hoping to stimulate further thought each time:

1.   Describe the elements that contribute to your own voice when you write (this a variation of the question I asked in the first class).

Asa: My personal voice developed...when I learned how to organize my thoughts on paper in a readable form.

I tend to be inquisitive and curious, and this is exemplified by the naivete of my works.

Marcia: I'm beginning to realize that the *me* in my voice will shine as long as what I'm writing is truthful.

Kristin: The *me* involved is inherent in all my writing, but shown in various degrees according to purpose, style, and audience.

Academic papers, where I take interest in the assignment, are the best in expressing my personal voice...they are more audience conscious and aimed to impress or affect someone.

Michelle: For the most part, her voice is conventionally intellectual.

I make sure we agree on several more general components of voice — that voice may include "structure" or "format" as well as value and style. And that it may include one's philosophical beliefs, what one stands for: I argue that there are some sentences I could not utter (racist, fascist, etc.) and that must include what we mean by voice as well as the length of words, sentences, types of metaphors, and so on. This is a hard one. Not everyone is buying it.

[2:15]   2. What do you want to find out about your own voice this semester?

Gail: To strengthen my voice, to craft it more carefully and let more of my personality through.

David: I wish I could hand in a paper with no name on it and have my professors say, "That's a David Smith paper if I ever saw one."

Mark: How to sound more polished but still be honest.

Jackie: Where it came from, how it got the way it is.

9/8 [1:45] I start class by asking which authors the students would like to investigate for their first papers. [This collective list is based on a homework assignment: Make a list of living nonfiction prose writers you enjoy reading and might be willing to analyze. Below is a portion of that list.]

- Gail Lawrence
- Russell Baker
- Ellen Goodman
- Erma Bombeck
- Mike Royko
- John McPhee
- Tom Wolfe
- Martin Luther King (not living, but current)
- Jesse Feldman (columnist for student newspaper)

9/15 [8:30 p.m.] In class today we examined closely one page of Loren Eiseley's prose from *The Immense Journey*:

> There are things down there still coming ashore. Never make the mistake of thinking life is now adjusted for eternity. It gets into your head—the certainty, I mean—the human certainty, and then you miss it all: the things on the tide flats and what they mean, and why, as my wife says, "they ought to be watched."
>
> The trouble is we don't know what to watch for. I have a friend, one of these Explorers Club people, who drops in now and then between trips to tell me about the size of crocodile jaws in Uganda, or what happened on some back beach in Arnhem Land.
>
> "They fell out of the trees," he said. "Like rain. And into the boat."
>
> "Uh?" I said, noncommittally.
>
> "They did *so*," he protested, "and they were hard to catch."
>
> "Really—" I said.
>
> "We were pushing a dugout up one of the tidal creeks in northern Australia and going fast when *smacko* we jam this mangrove bush and the things come tumbling down.
>
> "What were they doing sitting up there in bunches? I ask you. It's no place for a fish. Besides that they had a way of sidling off with those popeyes trained on you. I never liked it. Somebody ought to keep an eye on them."
>
> "Why?" I asked.
>
> "I don't know why," he said impatiently, running a rough, square hand through his hair and wrinkling his forehead. "I just mean they make you feel that way, is all. A fish belongs in the water. It ought to stay there—just as we live on land in houses. Things ought to know their place and stay in it, but those fish have got a way of sidling off. As though they had mental reservations and weren't keeping any contracts. See what I mean?"

"I see what you mean," I said gravely. "They ought to be watched. My wife thinks so too. About a lot of things."

"She does?" He brightened. "Then that's two of us. I don't know why, but they give you that feeling."

He didn't know why, but I thought that I did.

Loren Eiseley
The Immense Journey

First I read it out loud, then gave us about five minutes to write about what "characterized" the passage — what language features we could identify. After the writing assignment, I asked what people had found and made a list on a transparency:

- general words: "*things* coming ashore"/"*they* ought to be watched"
- simple language, few complex or multisyllabic words
- parallel structures, where one sentence balanced another
- careful sentence rhythms
- repetitions: "pays, pay, pay"
- metaphor: "oceanic vat"
- snatches of conversation: "They fell out of the trees, he said"
- passages that read like drama

These elements of style, we agreed, became Eiseley's voice when they began to convey his individual person (persona?) speaking uniquely to us. We begin to make inferences about his personality and values from his language.

This seemed to work well; I could tell that most were not used to doing this close scrutiny — being forced to ground their generalizations in very particular language (e.g., "Eiseley is a curious, speculative, sort of laid-back person." OK. Show us the words or phrases that demonstrate this).

9/17 [2:30]   Sarah and Michelle report to the class on what they have learned about Loren Eiseley's later work, after *Immense Journey* [they volunteered to do this at the last meeting]: they find things about his life that surface in his prose; they also spend too much time retelling his life and do not analyze how his written voice works.

I praise their class report, but push them gently for more direct connections to the written voice we hear on the page — all the students will have this problem as they write their first paper on a prose writer's voice.

9/22 [2:45]   We confront the issue of *style* versus *voice* head on and try to write out the distinctions. People (including me) extract sentences from their journals to write on the blackboard and we talk about these:

Carter: Style is the method, voice the man behind it, the shadow of the author.

Mary Cate: This paragraph is typical of my academic papers in that it contains a topic sentence, it progresses logically, it's clear, and it contains expressions I don't use in daily conversation.

Mark: My writing voice varies according to the audience I'm writing for—but really, isn't that just my style?

Barbara: Style is more mechanical, voice is more personal, and you can't really change it much.

9/24 [1:50] I ask students (in pairs) to investigate one resource to contribute to our understanding of voice and to make a 10-minute report to the class. I suggest working from this list of authors:

- Richard Lanham, *Style: An Anti Text*
- Joe Williams, *Style: Ten Lessons in Clarity and Grace*
- William Zinnser, *On Writing Well*
- Walker Gibson, *Persona* or *Tough, Sweet, and Stuffy*
- Ken Macrorie, *Telling Writing* or *Uptaught*
- Roland Barthes, *The Grain of the Voice*
- Erving Goffman, *The Presentation of Self in Everyday Life*
- Peter Elbow, *Writing with Power*
- Lionel Trilling, *Sincerity and Authenticity*

Marcia and Frank want to interview UVM professors on the topic of "personal voice," finding out how other academics view the question. I agree that this would be an interesting substitute for an oral report. They will investigate the possibility of videotaping their subjects.

9/30 [8:00 a.m.] Yesterday we talked about *An Alternate Style.* Or at least we started out to do so, identifying devices such as "crots," "lists," and "labyrinthine sentences" as typical of this "Grammar B" as Weathers calls it. But we ended up spending most of the period talking about the traditional academic style that does not permit such devices. I should have realized this discussion had to occur. We agreed that the conventional style looks as it does in order to promote belief in a stable, rational world. The academic disciplines assume a world that is (to a great extent) predictable, linear, and logical. It is rule-governed, and order can be found if we observe carefully enough with good instruments, etc. (Shades of Isaac Newton!) As such, the language that represents this world is likewise predictable, linear, and logical.

I could tell people were intrigued by this discussion, as we ranged over all sorts of political and philosophic reasons writers from Walt Whitman and e e cummings to Tom Wolfe and Hunter S. Thompson threatened this world view with their language. I'm sure some liked it because they thought it a digression—which of course it wasn't at all. But what it did for most was put into perspective the *reasons* they were asked to write term papers, lab reports, and essays in certain formats and styles—which few, even the seniors—had ever actually thought about.

10/1 [2:30] First writing groups (4 groups of 5 each) on first paper. Students have brought 3-page typed drafts to class, 5 copies each. I give careful directions about responding, limiting responses to two kinds: (1) What struck you as interesting? and (2) Where did you want more information?

I join one group, but stay away from the others. I think the group I am in gets used to me. I try not to say a lot, but find they are overly kind to each other, so I am often the one who wants "more information." Complete drafts (5–7 pages) are due a week from today.

10/6 [1:50] A quick note about attendance: it's quite irregular for some students. It's become common for several to waltz in 20–30 minutes late—even later—and join in. Part of me is angry, but part of me actually enjoys it: they are comfortable enough to do that in here, to come late, but still want to come and know that we'll notice but still welcome them. In this sense, I feel we've created more of a living-room community of writers than an academic classroom.

10/8 [7:30 a.m.] Papers analyzing prose writers are handed in for my response. These second drafts prove disappointing: too much summary, too little analysis, too casual. Two things happened here: first, their groups told them the papers were "just fine," which gave the writers a false sense of confidence; second, they thought that in *this class* they didn't have to be analytically rigorous—after all, we were studying *personal* voice, right?

[2:10 p.m.] I set them straight about my expectations: Look, just leaving a paper alone for a week—then coming back to it—will help you get some necessary distance from it; with feedback from peers you should have even more to go on; it doesn't help a writer to say the paper is perfect—I've never seen a perfect paper, or perfect published work for that matter. Etc.

I also explain that this course takes place within the context of the academic community—and so the expectations here are similar. Though our subject is personal voice, this paper was to analyze that voice in conventional academic language and form—the word analyze tips that off, doesn't it? We argue, but it's not hostile.

I project some passages from their papers (anonymously; only pretty good papers) [on the overhead projector] and suggest where I, as an academic reader, would expect more support, evidence, tightness, etc.

10/15 [8:30 p.m.] Discussion today of James Britton: very tough. They didn't read him carefully, and when I asked for definitions of Britton's terminology (expressive/transactional/poetic or spectator/observer) nobody was very sharp. Britton is conversational and digressive in that British style that sometimes Americans don't know what to make of; I like it more and more, but it's not the typical *American* academic style. He could be more to the point, but I think it a better representation of truth that he is not. I reassigned Britton for next time, and required journal writes that I said I would look at — along with some other j. entries.

10/17 [2:40] Collected "ten good pages" from their journals today — free choice on what to share with me, but they had to give me something on Britton. Since the journals are loose-leaf (most 7 × 10, some 8½ × 11), I gave everyone a small brass fastener to temporarily bind their pages and collected them. An easy way to demonstrate that the journals are important, but I'm not prying.

10/27 [Noon; Pittsburgh] Paper analyzing their own voices due today in 3 page draft to be read in writing groups. I am out of town, so the groups will meet on their own, share drafts, and leave copies in the box on my office door. By now they work well in groups, and I can trust them to work well on their own.

10/29 [1:45] In making the assignment to analyze their own voices, I asked students how many voices they had — a question that came up often in our discussion of "alternate styles." I now find many of their papers trying explicitly to pin that down, so I extracted these opinions from their papers and have duplicated them to share with the class:

Kim: I have several voices...the writing-home voice, the chemistry-lab voice, writing-to-boyfriend voice, writing-to-best-friend voice, freshman English voice, and journal voice. Each one requires me to author it, but my actual presence in the piece will be stronger or lighter depending on the topic.

Bobby: I think I have three different writing voices: one academic, one personal, and one that lies somewhere between the two. The ones I use most are the two extremes.

Lisa: I have three voices: the first is formal, a writing-for-the-teacher voice; the second is a letter-writing voice; the last is a train-of-thought voice....I am most comfortable with the last two—they are both like a real person speaking.

Gail: My three voices do have common elements, which is unavoidable since they all come from me—they reflect my fairly liberal, humanistic viewpoint.

Carter: Good writers or bad, we cannot change our voice from one moment to the next. We can disguise it with style, but...our voices will ring true.

Jen: My voice...always maintains, if not screeches, an egocentric notion of who I am.

11/5 [2:40] Discussion of voice in photographs: we look at Walker Evan's photos in *Famous Men.* We find these parallels:

- Photographers use light/shadow, perspective, arrangement, angle of vision, subject matter to *voice* their beliefs.
- Shades of black and white establish *tone* in a photo.
- A single photo is a matter of style; a sequence may be a matter of voice.
- Evans has a consistent voice in the same sense that Eiseley does; he even seems to value the same things, except they are social rather than natural.

11/11 [8:10 a.m.] Discussion yesterday of James Agee's voice(s): I did not leave enough time for this. (In fact I had not read Agee in 10 years and really sold short how much we could talk about in two allotted discussion periods...)

11/12 [2:00] I have projected a series of my own writing to the class on the overhead; I went back 8 years through my published writing and made a series of transparencies of my "evolving voice," even included some journal entries.

What we have concluded is interesting: that I have a more distinctive and personal voice in my published writing than in my journal entries. The journal entries are typically *expressive*—full of fragments and dashes and casual language, so much so that they more resemble other people's journal entries than they do my own published writing. In the published stuff, they say they really hear my voice and see me talking! I guess that in the formal language I worry over and revise and edit until I make my voice just right—which I do not do in my journal entries. They also notice that I am humorous in my published voice — the later pieces — whereas I am not in my journal (what for?) or in my earlier published pieces (less confident).

11/17 [after class]   Paper on open topic — second try (3-page draft, 5 copies).

About a third of the people are not well motivated for this — their papers are short and cursory and seem hastily written. Too many exams? Too busy to be open and creative? They have put this assignment on back burners in lieu of more fixed requirements and due dates in other courses. I think they're right — late in a 5 course semester is not a good time to explore your creative writing juices. Next time: move up earlier in the semester, make more focused (?), make collaborative (?), add local research component, model after *New Yorker* feature (?), make shorter.

Nevertheless, Gail's paper knocks me out. She missed class two weeks ago to attend her mother's funeral. She writes about it: her voice is strong, she puts us at bedside, we feel the cancer, she writes with telling detail and is not maudlin. (How wrong I was to interpret her silence these last several weeks as hostility.)

And Rebecca gives me a paper with a note on top: "Do not read out loud in class." It is about her emerging realization that she is gay — something she is still recognizing and reconciling, but has never written about. I respect her note.

11/19 [2:45]   Frank and Marcia's videotape report of professors' opinions about voice in writing: it's a sprawling, hour-long tape of people trying to articulate something about voice. It's funny, full of energy, poorly edited, overly repetitive, and ultimately wonderful. Reminds me of 1968, teaching at Wisconsin — students taking control of the medium of their instruction. And like 1968, it's full of good ideas, but loose, undisciplined, and ultimately too short of its mark to teach us very much.

12/1 [1:40]   First class after Thanksgiving break. I have scheduled a portfolio workshop class: students brought any piece they were working on or the whole portfolio so far. I am limiting at-desk conferences with me to 3 minutes each; people will work alone or talk to each other. But first I have asked each of us to write in our journals about what we plan to work on. These classes always work well with first–year students; the same will be true here. (Five are absent — a lot.)

12/3 [after class]   David led the discussion of the *New Yorker,* having concentrated on "voices" found in a series of issues. Frankly, I really blew handling this *New Yorker* assignment, always leaving it on the back burner and trusting that people were doing the reading. Will attend to if more regularly next year.

12/8 [9:30 p.m.] The *New Yorker* continued: everybody was supposed to bring the article that most moved them, and we were to share. Too late in the term — almost everyone brings in a copy of the latest issue. And I realize they've spent about as much analytical time reading *New Yorkers* as I have (they're piled high on my bedside table, me full of good intentions!). The students tell me not to worry, that it was worthwhile just looking at the cartoons every week. I tell them that people at *The New Yorker* call them drawings. I really don't feel too bad about this — I'll do better by this, too, next time.

12/10 Last class: I return after leaving for 10 minutes while they evaluate the class and me. I have real mixed feelings about what I'll find out — for some, like Gail, Mary Cate, and Jackie, I really think it's been a profound experience; for others, like Jen and Barbara, it's probably the most unfocused class they ever had.

I focus our last discussion around the question of change: What have you learned about your voice in studying it over the last few months? We write first, for 5 minutes in our journals, then volunteer answers:

Wendy: My personal voice has not changed significantly since fifth grade.

Wendy [also]: Changing one's personal voice is sort of like changing one's personality. . . . I see that as I grew older my writing matured, became more open, and developed in many ways I did myself.

Dan: At some point in my life. . .I'll concentrate more on drawing from past experience than on gathering new experience, and at that point my style and my personal voice will be more consistent . . .

Carter: The man with the perpetually constant voice isn't alive, he's memorex.

Kim: My personal voice has remained stable since childhood. . .it has not been held to any particular style, but is permitted to be free and natural.

Sue: Since freshman year my voice has changed considerably. It has evolved from self-conscious to self-assertive. . .Yet I know that behind every Woman's Studies paper is the little girl who wrote "I have a loose tooth," who feels as if she's still saying something exciting when she discloses something about women and society.

Mary Beth: I am now aware of who I am and what I stand for...I go out on a limb when I write.

12/20 Grades are turned in—mostly A's and B's. OK. The portfolios were good to read at the end—made the course make more sense *to me* as I see a fairly substantial body of work turned out by each student. In the end I am pleased—though I will change a dozen things next time I teach it, especially by providing more structure and more focus on the books we read. Some want me to keep the extra reports, some want me to drop them—same with *The New Yorker* and the free paper—but everyone liked analyzing a prose writer, analyzing their own voice, and the informal class atmosphere—though some questioned whether or not I knew at all times what I was doing. Here are some samples from their written anonymous evaluations:

- Keep the open class discussions; very comfortable class; free, open, usually interesting...didn't like the reports much.
- I still don't exactly know what I was supposed to come out with. I came out with a variety of things, but I can't tell exactly what you were after.
- Do a short analysis of voice form *The New Yorker* every week.
- Keep the open topic paper! How else would we be able to explore our voices if we are not able to have an opportunity to do so!
- I think I got a good sense of what my personal voice is and how I need to write in order to craft my voice so it comes across as I would like it to.
- I still do not know what personal voice is or what I should do with my voice (if I have one). At times I felt confused and I felt that the teacher was too. I don't know...I felt we were going around in circles.
- Studying other people's writing styles was useful in learning about who I was—what my own voice is.
- Don't digress so much!
- Maybe because the class was experimental I did enjoy it and found some useful analysis of my own writing.
- At times I thought the focus of this class was muddied, maybe it could be more clarified...Portfolio system is cool, keep it.
- I started the semester hating this class, but it became my *favorite!* Is there an "advanced personal voice" class?

Appendix
Revised Syllabus For English 172
Personal Voice

Because the course was new for me and because I wanted to teach it again next year and better, I revised my syllabus as soon as the semester was over. I acted on a combination of the students' perceptions and my own notes. It will be a much better course next time — more structure, fewer and different books, revised paper deadlines, more attention to the *New Yorker*. The resulting syllabus looks like this:

ENGLISH 172 will explore the notion of voice in writing. Normally, when we think of voice, we think of a person speaking, using oral language. But many of us also think we *hear* a voice when we read, think we hear someone talking to us, imagine what that person is like. That's style, you might say, *style*, you know, when a writer chooses certain words, rhythms, images to convey particular impressions. Well, yes, impressions are conveyed through all those writing conventions. But when I say *voice* I actually mean something different from style, something of which style is a part, something that goes beyond the visible manifestation that I think of as style. For instance, voice may include, in addition to style, one's beliefs, ethics, values — things less likely to change as one shifts from writing a memo to a letter to a close friend.

In 172 we'll examine several nonfiction writers with strong voices, look at scholars who have written about voice, and explore — as analytically as we can — our own voices.

Discussion Groups

Class will be divided into five groups that will meet together throughout the term (1) to read and comment on each other's paper drafts, (2) to study selected class readings, and (3) to collaboratively collect material for individually written research essays.

Reading

Persona, Walker Gibson
An Alternate Style, Winston Weathers
Style: An Anti Text, Richard Lanham
Let Us Now Praise Famous Men, James Agee and Walker Evans
The New Yorker (A 16-week subscription for $5.00!)

Writing

1. An ANALYTICAL REPORT based on your individual study of one living nonfiction writer of your choice. Write this in appropriate academic voice using appropriate academic logic, evidence, and conventions. [Duplicate copies of this for your writing group; limit 5 pages including references; 20% of grade.]

2. A paper tracing the DEVELOPMENT OF YOUR OWN WRITING VOICE. (In which you substantiate assertions with evidence from your own murky history as a writer.) [Duplicate copies for writing group; limit 5 pages; 20% of grade.]

3. A FREE TOPIC essay. This to be written in the voice with which you are most comfortable, but aimed at a real publication, for example, *The Burlington Free Press,* UVM *Cynic, The New Yorker* magazine. [Duplicate copies for your writing group, limit 5 pages; 20% of grade.]

4. A RESEARCH ESSAY after the fashion of those published periodically in *The New Yorker.* Topics to be agreed upon by each writing group; papers to be written individually or collaboratively according to your preference. [Duplicate copies for writing groups; limit 10 pages; 30% of grade.]

5. A JOURNAL exploring (1) the theoretical ideas discussed throughout 172, including readings, class discussions, oral reports, colleague's papers; (2) your own musings related to *personal* and *voice*—wherever they may come from; (3) your reading in *The New Yorker,* and (4) whatever else contributes toward your understanding of the concept of voice in text. [Selections of your own choosing to be handed in four times throughout the semester; see due dates in attached schedule; 4×=10% A.]

When our *New Yorkers* begin to arrive, somewhere around the third or fourth week, we will take turns recommending articles and essays in the current issue that are especially interesting in terms of voice; I'm thinking here of 5-minute recommendations each Tuesday and Thursday as we begin class, these to be volunteered for in advance.

9

Teaching Style in Advanced Composition Classes

Mary Fuller

Nowhere is our writing teacher schizophrenia more apparent than in issues of teaching style. Many teachers have abandoned teaching style altogether — and for some defensible reasons. They worry that helping students consciously and systematically craft language can interfere too much with their production of that language. They fear that by teaching style they might appropriate the student's text too completely or end up after vigorous lessons on *vigorous* sentences with very prescriptive advice and a few simplistic bromides: use more appositives and absolutes; avoid nominalizations; avoid too many passives. These teachers argue that through such advice we may well convince our students that we guard the Tower of Babel. And we will admit no one to our conversation who does not speak our language in our way.

Just such issues are thoughtfully attended to in Ian Pringle's "Why Teach Style? A Review Essay," a review of Joseph M. Williams' *Style: Ten Lessons in Clarity and Grace.* While applauding Williams's book as challenging, one necessary for all writing teachers, Pringle raises difficult questions for anyone wishing to teach style in a writing class — or for anyone writing essays about how she teaches style in writing classes. Williams's book challenges the profession, Pringle suggests, to consider two vital questions: "Is it really possible to teach style at all? And if it is, is the plain 'efficient' style the right goal for our students to aim at?" (92). Pringle warns that, just as there has been no empirical evidence that teaching grammar to students improves their writing, there has been no evidence that "teaching about style at this level of explicitness can improve style" (95). Even more worrisome, perhaps, is his suggestion that, as Hake and Williams demonstrate, "when student essays are relatively good, what typical judges of student writing value when they make their judgments is a complex style with heavier cognitive demands, and that, in both better and poorer papers they will find and mark more trivial mechanical and conventional errors in essays written in a plain style than in those written in a complex style, even if there is actually no difference in the frequency of such errors" (95). In essence, then, teaching students plain style may "focus students' attention on what is probably the least of the problems in their writing" (96) and even lead to lower grades for them. If we accept Hake and Williams's findings, then, we must ask ourselves why we spend time showing students how to avoid nominalizing their verbs and adjectives, how to suction sentences fat with noun and prepositional phrases, and how to, as Williams calls it, "control the sprawl." We must begin discovering if, in fact, the audiences to whom our students write value a spare, clean prose style as much as we do.

Pringle's fears are shared by many teachers, I think, who believe that attention to style is important in writing classes—especially in advanced composition classes. For those teachers, Pringle offers a suggestion, "It might make sense...to teach from Williams's *Style* at the end of the college years, or after them," recognizing that what our students learn in their first-year writing classes will surely not survive three years of development in writing ability, and that the techniques of "monitoring," which reading for style requires, could be detrimental to students' early writing efforts (98). Most of us agree, I expect, that we can anticipate stilted, passionless prose from first-year writers if workshops in finding ideas and developing fluency fall victim to endless lessons in style.

With such caveats I introduce my discussion of how I teach style to my advanced composition students at Miami University. I'm convinced after coffee room chat and near-brawl discussions with my colleagues that teaching style is not an easy issue for anyone. I have come to believe, however, that the students (most of them juniors and seniors) who arrive in my advanced writing classes are capable of attention to their prose style. I am convinced that writers who are confident and who have ample opportunity to practice writing for many different audiences begin to develop stylistic strategies and techniques to accommodate their growing sense of the conventional language of the genre or discipline for which they write. I teach varying styles as one of numerous writing options available as revising and editing techniques, not as preliminary invention or drafting behaviors, though I've seen that audience awareness often dictates my most experienced writers' styles and influences their earliest rehearsing and drafting.

Course Description

English 225, Advanced Composition at Miami University serves primarily three groups of students: approximately one-quarter of the students are English majors; about one-half of them business majors (who when closed out of our over-subscribed business writing class may fulfill the requirement in English 225); and the other one-quarter miscellaneous majors. I ask students in the semester-long class to practice writing in multiple forms, to write for different audiences, to share their writing with their peer group members as well as with me, and to start focusing quite deliberately on their own writing styles through a style notebook.

The course description, which I give to students at the beginning of class, describes the course requirements. I've excerpted several appropriate portions below:

English 225: Advanced Composition

Texts: Daiker, Kerek, and Morenberg, *The Writer's Options* (3rd Edition)
Richard Lanham, *Revising Prose*
Peter Elbow, *Writing With Power*

Requirements:

Portfolios: To receive a grade at the end of the term, you will need to give me a portfolio of your writing. In the portfolio you should have 10 completed essays (types of papers discussed below); rough drafts and notes from each; all in-class and out-of-class short writings, papers, or materials I assign. During the semester, try to keep up with *everything* we do in or out of class. (You'll save yourself scurry and hassle at the end!)

Style Notebooks: In your notebooks I will ask you to complete exercises and individual assignments from your textbooks, assessments of your own style, and analyses of your classmates' styles. I will make some of the assignments for all students in the class; I will make some individually. You will probably find your style notebook especially helpful as you examine your own writing process and as you analyze your favorite magazine.

Papers: Unless you arrange something different with me, you'll write the following kinds of papers for our course: (1) a story about yourself; (2) a paper about someone else, either alive or dead, whom you know or don't know; (3) a review of some event or experience around campus or town; (4) a paper that requires you to interview one or more people; (5) a piece of writing submitted to another class; (6) a paper in which you analyze your favorite magazine; (7) a paper in which you review a recent book—fiction or nonfiction; (8) a letter to the editor on a controversial issue; (9) a paper in which you descirbe your own writing process; and (10) a publishable piece (which you will mail to have it considered for publication).

Grades: You will receive oral response from me on all your papers — in conferences and on your cassette tape. In that response I will say what I like about your writing, what I think needs work, and how I suggest you improve your papers. At the end of the term, you will select three of your papers to revise and submit to me for a grade. Each grade will be worth 25 percent of your final grade. (If you are fortunate enough to have your publishable piece published, you will receive an *A* on that work whether it is published during the course or afterward. Who can argue with success?)

You will also receive a grade for class participation, based on your attendance, your style notebook, your completion of other short in-and out-of-class writings, and your willingness and helpfulness in class discussion and peer group work. Your class participation is worth 25 percent of your final grade.

I will be happy any time to discuss with you your writing, your grade, and your progress in the course. We will meet in scheduled conferences every other week—and, of course, in class.

At the beginning of the course students receive a packet of descriptions and sample papers for each of the assignments. The papers, some inspired by suggestions in Peter Elbow's *Writing with Power,* don't need to be written in any special order, though some are easier than others to write. Just as students are free to write the papers in any order that suits them, they're free to design their own projects if the assignments aren't appropriate to their tastes or interests. I do suggest to students that the interview paper might help them prepare for other kinds of papers—such as the paper about someone other than themselves. And I suggest to them that their style notebooks will help them considerably on their composing process paper which, therefore, might best be undertaken at the end of the term.

The class meets an hour and a half twice a week. During class, students draft, meet in their peer groups, and work in full-class revision workshops. In large group discussion, we discuss style primarily as it enhances or characterizes a specific student paper. We will, on occasion, have 5 to 10 minute lessons on some stylistic feature, but for those I select examples from the students' own work.

The Style Notebooks

In the style notebooks students complete a variety of activities. All students complete the basic pattern activities from the *The Writer's Options,* learning from those exercises to construct and control relative clauses, participles, appositives, absolutes, subordination and coordination, infinitives, and noun substitutes. The activities are short, offering an introduction and then a few sentences for practice. An assignment I make during the third week of class is typical of each unit: students read the introduction to appositives, construct the 10 appositives offered in the end-of-chapter exercise, and then move to their own writing. From their writing, they select one or two paragraphs, construct two appositives appropriate to the writing, and include them in their paragraphs. Then they write a 5 to 10 minute response to their use of the appositives. I ask them to read their paragraphs aloud and consider (1) why they selected appositives for the sentence; (2) what the appositive accomplishes grammatically and syntactically; (3) what other comments they can make about their stylistic selection of appositives; and (4) whether they liked their sentences more before they included the appositives and why.

Through such activities students begin to see that their stylistic choices can very much influence the content as well as the language of their pieces, even while they are working on vastly different kinds of papers. Beginning the fourth week of class, students meet in their peer groups for 45 minutes every other week for style sessions. I ask them to bring their style notebooks to those meetings and to be prepared to discuss something they've each learned about their own writing style. I also ask them to show to the group a sentence or passage where they have practiced a style of writing or attempted a construction new to them. Finally, I ask them to share aloud (and on Xeroxed handouts) a short piece of writing where they think their style of writing blends successfully with their content *or* where they've accomplished something in style they particularly like. As you can imagine the first meetings are halting, clumsy, at times uneasy. We are very unaccustomed, as a rule, to discuss our language use. And too seldom are students invited to find examples of their own *conscious* language use that please them.

Practicing the techniques espoused in Peter Elbow's *Writing with Power,* a text I recommend for any advanced writing class, could lead some students to believe that writing is somehow magical—that after the nonstop writing, the looping, the timed forced writings, there isn't much else to do. I particularly like the style notebooks because they encourage students to see how revising for style—even at the sentence level—asks more of them than a simple rip, patch, snip approach to writing. When they work with coordination and subordination, students discover that ideas create logic and momentum of their own, demanding coherence throughout a text. When they learn to construct appositives and absolutes, they must begin evaluating a piece for tone and for voice. In short stories and descriptions, absolutes abound; in letters to the editor, they can be obtrusive, even silly. So even as my students begin working with sentence-level stylistic activities, they are scrutinizing their own full texts and preparing for more detailed whole discourse activities later in the term.

When students have completed all of the basic exercises, I begin to diversify the assignments. Through individual conferences (10 to 15 minutes every other week), I find out which students enjoyed the exercises, which benefited from them, which hated them. I've also begun to see quite a bit of their writing and can determine where students could use work in tone (something that comes up often in the letters to the editor and the publishable pieces); where students could use work in something as basic as rearrangement or as sophisticated as repetition and emphasis; and—most important—where students could use considerably more time rehearsing and drafting and considerably less time revising and editing for style. As I said earlier, the danger for any of us who teach style is shoving students into the cart before they've even harnessed the horses. There are students who, for any number of reasons, are not ready for increased work in style or are well beyond it. These students make their short entries on style in their notebooks, but they do not work on any more style exercises until after midterm.

After midterm, I assign Richard Lanham's *Revising Prose* to everyone in the class. The sentence-combining activities provide students vocabulary for discussing language and their writing and afford them intense practice in various stylistic strategies. Lanham's book, offering its Paramedic Method for trimming lard and translating essays into plain English, gives students a handy, quick revision procedure to apply after drafting for ideas. It offers practice in some simple steps:

1. Circle the prepositions.
2. Circle the "is" forms.
3. Ask "Who is kicking who?"
4. Put this "kicking" action in a simple (not compound) active verb.
5. Start fast—no mindless introductions.
6. Write out each sentence on a blank sheet of paper and mark off its basic rhythmic units.
7. Mark off sentence lengths.
8. Read the passage aloud with emphasis and feeling. (100)

Through Lanham's book, students practice eliminating an overly nominal style fraught with too many prepositional phrases and too many passive verbs. They learn to start fast—with "no mindless introductions." And they discover their writing is language with rhythm, units of sound, and units of length. My students enjoy Lanham's breezy style and quite practical information.

We continue the style-group sharing throughout the semester, focusing less and less on the techniques of style and the apparatus of style exercises, and more on students sharing examples of their writing where the style pleases them. From midterm on I ask them to write a journal entry a week assessing their style in a specific essay, showing where they've tinkered or experimented with style in one of their papers, or examining the style of one of their classmate's successful pieces of writing. As lively as the peer group sharing and revision sessions, these entries provide students an opportunity to examine why writing *works* for them or it doesn't. In previous workshops where my students concentrated only on writing-responding–revising, they could not articulate their goals in their own writing nearly as well, they could not measure how their writing affects readers, and — most obviously — they could not discuss in detail why they enjoy some writing more than other writing. The style notebooks and style sessions foster such insights.

An Example

To show how the language of style and the awareness of style translate into improved writing and more sensitive responses to writing, I offer an example. Here is an early draft of an essay by Sheri, a junior business major, working on her seventh paper in the class. The assignment asks students to describe their favorite magazine and explain why they enjoy it. To write the paper they must examine their own reading tastes and, more often than not, popular culture as well. (*Glamour, Vogue,* and *Sports Illustrated* are the three most popular magazines with my students.) While the assignment is obviously an old chestnut — a variation of the rhetorical analysis popular in the 1960s and 1970s — it asks students to examine their preferences, their interests, and — as Sheri's paper illustrates — their values.

In early draft form, Sheri's paper does not successfully examine her interest in the magazine:

> Pushing the shopping cart through the checkout line at the supermarket, I'm dazzled by the wide array of magazines. Often after glancing at *National Enquirer's* headlines, I'll pick up a *Glamour.* Why? Because *Glamour* is geared to today's woman — whether she's "working, playing, or resting." Not only does it aid a woman to become more glamorous, it also can give tips on how you survive the brutal everyday life of dressing right and handling the trials and tribulations of men.
>
> After I dig out *Glamour* from between the cheese-whiz and pop, I flop on my cot and "take off." The women in *Glamour* never look like they shop at Kroger's (I don't think they ever eat anyway). In last September's issue, *Glamour* ran their usual "back-to-school" bonus, complete with fashions every college girl needed to make it in "an active college life." Ralph Lauren sweaters, only $320, Anne Klein blouses, a mere $150, and Ilena Italian flats graced the pages. I probably like *Glamour* so much because it's so optimistic. It believes with the right clothing I'll look just like those skinny, gorgeous creatures who I'm sure worry about exams and finding someone (anyone) for next Saturday's date party.

Over half the ads in *Glamour* are for make-up. In the September 1986 issue, there are 56 make-up ads in all, from Maybelline, Cover Girl, and Revlon up to Estee Lauder and Lancome. Of course all the models are gorgeous, and I sit and fantasize that once I have "mascara that lasts 29 hours" or "eyeshadows that cause a man to propose," I will look just like them. I don't usually do more than browse through the make-up ads, but I must admit that once before a special date I spent time with *Glamour's* "before" and "after" make-over section, trying to transform myself with the help of $65 dollars worth of make-up and their tips on "how to go from plain to pizzazz!!!!!" in 20 minutes. It was more a case of from "dull to desperate," I decided after washing my face three times and starting over.

Another thing I really like about *Glamour* is its confidence that I'm going to shape-up, diet, run, start a new diet each month (because there's always at least one featured). They usually place the diets right next to their latest recipes for "late-night linguine for lovers." In last year's Valentine's Day issue, they placed a recipe for giant, heart-shaped chocolate chip cookies entitled "the way to your own sweetie's heart," two pages after a spread on trimming down your tummy and thighs after the holiday eating blitz.

If I'm honest, I have to admit my favorite part of *Glamour* is reading about men. (Add articles here)

I guess I enjoy *Glamour* because it allows me to fantasize with some perspective. If the truth be known, people who eat half a jar of cheese whiz at one sitting have difficulty seeing themselves with mohawk haircuts in Guy Laroche satin slips and blue nail polish like the women in *Vogue* and *Harper's Bazaar*. But with *Glamour* I can close my eyes and pretend that my boyfriend Freddy will maybe someday look at me with smoldering lust and sail me away on a cruise down the Nile, billed in *Glamour* as a "dream vacation for the most romantic."

After peer group sharing, Sheri received the following letter from Miranda, one of her peer group members. The letter was not one intended to focus on style. Sheri is too soon into the paper to need stylistic suggestions or comments

Dear Sheri,

As I read this paper I could relate to it. In the check-out line I do the same thing. I flip through ads and stare at the models and wonder what their parents look like to make a product like that! It's the same kind of magazine I read, so I can understand what's in it and what's appealing.

The writing seems to be about what *Glamour* magazine has to offer and what you like to look at in it. I wasn't too clear by the end, though, if that was the main point. It seemed like you should talk as much about what *Glamour* offers as what you got out of it. Maybe that's one of the things you should think about.

I can see myself flipping through the magazine just like you, eating cheese whiz, then turning to the diet of the month. I think I saw the same Valentine issue you mentioned!

I liked this paper more than any other I read because it's funny, and I loved that line about "from dull to desperate" and the part about Freddy. (Is he a regular? I know a Sigma C. who's on the loose!)

I guess my two suggestions are to add more funny stuff if you can think of any and to figure out the focus.

The end!

Best regards,
Miranda

Quite good for what it is, Miranda's letter illustrates how thoughtful students and honest readers can help writers as they explore ideas and as they draft. Sheri did need to find a focus for her paper, and she later made a good paper sing when she added "more funny stuff." Compare, however, Miranda's letter and its advice with the detailed analysis of style that Jeff offers Sheri after her second draft. I ask students when they write their analyses of style to attempt to be descriptive more than prescriptive, pointing out style that works well in the paper, commenting on what features are most prominent in a writer's work:

Dear Sheri,

Whew! I liked your paper "To Be or Not To Be...Glamorous." I went through and circled the first words in all of your sentences and figured out that you use adverb clauses or phrases most often or nouns as subjects second most often. That's starting fast. I also liked the repetition you used. The listing in the second paragraph, "sweaters, blouses, shoes," was good. My favorite sentence had repetition, too, in the last paragraph: "I can close my eyes and pretend that my boyfriend Freddy will maybe someday look at me with smoldering lust, throw me bodily into his candy-apple red Porsche, and spirit me off for a cruise down the Nile (a 'dream vacation for only the most romantic')". I liked the way you put your funny material in parentheses or set it off in dashes. "From dull to desperate" was terrific. I guess that is style. When I tried to be funny in that restaurant paper it fell flat (ha!). Yours worked though.

Jeff

Both letters show how mutually reinforcing the responses are, while offering different information and advice. Sheri receives reinforcement for what she does well in both content and style, and Miranda and Jeff offer Sheri a chance to consider her writing in two different, yet overlapping ways. Interestingly enough, Miranda likes Sheri's paper for its humor, something Jeff recognizes (quite appropriately, I think) as style. Such response from her readers helps Sheri to write a fine last draft:

To Be or Not to Be. . . .Glamorous

Pushing the shopping cart through the checkout line at the supermarket, I'm dazzled by the wide array of magazines. Often, after reading the headlines on the sleazy pulps — how many alien invasions can anyone stand? — I'll pick up *Glamour*. Why? Because *Glamour*, more than any other magazine I know, is geared to the kind of woman I like to think I am. It claims that it's for "today's woman," whether she's "working, playing, or resting." I know when I plunk down my hard-won three dollars (hey, allowance doesn't go as far as it used to!) that I'll earn a quick but sure-fire escape into the world as I want it to be.

As soon as I'm back to the dorm, I dig out my *Glamour* from between the Cheese-Whiz and diet-Pepsi, flop on my cot, and "take off." The women in *Glamour* never look like they just got back from Kroger's in worn-out Nikes and an over-sized sweatshirt stolen from an older brother. In last September's issue, *Glamour* ran their usual "back-to-school" bonus, complete with the fashion every college girl needed to "make it in an active college life." Ralph Lauren sweaters, only $320, Anne Klein blouses, a mere $150, and llena Italian flats graced the pages. As I devoured the pages (and my Cheese-Whiz), I noticed that four-inch wide leather belts (costing as much as most skirts) were what I needed "to cinch" my campus look. I probably like *Glamour* so much because it's so optimistic. It believes that with the right clothing I'll look just like those skinny, gorgeous creatures who I'm sure worry about calculus and Western Civ exams when they're not modeling.

Over half the ads in *Glamour* are for make-up. In the September 1986 issue, there were 56 make-up ads in all, everything from Maybelline, Cover Girl, and Revlon for the more economical girl, all the way up to Estee Lauder and Lancome for the more self-indulgent among us. Of course, all the models are gorgeous, and I sit and fantasize that once I have "mascara that lasts 29 hours" or "eyeshadows that cause a man to propose," I won't need to worry about much else, especially if that special man spirits me away to his Italian villa, pictured in my favorite Jontue ad. I don't usually do more than browse through the make-up ads, but I must admit that once before a special date I spent time with *Glamour's* "before" and "after" make-over section, trying to transform myself with the help of $65 dollars worth of make-up and their tips on "how to go from plain to pizzazz!!!!" in 20 minutes. (It was more of a case of from "dull to desperate," I decided, after washing my face three times and starting over.)

I do more, of course, than browse the advertisements. I love the monthly columns, located always after the first flurry of perfume ads — generally around page 22. In one column, "Can This Be Love,"

I get to see other people as confused about boyfriends as I am. In "How to Do Anything Better," I've gotten tips on managing money, keeping pets in a city apartment, and landing an executive job with a top-flight accounting firm. While I've never ordered from "Shop by Mail," I plan to as soon as I graduate. My first choices are Pheremone perfume, direct from Marilyn Miglin in Chicago, at $350 an ounce, New Hampshire maple syrup squeezed fresh from the tree for $21, and a Kilgerry blue, hand-knit fisherman's sweater direct from Ireland—a steal at $221. (Most of the suggestions are clearly for women who've already landed their jobs with the accounting firms, but there are the occasional "bargain" foot massagers and rhinestone halters "for that daring evening out.") Probably my favorite column, after the monthly horoscope, is "Women Right Now," which each month features someone involved in "a dream job" or occupation.

Another thing I really like about *Glamour* is its confidence that I'm going to shape-up, diet, run, start a new diet each month (because there's always at least one featured). They've got more faith in me than my mother! In fact, in last year's Valentine's Day issue, they placed a recipe for giant, heart-shaped chocolate chip cookies, entitled "the way to your own sweetie's heart," two pages after a spread on trimming down your tummy and thighs after the holiday eating blitz. Obviously, they trust that none of us ever lick the bowl or sample our own cooking.

Finally, I guess, if I am honest, I have to admit my favorite part of *Glamour* is articles about men. I realized at about age 15 that men are impossible to figure out and I've not met any since to change my mind. *Glamour* understands that. They've run articles like "Why Half the Men on the Face of the Earth are Geeks," "How Often Do Men Tell the Truth?" and "Real-Men: The Endangered Species." Even though I haven't yet unraveled the mystery of the opposite sex, I expect to start soon. And while I'm working on it, I won't suffer any male shortage because I've read "100 Ways to Attract that Man You've Been Eyeing."

Finally, then, I guess I enjoy *Glamour* because it allows me to fantasize with some perspective. People who eat half a jar of Cheese Whiz at one sitting have difficulty seeing themselves in Guy Laroche satin slips and blue nail polish, typical of the spreads in *Vogue* or *Harper's Bazaar*. But, with *Glamour*, I can close my eyes and pretend that my boyfriend Freddy will maybe someday look at me with smoldering lust, throw me bodily into his candy-apple red Porsche, and spirit me off for a cruise down the Nile (a "dream vacation for only the most romantic"). It's a way to dream realistically!

Sheri's essay is effective for a number of reasons. She has found the focus for her essay—how *Glamour* allows her to dream within some realistic parameters, parameters that she can gently spoof, even as they entice her. Her humor sparkles and thanks, in part, to Jeff's appreciation of "the way you put your funny material in parentheses,"

Sheri adopts that strategy to real advantage throughout the essay. Choosing to alert her readers through punctuation that "I'm saying something funny" is a sophisticated stylistic feature that Sheri may not have exercised without Jeff's comments. Miranda likes "the funny stuff," but Jeff has noticed and encouraged something that helps scaffold and intensify such "stuff." His remarks about style have shown Sheri something of the skeleton beneath the flesh.

And the skeleton is well worth the praise. Sheri practices a full repertoire of stylistic strategies in her paper. I am less impressed than Jeff with her adverb clauses, not especially notable constructions in themselves; however, I am dazzled (to use Sheri's phrase) with the variety of her techniques to add detail. Notice the ease with which she uses free modifiers: there are four used effectively in the first paragraph alone and an equally impressive series in the sentence, "My first choices are Pheromone perfume, *direct from Marilyn Miglin in Chicago, at $350 an ounce*, New Hampshire maple syrup *squeezed fresh from the tree for $21*, and a Kilgerry blue, hand-knit fisherman's sweater *direct from Ireland—a steal at $221*" (paragraph 4). The paper is not only rich in repetition, as Jeff points out, but varied in sentence length. Consider the successful one word question "Why?" in paragraph one; the acerbic bite of "They've got more faith in me than my mother!" in paragraph 5; and the brief sentence concluding the essay, one which reinforces the paper's central idea. The short sentences balance and punctuate the long, graceful sentences that mark Sheri's style. And lastly, one needn't look too hard for concrete and specific diction, such as "sleazy pulps," "worn-out Nikes," "first flurry of perfume ads," and "candy-apple red Porsche." Her use of the articles' titles alone provides a good bit of the paper's humor.

I would argue that essays as sophisticated in style as Sheri's are no accident. Certainly, she may have been a good writer when she started the class; many students entering advanced writing classes are. Writers made conscious, however, of a full range of stylistic strategies prosper, I believe, more quickly and more fully than those who aren't offered such information. Through *The Writer's Options* and *Revising Prose,* students learn the *language* and tools of style. Through the style notebooks, they question, explore, and practice what the textbooks offer, sharpening their personal writing tools. They begin to choose what feels comfortable to them and to articulate why they make such choices. Finally, through reading one another's papers for style, they accustom themselves to see meaning as inextricably interwoven with language use.

Conclusion

According to Ross Winterowd, "there is no way to answer the question of why a writer chooses his or her own subset of syntactic gambits, but it is not unreasonable to suggest the influence of cognitive style, reading background, education, and general culture" (83). Given that assertion, it makes more sense to begin educating our writing students about their own styles than it does to abandon the effort altogether. It is reasonable, I believe, to expose students—especially advanced writing students—to a full range of stylisic strategies and possibilities, to invite them to practice those strategies, and to examine quite carefully how those strategies affect their writing. When students can recognize, control, and enjoy those possibilities, they are well on their way to becoming really *advanced* writers.

Works Cited

Daiker, Donald, Max Morenberg, and Andrew Kerek. *The Writer's Options: Combining to Composing.* 3rd ed. New York: Harper, 1986.

Elbow, Peter. *Writing with Power.* Oxford: Oxford UP, 1981.

Hake, Rosemary T, and Joseph M. Williams. "Style and Its Consequences: Do as I Do, Not as I Say." *College English* 43 (1981): 433–51.

Lanham, Richard. *Revising Prose.* New York: Scribner's, 1979.

Pringle, Ian. "Why Teach Style? A Review-Essay." *College Composition and Communication* 34 (1983): 91–98.

Winterowd, W. Ross. "Prolegomenon to Pedagogical Stylistics." *College Composition and Communication* 34 (1983): 80–90.

10

Letters on Writing— A Medium of Exchange with Students of Writing

Sam Watson

Reflecting on what we do while we do it, we come to do it differently. And we come to do it better, sooner, than we would without the reflecting. Our writing improves our learning; it obliges us to reflect on what we are learning, and it invites us to reflect on how we are learning it.[1] If that is true generally, are there some modes of writing that may particularly help the writer learn—writing?

"You learn to write by writing." That old saw may be one-half true, but the other half is merely convenient. It can warrant our simply imposing writing upon students, thoughtlessly, and it can invite our students to respond in kind. Not all writing is equally effective in improving writing; some may actually be counterproductive. It may be that writing about our own writing, as we are doing it, can help us improve *as* writers.

The Problem

For years my classes have endured a standard sermon; that any writing is done within some social context, which shapes and constrains both the act of writing and the text(s) produced; that writing is a *process* before it is a *product*; that both the acts and the artifacts of writing are *situated* in some one or other distinctly human world with the presence of real persons who have real intentions. And I have realized that a major difficulty with school writing, hypothetical case situations notwithstanding, is the absence of any real context within which school writing is done.

133

It has taken me longer to realize that a real context is immediately at hand, one that students and I jointly inhabit. It is the context of the class we share and the varied intentions we bring. Writing is not only *done* within social contexts; it is *learned* within them as well. How we shape our classroom contexts influences powerfully — probably more powerfully than what any of us explicitly say — how and what our students learn of writing.

Now in my classes, an important part of our shared context is a mode of writing intended to give students and me access to the contexts of our work. Writing about writing — a semester-length series of letters between each student and me — now forms a continuing medium of exchange and mutual reflection.

Initially, I was spurred to develop this mode of response to student writing by a real difficulty in my own writing: I was unhappy with what and how I was writing on student papers. Despite the process orientation I was espousing, my traditional mode of response seemed to be reenforcing a familiar emphasis on finished products. In marginal and extensive end-note comments, I was trying to be supportive, insightful, critical, all at once. I found it difficult and tedious to write these comments, and in students' subsequent work there was little reason to believe that my labored responses had given much help.

It was as though certain critical dimensions of the social context, which should be shaping and constraining my responses, were inaccessible to me. For instance, from a paper only, I could rarely tell much of what the student thought of that paper. I couldn't know what had gone into the writing; what issues the writing had uncovered for that student; what potentials the student felt still lying somewhere "behind" the text, as yet unrealized within it. It was as though I was writing my comments — and my students were reading them — in a vacuum.

I began to suspect that the same vacuum that was giving me difficulties in my writing was giving my students difficulties in doing theirs. And — since a vacuum *will* be filled — that students probably saw me as having some ideal text in mind against which theirs would be measured, an "ideal" that I might describe to them were I more articulate or less perverse.

The Course

In recent years, I have attended to the social context that is our course. I want to situate us — students and me — as a community of learners, brought together by our common interests in developing our own writing. As the hollowness of those words suggests, this is a relationship that cannot be established by just talking about it, and it is one quite different from much school practice. Central to this relationship is the unfolding dymanic of the letter exchange I engage in with each student. My letters have become my mode of responding to student writing, one that has replaced virtually all marginal comments and is still evolving within a course I teach virtually every semester. It is a course in expository writing, taken by upper-division and graduate students at University of North Carolina—Charlotte. In that course we write frequent short papers—a dozen or so in a semester. Assigments tend to specify an audience (often it's "us," the other members of the class) and hint at some purpose, but they only rarely stipulate a subject. I put no letter grades on papers—or in any secret grade book. From the beginning I tell students, in print:

> If you ever feel yourself getting particularly anxious about grades, let me know that (for instance in one of the letters you're writing to me), and we'll develop a way for you to get a grade evaluation of your work to that point. At midterm, I'll give you a provisional grade. You do have to get a grade at the end of the course. That decision has finally to be my responsibility, but I will doubtless be asking your advice on what grade you have earned. (There will be no "grading curve" in this course, so you are not in competition with each other for good grades.) Stated very generally, it strikes me as appropriate to consider these things: (1) signs that you are growing, as a writer and as a learner; (2) signs that you are reflecting on what you're doing; and (3) signs that you are contributing to the growth of others.

In the course, my central task is not to evaluate developed writing but to help writers develop. Grade assessments need to be based fundamentally not on the qualities that finished texts exhibit but—what often amounts to the same thing—on the quality and depth of insight a student develops through and within her/his work.

How and Why We Now Exchange Letters

Dear fellow writer,

You are currently engaged in doing some specific writing task. As you go about that task, what do you notice yourself doing? Are there any quirks or habits you find yourself using that seem to be helping, even if (maybe especially if!) they have little in common with what you've heard from texts and teachers about ways one "ought" to write? (Those "ought"'s have little to do with the ways *I* write, and I've never been able to make myself believe in them!) As you keep writing, what do you notice your text doing—even if (maybe especially if) it seems to be doing something you hadn't expected or wanted it to? What would you like it to do, that maybe it's not doing yet? From what you notice going on in your own writing—both the "how" you are going about it and the "what" that the text seems to be doing, what questions are you forming that I might be able to help you grapple with? Please write me a letter as full of your observations and questions as you can, and say anything else that you'd like me to be thinking about. (That's a marvellous thing about letters; they can "follow" wherever our minds go; they don't have to be "organized" in advance!) Leave with me both the letter and the text you're working on; I'll write you a letter in return, before we meet again.

Sam

Given the silent protocols of printed texts, doubtless I will not be getting reply letters from readers of this essay—though to be proven wrong would no doubt delight me into responding. The letter above both sets the context for our letter exchanges and illustrates the dynamics of these exchanges. In students' letters I am not asking for evaluation or self-critique; I am asking for *description* instead, description of how that student finds her/himself working, description of how the emerging text is shaping itself in light of a particular intention— which may itself be emerging with the text. What I most hope to read in students' letters to me is self-awareness that opens toward speculation.

Whether or not a student's letter is descriptive in ways I would wish, it always gives me a perspective for useful response that a paper by itself does not. At the least, I can read that student's engagement and attitude—toward the act of writing she has just engaged, toward the resulting text, toward our course. From how the student's letter is shaped and from what it says (and does not say), I can usually read a set of assumptions about writing and (often) about education. A student's letter allows me to see writing through that student's eyes— or it tells me that I am not yet privy to that vision.

My response is no longer being written in a vacuum. It is, quite simply, a letter to that student, guided by the letter I have just read. Taking her/his letter as my point of departure, I follow my thoughts wherever they seem to want to go. In a sense, that is all there is to it; I am no longer critiquing a text, I am responding to a person.

Responding *to* a person obliges me to respond *as* a person. I write quickly, almost never revising or correcting as I go; students will see my misspellings, grammar mistakes, and (I'm sure) connections that seem (or are) illogical. I frequently shape questions that might guide that student's (or my) future reflections, as we continue trying to deepen our understanding of how writing gets done and how texts work. Writing these letters gives me needed practice in developing fluency and in writing my way toward new understandings. It gives me ideas that I will bring to class and to my scholarly work. As letters will, mine often become excursions into thoughts of my own that are trying to form themselves.

I enjoy writing these letters. My sense is that my responses now are both longer and more quickly written than they used to be. Certainly they are easier to write and more individual. And knowing that I must write the student a thoughtful letter makes the student's writing more interesting for me to read. It also provides a continuing challenge that I need: when I must write that student a letter, I must really *read* and think about what the student has written; I can't get by with vague, innocuous, and unhelpful comments (e.g. "good paper").

I don't know whether it is essential, but I write all my letters on computer. That gives me practice at keyboarding skills (something else I need), and it means that students need not decipher my awful handwriting. The computer also makes it easy for me to occasionally incorporate into a letter some excerpt from my own writing which that student might find useful or interesting. And with the computer, I have ready access to all the letters I have written that student through the semester; I usually scan my most recent letter before writing my next one.

Early in the semester, students' letters are often defensive and vacuous. That is a time when I especially need to be reassuring, to share some of my own frustrations with writing, to urge students to let me hear their voices by inviting them to listen to mine. As the semester unfolds, so do many of my students. They begin to develop tentative, promising insights into their own writing processes. They start identifying difficulties as well as achievements in their own texts; I am spared both the tedium and the negative stance of painstakingly describing some problem that a student in some measure already *sees* in her/his text. It feels a lot healthier all around to be able to write "Hooray! What a fine problem you're seeing!" and to take it from there. The exchange of letters enables me to become more nearly coach and collaborator than critic.

Despite my written, private, repeated, and increasingly strident requests for more thoughtful letters, some students' letters remain a mere afterthought, a quick note dashed off hurriedly. I have begun experimenting with some strategies that may help. This semester, for example, I began the course by giving students an open letter about my writing and asking for a letter about theirs, without any accompanying text. I also am trying some modeling of what I am asking from students: giving them something I am working on, accompanied with a letter to them. When I give my letter responses to students now, I try to allow a few minutes of class time for them to read my letter and quickly jot what they find themselves thinking or feeling — comments that I hope might feed into their next letter to me. And I often allow some classroom time for students to add a postscript to their letters to me, once they have participated in a writing group discussion of the piece the letter accompanies. These are a few strategies intended to help students more quickly see the sorts of reflection I am asking for in their letters. I would like to develop still others, especially some that would help students meaningfully read an emerging draft of their own and describe the potential ways the draft or some portion of it is or is not working.

My aim of course is to engage each student in a semester-length written dialogue, whose subject is that student's writing—and whatever else comes up as we try together to make sense of writing. We have a private channel of communication between student and instructor, and the channel runs in both directions. There is always another letter to be written; students always can respond to my responses. As one student puts it, "I need to be able to say to you what I feel about what you have said to me."

Illustrative Exchanges

By definition there is no such thing as a model letter, but the following excerpt from a letter accompanying some academic-sounding assignment, which Robin wrote late in the semester, illustrates some dynamics that I welcome:

> Dear Sam,
>
> [In this paper] I just put down the facts where I thought they were most appropriate. [It was] not like using a thesis, opening (intro.) paragraph, then the body, and a conclusion. My words just flowed on and on until I felt it was through...In any paper, would it be acceptable to write your own thoughts at the beginning as I did? After putting in the facts, is it good taste to comment on them right then, or [should you] wait and put [the explanations] in as a conclusion? I felt I was writing lines that weren't relevant. Almost as if I was talking to myself about what I read. You said this was o.k., but any other English teacher would throw the paper away because they want strictly facts from sources and nothing but the correct structure for putting it in.
>
> Robin

Robin's letter to me reflects sensitively on her writing process and her text. Her work also illustrates two turns I often see simultanously in the efforts of successful students. The first is a qualitative growth in the richness of the text their letter accompanies. The other is their new feeling, expressed in their letter, that they must be doing something wrong. Though most of them are not as articulate about this discomfort as Robin, their writing no longer *feels* like the writing they have done under a paradigm of rules, which (Robin's letter illustrates this too) have, at best, been misunderstood.

Here is my letter in response, just as I gave it to Robin:

Dear Robin,

I've enjoyed reading the paper. I do want to raise one point (not a criticism) about documentation, then respond to the thoughtful letter you wrote.

On documentation, keep this general rule in mind: you give specific citations anytime the information (a) is specific and (b) is not common knowledge among those who know something of your subject. You're not giving "specific citations" through this paper, and I think that is appropriate, under (b), but I wanted to point out the rule for your future reference. (Just to be complete, of course you ALWAYS give specific citations when using direct quotes.)

Now, on your letter, I want to say two things, which may SOUND contradictory to each other. First (and most important), assuming that ANY paper is more than a fill-in-the-blanks exercise, what gives it shape IS the writer's thought. There just isn't any other way. Attempts to suggest something about the "shape" of a thinking process ("intro. body, conclusion" is one such attempt) often get treated as formulas to REPLACE thinking, as you're suggesting here. The thinking is what's central, to the shaping of a paper as a whole AND to the shaping of sections and smaller parts. It's like the thinking is what gets you from one thing to a next one; at the very least, it's the "glue" that puts "facts" into a meaningful mosaic. That much is true for ALL writing. It is just about the most insidious thing I know of, that we have managed to teach writing in such ways that students believe that their own thinking is not appropriate to that writing. NO WONDER they find it difficult to write—or to learn. The second point is really just a qualification of the first: Though thinking always GUIDES the formation of a text, whether or not the thinking ought to be represented IN the text depends on the purpose OF that text. Imagine yourself reading a phone book, for example. You won't want to know how the phone company thought it through, decided who should get which number, etc, or how to collect all the information; you just want to find the right number. But a lot of thinking had to go INTO the formation of the text, even one as "straightforward" as a phone book. See what I mean? It's just a qualification to the point, the REALLY IMPORTANT one, I was making above.

Sam

Representative papers from another semester illustrate still other dynamics. A month into this semester I was asked to conduct a workshop on writing for university faculty in Alabama. Before the workshop, these professors jotted concerns and questions to which my expository students might respond. I gave out typed copies of these and—with only two days' notice, I'm afraid—asked my students to write a response to those professors, accompanied by a letter to me, to which I then responded. The resulting writing illustrates a range of student work—and of my letters to them. Unlike most of our work, these student pieces also suggest how my students' writing might read when its intended audience is other professors.

Following are: (1) excerpt of a student's reflection to the Alabama faculty, sufficient to give a sense of how that piece is developing; (2) excerpt from that student's accompanying letter to me; (3) my full letter in response to that student. I spent just over 10 minutes, on average, reading both letters from a student and writing my response. The typos in my letters are born both of hurry and the sound rhetorical sense that not all writing needs to be corrected. As you read, I invite you to reflect: (1) If you had *only* the letter for the Alabama faculty, from which the first passage is excerpted, what would you write this student? On a spectrum running from *critique* to *response,* where would yours fall? (2) Now that you have read that student's accompanying letter to me, what/how/why would you write to that student? (3) How does your response compare to the one that I wrote? In comparing your responses with each other and with mine, I'm inviting you to *describe* rather than to *evaluate.*

In Alabama, incidentally, I did ask each faculty member to read a student's letter addressed to the group and to write a response to that student, which they did—appreciatively. I then asked faculty to take another student's letter, write a *critique* of that one, and then show the critique to the colleague who had already *responded* to that student. Several faculty reported finding themselves offended as they read the critiques their colleagues had just written. There is no question that critiques work very differently from responses. There is need for both, in a classroom world, but it may be that critiques are more effective when set in the larger context of response.

Dear Faculty,

Allow your students to write. It is a privilege and a pleasure to be able to explore the freedom found in writing. Explore all kinds of writing. Begin with free writing (freedom from criticism—grammatical or otherwise) for writing's sake. This gets the mind moving and the thoughts stirring...

After you have generated some ideas begin to focus on a specific idea or phrase or thought. Focusing helps a student to concentrate on a subject. Focusing or concentrating on a subject requires discipline...

Dorothy

Dear Sam,

....The most valuable thing I have learned in my writing experience is that if I will only put down on paper what is flowing through my mind, I can bring my thoughts (those misty forms) into something more concrete or solid. I can begin to see (on paper) my thoughts taking shape...I used to be afraid to write. Now I feel free to write and usually have more than enough to say on a paper.

Dorothy

Dear Dorothy,

What utterly fascinating contrasts, between your letter to me and the one to the Ala. folks; and both all filled with such good sense! In the Ala. letter, from the start you're giving advice — the imperative verbs show that. That is, your stance, though informed by your own experience, is that you already share a context and purpose with your reader and that s/he's ready to begin trying to act on what you say. The letter to me — so different, in that there it's your reflections on your own experience that's at the fore. What a different set of assumptions/ re your relations with your audience! What fun!! (As you see, I'm sharing the excitement you express!)

Sam

In Dorothy's letter I see potentially liberating awareness of process; in Erin's, which follows, reflection on genre and emerging intention.

....The classes which have encouraged discussion and, even those which have encouraged writing, I have gained more in them. I felt as though the professor appreciated my thoughts and wanted me to "succeed in learning." For in fact, those which I had to do out of class writing, I learned more and that knowledge seemed to stay with me even after the class was finished.

Writing and being able to speak properly is an art. Like all artists, they must paint more than one picture to gain the experience. Students need the experience...

Erin

Sam,

I had so many ideas — I wish I would not have been the procrastinator that I am. I think that I could have kept "on-a-writing." My only problem, I seemed to have a hard time connecting everything I wanted to say. I wasn't trying to, but after I finished the letter I felt as though I had written an editorial. Problem is, I'm not sure that was what I wanted to do. Then again, maybe it was!!!! I seemed to take a turn at "writing...is an art." This is when I wanted to make all my ideas connect. I couldn't so I just took the easy way out and didn't write much more. How can I do this? Am I just giving up too soon? How can I help myself learn to connect? Thanks. Have a good trip.

Erin

Dear Erin,

Well now, between Tuesday, when I gave the assignment, and Thursday, when you responded, there wasn't much TIME to procrastinate! (One thing that's always struck me — how it often is, that the more time students have, the worse the papers get. I DO wish we'd had more time here, though!)

"Only connect." That's the motto, too, of one of E.M. Forster's novels. The first step, I'm sure, is to have things (must be things — plural) TO connect — as you clearly do here. Then, to look for possible connections that those things suggest, as I also think you're doing. And a "frame" that further suggests connections — as your references to the business world function for you here. So, I think the issues of 'connectiveness' are ones you've largely solved here, though maybe we'll see what our Ala. friends think. The level I see that might best use attention — oh, for the extra time I wish we'd had! — is in sentences and sometimes paragraphs; there seem places that take "2 readings" where, with a little reshaping, they might require only one.

Sam

Kyle's work shows a well-developed strategy in light of the rhetorical situation:

From what I have experienced in my classes at UNCC, I suspect the most undervalued potential for student learning on this campus could be through the use of informal writing assignments. It seems to me such a technique would help students synthesize what is already being covered in class.

An instructor is already aware of the organization of his/her material and how it fits together. But unless a student goes thru some sort of integrating process, the entire body of knowledge remains a jumble of individual facts. By themselves these ideas are easily lost in the data banks of the mind once the exam is over. Having to write a few paragraphs tying the main ideas together at times in the semester has helped me. I gain a better perspective of how the pieces of information fit together, and I feel more confident about my grasp of the material . . .

Kyle

Dear Sam,

What helped me most in developing content for this letter was reading the expectation blurbs on the sheet you gave us. It pointed out what questions my readers wanted answered.

I right away decided to direct the letter toward the hard core lecturer who is convinced writing has no relevance to his or her class. I figured those already sold would come like sponges wanting to soak up whatever you offered, and so I could be most effective as a sales tool to the skeptic. So I wanted to stick to facts and not get flowery (in keeping with my perception of what language is best understood by my audience).

You'd be proud of the number of paragraphs that aren't in the final version of this thing!

It's sounding very particular at this point. But I think I'd rather cover all the aspects of one idea in a letter like this than to try to say all the things that could be said on this topic.

I've debated on whether or not to mention that as a philosophy student I get a lot of this kind of thing and find it very helpful. But I think maybe my target group would use it as a means to discredit its applicability to other disciplines. Better left unsaid.

Well, if it didn't mean copying the whole letter page over I'd change that 1st sentence. It sounds long and clumsy, and neither "is" nor "are" sounds right to me. The curse of long hand. (My kids messed up the margins of the typewriter or I would type it.)

Anyway I've tried to write this letter about that paper as I went and I hope it contains some of what it is supposed to.

Kyle

Dear Kyle,

I'm proud to see the sense of strategy that your letter to me shows—and so does you open letter to the Ala. folks! Your consistent reading of your audience is guiding your choices of what to say and how to say it. And your own experience is just "behind" or "beneath" the text of your letter—not so far removed from it that you seem to be playing "God," and not so immediately "present" that it would allow you letter to be discounted by those who don't appreciate the value of philosophy. It's a confident tone without being overbearing or "preachy." Good going!

I'd love to know what paragraphs got left out. Could you show them to me sometime?

Re/ the "is/are" question. Depends on whether you're going here by ear or strict "grammar." A linking verb, used to join two nouns, one of which is singular while the other's plural—that's what's giving you the uncertainty. The subject is singular, so the verb "ought" to be "is." But the verb is closer to "assignments," which makes it sound like "are." Which to use? I'd say it depends on the tone, the formality, of the piece.

Sam

The work of Madge shows instructive shifts of language, between the formal reflection to the Alabama faculty and the accompanying letter to me:

Distinguished faculty:

The views you have expressed concerning incorporation of writing by students into various disciplines are also major concerns of students. As future educators, administrators, business executives, engineers, etc. there are concerns about job performance that will ensure that these positions be maintained. While many of these roles have not traditionally required extensive writing skills, there is a new trend pushing toward coherent communication through proficient writing...

Madge

Dear Sam,

Writing this letter helped me deal with some of the major quarrels I have had with educators concerning attitudes of society as a whole toward writing...

Dear Madge,

In BOTH letters—the one to me and the one to the Ala. "Distinguished faculty," you are getting at SUCH important things! I want you to notice some important differences between those two letters. The "situation" is very different, of course. You know me, and you haven't met them. But notice too the difference in your language. In the letter to me, it's so very clear and direct. In the other letter, there are times when the language becomes "distinguished"—so much so, that it may not be possible for readers to tell just what you're saying. See what I mean?

Maybe the lesson here—and it's SUCH a crucial one!—is how necessary it is to trust yourself, to give yourself the confidence to say what needs saying—even if you DON'T know the readers; even if they ARE "distinguished."

Sam

The language differences in Madge's work were characteristic of many of these students. In the reflections to the Alabama faculty, language is often so formal that it restricts what can be said or developed, while the greater informality of the accompanying letter shows that the student *is* thoughtfully engaged. The dynamic illustrates an irony that I see virtually every day: students tell me that professors do *not* want to see students' thinking in their writing, while faculty complain that they cannot *get* students to show their thinking in their writing. Perhaps we have all misconstrued what *thinking* is and how we do it; certainly, it is as though we were ships passing silently in the night, seldom really making contact with one another.

Effects My Students and I See

My students may have written *for* teachers all their lives. If they have ever written *to* a teacher, they have not considered it writing. Perhaps largely because of the overwhelming student loads that many teachers face, my students have almost never received responses *from* teachers. That is clear, from written reflections by my students on the effects of our letter exchanges, reflections I don't see until our course is over. My students perceive that from other teachers their writing has received "corrections" (the term my students use time and again to describe what teachers do) or (occasionally) praise. Writing, it seems, is either "right" or, more usually, "wrong." Period. And the task of teachers is to "right" what is "wrong." With what effect? One student says: "I rarely read the criticism of poor papers. I just toss them. Very little is written on good papers."

Within the mindset of writing as right or wrong, it is inconceivable that students could have anything to say about their writing; nor is reflection on what they are doing a possibility. At this stage of development their letters to me may be merely brief notes, quickly dashed off, or they may express frustration, saying in effect that if they saw any way the paper *could* be better, it *would* be better: "It was very difficult to think what to say to you in the first few letters I wrote. I wasn't used to looking at my own writing." The presumption is that papers stand alone, independent of social contexts — audience and intentions — that are always present within writing contexts. *No* text stands alone; the presumption that theirs should is one dimension of the vacuum of context that I think accounts for much vacuousness in student writing.

Students who have not gotten responses from other teachers initially have difficulty seeing the letters I write as responses: "At first it drove me crazy that you didn't give us letter grades but wrote me a letter that I really couldn't understand." "I am somewhat troubled by the lack of CONCRETE feedback from Sam. He says things that help me, but I am dying to know what he is putting down in his grade book. Does he grade our papers?"

Over time, I see these attitudes begin to shift for most students: "The letters have put the class on a more personal basis. Through them, I feel more comfortable asking for help. The letters make us, the teacher and student, friends. I certainly feel more at ease asking help from a friend than I do a Doctor of English." "It is so much easier to write a paper when you know at the end you can write a letter and explain exactly what you would like the teacher to know. It's more like writing to a friend than a person with a grade book and a big red pen. . . . I look forward to these letters because they make me feel as if a real person has read my paper — not just a teacher."

The letters encourage new relationships between students, texts, instructor, and responses: "Previously, I had learned to be helpless. Most teachers just gave back a paper with a grade on it. I became defensive and just tried to argue about the grade. [Our letters] made me feel more like a real writer instead of a tape recorder to play back what the teacher said." "At first I found the letters frustrating and had to try to figure out what you were talking about. But, then, I'm an instant gratification type of person, so I would want to see immediately ...through comments on the paper beside the section that the comment is about — the feedback from you. Instead, I have had to read back through my letter to you and whatever it was that I wrote to find what you were talking about. This has produced some discipline in me, I think." Later, the same student wrote: "I'm surprised. I don't sense the frustration that I thought was there at that point in the semester."

That student, like the one following, notes a very important point: like any other letters, mine do not "stand alone," outside the context of the situation. As a result, students must contextualize what I say globally, rather than (as with marginal comments) seeing my responses only within the narrow context of a particular sentence or short passage: "Often when I received a letter from you I would take the time to re-read my story, then my letter, and then your response. That way I can see again what my questions to you were and what your thoughts were in relation to those questions. Then you usually raise a new question, thought, or perception that stimulates my thinking because I re-think my story and letter and try to understand the new points you raise in your letter." There is, as one student put it, "more to writing than just writing."

Some students see the letters as a kind of "written talk" which may be more beneficial than conferences: "The letters allow me to express my thoughts and ideas to you and I can get your feedback. What is better with the letters is that they are written. You can read them as often as you need to really understand what is being said. They also offer that tiny bit of 'distance' where we can be honest without having to face each other."

Students come to realize that my response is cued by their insights, questions: "Consistently, I am finding that whenever I write you a long letter, I receive a long response in return, and the opposite whenever I write you a shorter letter. I wonder if you are aware of this. I am beginning to write longer and longer letters just to get more wisdom out of you." "My letters to you enable me to discuss my problems and approaches to writing with you and get feedback that might help me on my next writing attempt. [Marginal] comments don't allow me the opportunity to get that type feedback on my *own* questions."

Recognizing one's own questions can be disquieting, and I frequently see students suffer a crisis of confidence — which usually accompanies a greater depth in their writing. "Often it seems as though your responses are aimed at the letter I've written instead of focusing on the piece of writing. Having realized that, I am beginnng to slant my letters to you in such a way that you are having to address my questions about the writing itself....I feel less confident about my ability to write anything of value than I did on day # 1." From the same student, in December: "Rescind that statement! My confidence is greater because my knowledge of what makes *me* write and what sounds good to *me* is greater. Actually, what is happening is that I am thinking!!"

Students are learning to think. Their anticipation of the letter they will write to me encourages their heightened awareness *while* they write. "I can no longer just pick up the pen and go at it. I know that in the Dear Sam letter I have to tell how I went about the piece, so, I begin planning my attack before setting out on my mission. This made the writing much easier because I always knew which direction I was going. I also realize now that the thinking process before the work is a major factor in determining the work's success." "Asking you specific questions about what I wrote and how I went about writing it, and then getting replies to my questions helped out tremendously....I find myself asking very important questions in my letters, and then answering them or stumbling onto new answers or possibilities as I go on writing." "Writing is more of a relationship between writer and reader rather than as assignment for a class."

The presence of the letters encourages effort and risk in students' writing: "Sometimes I work really hard on a paper and the final result stinks. A letter lets us tell you what difficulties we ran into and enables us to ask for help." "[The letter] provides a place to voice what I would have liked to have done with my paper, but could not." "I no longer see the piece as 'completed'."

The important dialogue, which the letters encourage, is the one that students begin to have with themselves: "While writing to you, I feel like I'm writing to myself." "It is the understanding that comes with thinking about the process that allows writing to become more than just putting words down on paper." "Knowing I have to respond makes me more involved in my own writing....To have to reflect on your own work, the processes that formed it and the experiences that gave birth to it, requires the ability to make writing a personal activity. ...If there is no right way of writing, then I must face the responsibility that I must find the best way in me to express what I want to express....I think this responsibility, this respect for our views throws a lot of students. I have heard many complain about the letters, but I see in their complaints the same thing that I see in my vague letters—fear of discovery."

The letters we write imply a particular orientation to what texts are and are not. Texts do not exist in a sea of silence. They are rooted in and surrounded by languages beneath and beyond the explicit text. Our letters give us some access, in ways that do not call attention to themselves as "writing" at all, to these languages. At the same time, our letters model a peculiarly linguistic kind of learning: we articulate what we know and what we wonder, so that we may build upon it. Our letters open an area bounded by a text, the context of its production, and the writer's intention for it. In just such ground, it seems to me, writers grow.

The growth of writers — that is really the point of our course, our letter exchanges, and this essay. As students engage with me in a semester-length reflection on their own writing, they begin tapping their resources — both social and personal — from which writing springs. The most important function my letters probably serve is this: through them I am acting as midwife to a continuing dialogue of a sort that writers have with themselves — dialogue with a self worthy of dialogue, which animates both the acts and the artifacts of worthy writing.

We know how important it is that writing draw somehow on the writer's own experience — and we know how often students' writing fails to do so. We also know that writing functions to give a reader access to matters that otherwise would remain inaccessible — another difficulty our students face, one that seems built into the situation of much academic writing, where the writer knows less about the subject than the reader, who is an expert of sorts. Letters from students give me access to what otherwise would be inaccessible to me, and they are each grounded in an experience — a writing experience — that is immediate and personal and on which she or he is undeniably more expert than I.

Writers find themselves cultivating certain kinds of self–awareness. For example, Don Murray urges, "Listen to yourself as you write" (23). Writers need to have intention(s) behind their texts; often students' sense of intention is weak, but the requirement of an accompanying letter may encourage them in some manner to develop intentions for their writing. It may act also as a kind of conversational scaffolding for the text it accompanies — the sort of language that writers use often in talking, which surrounds an emerging text and sometimes feeds into the text itself. The letter requirement certainly encourages students to realize what they would like to say but that refuses to fit into their current draft. They begin to develop a healthy sense of how a text assumes some shape, taking cetain directions and at the same time developing constraints within which not everything can be said.

I think the letter exchange also implies a sobering orientation to what texts really are and are not. We sometimes say to students that their texts should "stand alone." Despite the pedagogical usefulness of that injunction, it has hazards. No text stands alone. As readers, we always make sense of texts in light of the person(s) and intention(s) we construe to be behind those texts. As writers, it's important that we stand by (or behind) our words. James Boyd White says, "The writer

asserts control over a language by taking a position outside it...
The writer, that is, speaks two ways at once: using a language and at
the same time recognizing what it leaves out" (71). White's concern is
the education of lawyers. Students of all sorts will become better
writers as they assume the kinds of control he describes, and letter
exchanges encourage students to consider what their texts necessarily
leave out.

Throughout this essay, I have been urging self-awareness born of
reflection in the context of written dialogue. What are the limits of
such reflection and of the claim with which this essay began? When
does reflection on some action lead to self-conscious paralysis of that
action? That question deserves serious consideration. My students
sometimes say that writing reflective letters to me makes their other
writing more difficult to do. But often these difficulties seem to be
useful, generative ones. In students' work I have seen little sign of
paralysis, probably because I don't insist that they try to tell me
everything in their letters. Articulation seems not to paralyze — when it
is articulation to (and perhaps with) some actual person. We often
assume that to reflect is to remove oneself from the object(s) of
reflection. But the assumption, which would make of self-reflection an
exercise in alienation, may be a mistaken one, which serves to close us
off from reflection. The potentials and limitations of self-reflection
deserve explicit treatment in other essays, though they have been the
implicit theme of this one.[2]

Notes

1. Donald A. Schon (1987) sketches an "epistemology of practice...,
based in knowing- and reflecting-in-action," toward development of an "art-
istry" that inherently resists formulation into "rules" (303). That seems to me a
useful characterization of the situation within which writers, including student
writers, find themselves. It may also be that Schon's epistemology, though it is
not directly concerned with writing, will help us better understand the potential
contributions of students' writing to their learning. Meanwhile, the goal of
reflective practice, for Schon, is that students begin "thinking like a [lawyer,
or doctor, or architect]." In my courses, a central goal is that students begin
"thinking like a writer."

Judith and Geoffrey Summerfield (1986) speak of "a fundamental dialectic
of text and metatext: we insist that students write not only texts but com-
mentaries [or reflections] on their texts....This immediately involves them in
the writer's dialectic of participation-spectator: now 'inside,' now 'outside';
now writer, now reader; first impulse and second thoughts...[W]e are now
convinced beyond any reasonable doubt that our students' reflections (meta-
texts) are among the most valuable texts they write — valuable both for themselves, in the discovering of meaningfulness and of ways of faring forward, and
for those of us who wish to enable" (260–1).

For an orientation to response, which in many respects is similar to my letter exchanges, see Sommers.

2. William H. Poteat charts important territory in this regard. The task he sets himself is to reconstrue his own thinking, and human thought in general, as embodied and situated.

Works Cited

Murray, Donald M. *Read to Write.* New York: Holt, 1986.

Poteat, William H. *Polanyian Meditations: In Search of a Post-Critical Logic.* Durham: Duke UP, 1985.

Schon, Donald A. *Educating the Reflective Practitioner.* San Francisco: Jossey, 1987.

Sommers, Jeffrey. "The Writer's Memo: Collaboration, Response, and Development." *Writing and Response: Theory, Practice, and Research.* Ed. Chris M. Anson. Urbana, IL: NCTE, 1989.

Summerfield, Judith, and Geoffrey Summerfield. *Texts and Contexts.* New York: Random, 1986.

White, James Boyd. *The Legal Imagination.* Abr. Chicago: U of Chicago P, 1985.

11

The Role of Theory in Advanced Writing and Tutor Training Courses

Tori Haring-Smith

We offer two kinds of advanced exposition courses at Brown, representing two different approaches to advanced composition. One of them presents advanced writing as a natural extension of a standard writing course and the other, a training course for peer tutors, provides students a new perspective on the writing process. Although these courses have very different audiences and purposes, they are linked through their emphasis on theory. These two advanced writing courses also share a teaching methodology that stems from their basis in theory. In both courses, students are expected to read theory and attempt to understand and apply it before coming to class. They cannot simply wait for the teacher or other class members to do their critical reading for them. Because students come to class having read and applied theory, they are prepared to discuss its strengths and weaknesses with little input from the professor. As a teacher of this course, I see my role as facilitating discussion in a truly collaborative atmosphere where everyone can and does contribute at a sophisticated level. Such high expectations of students also define these courses as advanced.

In one advanced class, Persuasive and Argumentative Writing (English 14), we offer students a more sophisticated examination of the building blocks present in any exposition course: thesis, organization, argument, style, and grammar. Our standard course assumes that students need to build skills in organization and style; it teaches students how to write a thesis, how to organize an essay, and how to write clear, coherent sentences. This advanced course, on the other

151

hand, assumes that students have these basic skills and builds upon them; it explores how different placements of the thesis, different organization, and different styles can affect readers. In other words, this course teaches students to use their fundamental writing skills with more flexibility and self-awareness. Teachers of this course do not ask, "Is this paper organized?" but rather, "Does the organization of this paper best suit the writer's goals? Are there alternative organizations? How would they alter essay?"

Although this kind of course may sound like a mere extension of standard, first-year composition, I would argue that it is quite different. In this course, students read model essays and student work, but they also consume large amounts of primary theory—semiotics, philosophy, rhetoric, linguistics, psychology, and aesthetics. They discuss the work of people like Aristotle, Carl Rogers, Roland Barthes, Michel Foucault, Stephen Toulmin, Carol Gilligan, Chaim Perlman, and Kenneth Burke. Of course, all these theorists may inform a standard composition course, but their work is not the subject of it. In other words, in Persuasive and Argumentative Writing, composition is *not* taught as processes to be emulated, dicta to be followed, archetypes to be imitated. Instead, students are encouraged to place their writing in a larger context. They become comfortable with the theory as well as the practice of writing.

This emphasis on theory reflects my general concern that students at an advanced level need to discuss not only writing practice but the theory that informs that practice. I believe that teaching is much like parenting—its methods need to change as its audience changes. At first, we simply direct our children's activities. ("Don't touch that stove!") Later, in response to our children's incessant "why's," we explain the reason or elementary theory behind our adages.("Don't touch that stove because you can't be sure if it's hot or not and you might burn yourself.") Finally, when the child's "why's" persist. we move to a new level and discuss openly the value system that generates our advice. ("Don't touch that stove—you know it could be hot and masochistic risk-taking is not valued in this household.") In composition, one could trace a similar growth in teaching methods: "Don't write incomplete sentences" becomes "Don't write incomplete sentences because they distract and confuse your reader" which in turn becomes, "Don't write incomplete sentences because they distract your reader and we value clarity and efficiency in this kind of prose." Without this kind of growing perspective, students may practice skills and improve them within a narrow range, but never see the limits of their understanding. Like actors trained only in realistic theatre, they may learn to perform well in one style but be unable to expand their repertoire.

Theory is also at the core of our undergraduate Seminar in the Teaching of Writing (English 195), which is designed to train the peer tutors (called Writing Fellows) who are the heart of our writing-across-the-curriculum effort. Established in the fall of 1982, the Brown University Writing Fellows Program employs each year about 80 undergraduate peer tutors, who serve as first readers for about 30 courses each semester ranging from anthropology to art history, biology, or history. About two-thirds of the Fellows are assigned to courses serving primarily first- and second-year students, while the remaining Fellows work with students in their last two years of undergraduate study. All told, the program provides individualized instruction in writing for 2,500−3,000 students each year. In order to understand the training course and its function, it is necessary first to describe the Writing Fellows Program in more detail.

Writing Fellows are sophomores, juniors, and seniors chosen from throughout the college—from comparative literature to computer science—for their interpersonal and writing skills. They compete vigorously for the opportunity to serve as a Writing Fellow. In the summer of 1988, for example, 160 individuals applied for the program's 40 open positions. The selection committee (composed of the director, associate director, and several Writing Fellows) evaluates applicants on the basis of a formal interview, a review of the applicants' coursework and extra-curricular experiences (that often include tutoring or counseling), and an evaluation of three samples of their prose. Once chosen as a Writing Fellow, students agree to continue in that position until they graduate—with the exception of semesters abroad. For their work as Writing Fellows, students receive an honorarium of $400 per semester.

Each Writing Fellow is assigned to 20 students in a given course. In some small courses, Fellows may work alone, while in classes of 200, they are one of 10 Fellows working with the course. The presence of the Writing Fellows does not change the nature of the instruction provided students; the program dictates only that the course include at least two significant writing assignments and requires students to revise each. For this reason, each paper assignment has two deadlines: one for the first version to be read and commented on by the Writing Fellow, and another about two weeks later for the first version and a revision to be submitted to the professor. All students submit their work for review—instruction is not reserved exclusively for those students with writing difficulties. This policy is designed to combat the students' belief that revision is a punishment meted out to poor writers, rather than an integral part of any writing process. The program also demonstrates that all writing (even "passable" writing) can be improved.

Two or three times each semester, then, each Writing Fellow comments in writing on about 20 students papers. Fellows work consistently with the same students so that they can foster on-going improvement from paper to paper. The kind of written comments that Fellows make are quite different from those traditionally made by faculty. We call them *readerly* as opposed to *teacherly*. A teacherly comment judges; a readerly comment reports reactions. Where a teacher might comment, "This is disorganized," a Writing Fellow would say: "You discuss acid rain on page one and increasing world population on page two. How are they connected in this paper?" Seeing a set of papers that all respond to the same set of readings and lectures helps the Fellows get a sense of the course's concerns, for Fellows do not attend the class to which they are assigned, nor are they necessarily majors in the field. Often, it is useful to assign Fellows to courses well outside their area of interest so that they can ask questions like "What does this word mean?" or "How are these ideas related?" and really be sincere. (Obvious exceptions to this general practice are courses that rely on highly specific or technical vocabulary [e.g., the physical sciences and language courses], where the associated Writing Fellows must have a working knowledge of the field.)

The Fellows generally have one week to comment on these 20 papers. The papers are then returned to the students and the student and Fellow meet for an individual conference to discuss the paper. This conference gives the student an opportunity to contest the Fellow's comments, to get reactions to specific revisions, or to request further feedback and explanation. During the week in which conferences are held, students revise their work so that they can submit both versions (the first with the Fellow's comments and the revision) to the professor, who reads and grades the final version. Students are asked to submit both copies of the essay in order to assure the faculty that the Fellows are not misleading students or acting as ghostwriters for them.

At the end of each semester, every Fellow's work is evaluated by the students whom the Fellow has tutored. These evaluations have shown that while students are initially fearful and defensive about showing their writing to a peer, they are converted to appreciating the program after they receive their first comments from the Fellows. Then they realize that the Fellows are "on their side," that they are helpful rather than judgmental. End-of-semester evaluations indicate that over 90 percent of the students served consider the Writing Fellows' comments to be helpful and valid, and 75 percent report that the Writing Fellows helped them improve their writing skills.

The program is successful because it responds to several needs. It increases the amount of writing that students do without increasing the number of papers that faculty grade, and so it allows faculty within any discipline to emphasize writing without becoming writing teachers themselves. Whereas most writing-across-the-curriculum programs ask the faculty involved to spend a lot of time being retrained and grading papers, this program offers a service to the faculty. When faculty participating in the program receive student papers, they can be assured that these essays were revised at least once. As a history professor noted, he can now detect and comment upon students' errors in historical methodology that used to be masked by writing problems. Furthermore, the program makes writing an active concern of the entire academic community. Rather than changing only faculty attitudes toward writing, as many writing-across-the-curriculum programs do, this program changes students' attitudes, too. It demonstrates that some students do write well and care about helping others learn to write.

Obviously the Writing Fellows are skilled writers — advanced composition students in every sense of the word. And the training they receive constitutes a form of advanced composition. The Writing Fellows take the Seminar in the Teaching of Writing (a full-credit, departmental course) during their first semester in the program — that is, while they are commenting on 20 other students' work for the first time. This course must therefore be both efficient and sophisticated.[1] Although this course is designed specifically to suit the Writing Fellows Program, it could be adapted to serve advanced composition students or peer tutors working in a dormitory or writing center.

The course introduces the students to many different areas of theory and asks them not only to discuss the theories' intrinsic strengths and weaknesses but also to apply those concepts in practice. Through this advanced course we hope that Fellows will both improve their own writing and also acquire the tools necessary to recognize and describe a wide variety of writing problems — all within the context of one student talking to another. Fellows are highly motivated in the course because they can immediately apply the material they are studying. In this way, theory remains rigorous and never becomes irrelevant philosophizing. Theories must not only be understood but also applied.

The course begins by helping students to reflect upon the politics of composition instruction. Reading Richard Ohmann's *English in America,* articles on the academic audience, and essays on collaborative learning and peer tutoring, students gradually realize that language use and instruction are powerful political tools. In practice, these first weeks of the course allow students to see the academic landscape with new eyes and to define their position as peer tutors within it. The class operates in an open manner, and students are encouraged to weigh theories and practices without feeling pressured to conform to a group consensus or a teacher's point of view. With this educational theory under their belt, students arrive at a variety of tentative definitions for their role as peer tutors.

Of course, these issues do not disappear after two weeks, but rather they inform our discussions for the rest of the semester. Specifically, they are crucial to the next section of the course, which looks closely at the process of writing and the role of the peer tutor in commenting upon student writing during its composition. Reading seminal essays like Linda Flower's "Writer-Based Prose: A Cognitive Basis for Problems in Writing," Nancy Sommers's "Responding to Student Writing," and Joe Williams's "The Phenomenology of Error," students come to appreciate the complexity of the writing process and the need, therefore, for intervention to be careful and informed. During this period of the course, students receive copies of three different student essays and are asked to provide comments on them. They then compare comments, examining not only their accuracy but also the kind of relationship that they establish between peer tutor and tutee. Tutors want to be sure that they have been precise and helpful without robbing the students of authority over their own texts. They discuss ways of determining which features of the text deserve comment and how these comments might be worded. They examine each paper as evidence of a stage in the writing process and learn to adjust their comments to the writer's level of performance. This period of the course brings together aspects of cognitive theory, rhetoric, and pedagogical theory, and explores their interaction in practice.

Having discussed the role of the peer tutor within the writing process, the course now follows a relatively standard progression of topics for a composition class. The difference is that in English 195 we discuss prewriting, thesis, organization, paragraphing, argumentation, revision, style, diction, and grammar from the point of view of the teacher/researcher. In this section, the students encounter theorists like Donald Murray, Mina Shaughnessy, Robin Markels, William Perry, Carol Gilligan, Stephen Toulmin, Carl Rogers, Peter Elbow, Richard Lanham, Ed Corbett, and George Orwell. These students read articles and books written primarily for college teachers — a rhetorical situation that is productively unsettling. Instead of reading composition textbooks in which the the process of writing often becomes a series of unrelated suggestions, these students learn the theories that lie behind guidelines for good writing. This knowledge is especially helpful in conferences. If a tutee does not understand a given suggestion, the Fellow can use knowledge of the theory behind the suggestion to describe it more fully or with new language. The conversations that occur during these conferences are obviously crucial to the success of the program. I frequently explain this course by saying that it gives students a wide variety of tools for discussing writing. Some Fellows will find some tools naturally more comfortable and use them more often. They will learn both how to hammer a nail and the physics behind hammering nails. Then, if the hammer they are using doesn't work, they can either adapt its use or select a new tool intelligently. In other words, when they complete this course, Fellows can listen to faculty or students discuss writing and understand not only what is said but what is not being said—the unstated assumptions of the speaker.

The written exercises completed by the Fellows during this section of the course also function quite differently from those in a standard composition course. Whereas students in first-year composition may be asked to correct the grammar in a set of sentences, to generate useful theses, or to outline an essay, Fellows are asked to explain the logic of a sentence; to understand the many kinds of theses found in academic prose, and to recognize their possibilities and their limitations; and to be able to describe the organization of a paper using a variety of visual and verbal metaphors, being cognizant of the emphases and gaps inherent in each of them. Frequently, Fellows are asked to read a theorist and then analyze a piece of prose as the theorist would. In other words, they move directly from reading theory to applying it through written exercises.

The course concludes with a return to the problems specific to academic writing, most notably the new research on disciplinary differences in academic writing. This theory brings us back to explicit discussions of the politics of authority in language instruction and the role of peer tutors who move from discipline to discipline and must adjust to each situation. Here a typical assignment asks students to gather several recent assignments given to them or their friends in widely ranging disciplines. Students then copy and share these assignments, attempting to decode the disciplinary assumptions hidden within them. This exercise frequently leads students to interview faculty about discipline-specific expectations for writing. At the end of this week of study, students have generated a guide to what Greg Colomb calls "disciplinary secrets."

For their last written assignment, students step back to review their developing sense of themselves as tutors. Some of them reflect on the revision process that they themselves used on a paper written during the semester, and others analyze their evolving strategies for commenting on students' writing, using specific examples from their work as Fellows during the semester. In all of these assignments, students are put in the position of teacher/researcher, knowledgeably and self-critically examining their own teaching and writing practices so that they can understand and improve them. By the end of the course, Fellows have become truly advanced writers.

After completing the training seminar, Writing Fellows continue to work in the program until they graduate from Brown. They are not required to take any further courses in the teaching of writing, but their work is supervised by the program's associate director (an adjunct faculty member in English) and its assistant director (a senior Writing Fellow). Talking with these experienced teachers and tutors, Fellows have an opportunity to continue discussing the theories they worked with in English 195. In addition, retreats and national conferences provide opportunities for large groups of tutors to learn about new research emerging in the many fields relevant to their work as Writing Fellows.

We could, of course, streamline this intensive seminar and simply refresh the Fellows' minds about the standard wisdom on composing. But we feel strongly that the presence of theory in the course enriches the student's experience of composing and tutoring. Advanced students need to stand back from the act of writing to consider it in a larger intellectual context. This more sophisticated perspective should prepare accomplished writers to appreciate the richness of the field of composition and its links to other fields like psychology, semiotics, and philosophy. As Bertolt Brecht said, "A man with one theory is lost. He needs several of them, four, lots! He should stuff them in his pockets like newspapers, hot from the press always, you can live well surrounded by them, there are comfortable lodgings to be found between the theories. If you are to get on you need to know that there are a lot of theories."

One benefit from the new perspectives provided by theory in advanced composition courses may be that bright students who appreciate the field of composition may become interested in teaching it—a benefit that we should increasingly value as we enter the period of teacher shortages that is forecast for the 1990s. For these reasons, I recommend a direct examination of theory in advanced composition classes, whether they serve peer tutors, a small group of advanced English majors, or a wide spectrum of experienced writers from across the curriculum.

Note

1. I am deeply indebted to Dr. Rhoda Flaxman, the Associate Director of the Writing Fellows Program, for her help in the on-going development and teaching of this course.

Works Cited

Brecht, Bertolt. Diaries 1920–22. Trans. and ed. John Willett. London: Eyre Methuen, 1979. 42.

Flower, Linda. "Writer-Based Prose: A Cognitive Basis for Problems in Writing." *College English* 41 (1979): 19–37.

Ohmann, Richard. *English in America.* New York: Oxford, 1976.

Sommers, Nancy. "Responding to Student Writing." *College Composition and Communication* 33 (1982): 148–56.

Williams, Joseph. "The Phenomenology of Error." *College Composition and Communication* 32 (1981): 140–58.

12

A General Theory of the Enthymeme for Advanced Composition

John T. Gage

Argument as Responsible Inquiry

As this volume itself demonstrates, there is no consensus about what *advanced composition* means or ought to mean. In thinking about the question, I often find myself in a paradoxical position. If *advanced* is to have any meaning, it must signify something that goes beyond what one finds in the *regular* composition course. But when I try to imagine what this might be, or when I read others' descriptions of it, I react by thinking that this so-called advanced approach, or this theory for advanced writing, may be precisely what all composition students (at least at the college level) need. Anything that I might imagine as saving for the advanced student always strikes me as something of which I would be depriving the student of composition who is not advanced. Consequently, I think we must view any distinction between composition and advanced composition as one of degree, and not one of kind.

So, what assumptions have guided my own inquiry, here, into the appropriate content for advanced composition? One is that advanced composition will not differ in substance from regular composition, but will present the student with that substance in a more sophisticated context. A second is that it will challenge the writing student to attempt higher levels of thinking, even if this means using writing techniques that are not in themselves restricted to advanced writers. A third assumption is that the advanced composition class cannot minimize the difficulty of any issue nor simplify the application of any technique for the sake of making an issue easier to understand or a technique easier to learn. If advanced composition does not confront students with the intractable ambiguities of language and the difficult relations between language and knowledge, chances are that no other writing course will. Thus, I suppose my own view of advanced composition, finally, is that it must encourage students to write responsibly.

In advanced composition, students should be invited or challenged to take on the highest degree of responsibility for their writing. All writers who are doing more than practicing discrete skills must acknowledge that the desire to use writing to communicate ideas brings with it the responsibility to communicate those ideas well, and to offer their readers honest and reasonable grounds for assenting to those ideas. But there is a deeper, more difficult aspect of responsibility that writers share with readers: the responsibility to know when to adjust their own beliefs — the ideas that they choose to communicate — to the world of available knowledge. Students who are asked to write responsibly, in this sense, can only do so when confronted by real issues and when they must find their own positions in regard to those issues and generate writing that does justice to those positions for an audience of mutual inquirers. This implies, I think, that there will be no essay models or formulaic processes offered for imitation and practice, no hypothetical situations offered merely to practice techniques, and no imaginary audiences that place only imaginary demands on the writer. Such artificial constraints might apply to composition at the college entry level, if they apply at all, but inevitably reduce the responsibility that writers face when they write about their own ideas for real audiences. The context for advanced composition that I advocate is one in which students experience the rhetorical options that become available only when writers find themselves in real rhetorical situations; in other words, when they are compelled to *earn* their ideas for an audience that has ideas of its own.

What is practiced, and learned, in such a context is not an empty form to be filled in with content, nor a technique for inventing ideas, nor a process for composing, but the activity of critical judgment. By *judgment* I mean the intuitive — but controlled — act of making choices for which no rule or formula or model is adequate, simply because real rhetorical situations are not easily reduced to approaches that have worked for others in other rhetorical situations. Responsible writing is that in which the writer has attempted to satisfy the unique demands of a rhetorical situation by thinking about her own ideas, those of her audience, and the quality of the reasons she might use to bring her readers and herself into earned agreement.

Thinking critically about such matters is not a process that can be reduced to formulae but one that involves intuitive acts of assessing reasons. In an essay called "The Uncritical American, or, Nobody's from Missouri Any More," Wayne Booth defines critical judgment as the act of assessing "the adequacy of the *case made* to the *conclusions,*" or knowing "how to match the degree of [one's] convictions to the quality of [the] reasons" (65, 73). I wish now to make several observations about this definition.

First, as Booth points out, the necessity of making this kind of judgment is our "common lot." All of us, teachers or students, females or males, romantics or rationalists, poets or scientists, are constantly engaged in the activity of either creating or consuming, and therefore of judging, reasons. Without a reliable definition of what makes a "good" reason, we nevertheless apply criteria implicitly whenever we accept or reject a reason, whether it is one we hear or one we might choose to offer.

Second, we all understand somehow that it is possible to judge reasons well or to judge them poorly, and that we are all equally guilty of doing both on occasions, depending, for one thing, on the degree to which we *want* to accept a conclusion. We all know, then, that since we have been wrong about such judgments in the past, the possibility of being wrong about them again is ever present.

Third, we have learned whatever we know about this process by doing it. We do not apply a memorized rule each time we make such a judgment. We apply instead a set of tacit standards that are in fact very complex and that we have learned just as we have learned the so-called rules of grammar: by active participation in the activity of making sense of our own and others' arguments.

Fourth, this definition denies the possibility of closure in the discussion of most issues. If we are obliged to measure the *degree* of our convictions against the *quality* of the reasons offered for them, then we have defined conviction as subject to degree. Many are accustomed to thinking of conviction as if it were a light switch having an "off" position and an "on" position: I either hold a conviction or I do not. But this shift toward judging reasons according to their adequacy and their quality makes that analogy inappropriate. Convictions, according to this way of thinking, resemble a rheostat more than a switch. Assent is possible *up to a point,* or *insofar as* the reasons are adequate. This attitude yields judgments that are real, but nevertheless subject to change (in either direction) if better reasons come along. It assumes that new reasons with the potential to change the degree of our convictions are always possible. This attitude enables one to *consider* the reasons of others when they are offered to us, justifies our willingness to inquire further into issues on which we already have convictions, and promotes the free and tolerant exchange of ideas and reasons between people who hold different convictions.

Fifth, and finally, Booth's definition of critical judgment reorients us to the idea of knowing and what it means. We are accustomed to think of knowledge in absolutist terms (and I do not reject the possibility of such knowledge in some areas), as a *commodity* that can be packaged and traded and remain essentially stable in the interchange of minds. But what I have been describing seems to me to transform our understanding of knowledge from a commodity to an *activity*. That is, as something that we *do,* rather than something we *possess,* and that we do together, in discourse, when we reason. In other words, the kinds of reasons we create and the degrees to which we accept them are not conditioned solely by rules and private understandings but are subject to the convictions, reasons, experience, and values of those other members of the discourse community in which we interact. So that what one believes is a result of the thinking that we have done together.

Because I think writers in advanced composition should be learning to practice critical judgment and inhabiting the necessarily ambiguous realm of reasons that it implies I advocate devoting such a course to argumentative writing. Argumentation need not be made to wait for advanced composition, of course, but it certainly cannot be postponed in advanced composition. Most approaches to composition accord argument a superior position, as in the teaching of modes of discourse in which students might progress through different kinds of essays and eventually attempt an essay of the "argument" kind. If such an approach results in the students putting off writing arguments until they have mastered other forms, the result can be less attention to argument than its alleged position in the hierarchy of modes suggests is needed. Or it may result in putting off argument indefinitely, since mastery of the modes preceding argument will always prove elusive. Consequently, if advanced composition is truly advanced, it must take on the difficult, but also elusive, challenge of writing arguments in which the quality of reasons is subject to assessment by the audience. In so doing, all the techniques and strategies that may be learned in the context of other kinds of essays will come into play: personal, narrative, analytical, causal, comparative writing, and so on provide means of achieving argumentative ends. But their place in a composition course devoted to argumentative writing will not be as techniques to be mastered but as potentially available means that may or may not be appropriate, according to the writer's judgment, in the context of a particular argumentative situation.

Argumentative writing provides the best opportunity for encountering what I earlier called "the intractable ambiguities of language and the difficult relations between language and knowledge." This depends, however, on how argumentative writing is approached. It is possible to avoid these ambiguities and difficult relations if the argumentative writer is required to have a thesis, but is not asked to develop that thesis in response to real issues on which serious thinkers genuinely disagree. It is possible to avoid them by asking the writer to give three reasons for the thesis, and devote a paragraph to each, without asking whether they are good reasons, or for whom they are designed to work, or even what makes a good reason; and it is possible to avoid them by testing reasons according to the objective, formal validity criteria of symbolic logic rather than to treat reasons as qualitatively dependent on the assumptions of one's audience, the language in which they are expressed, and the emotive values they necessarily connote. Argumentative writing, in other words, can be as formulaic, sterile, and passive as any other kind, and it is the challenge of teachers to try to find ways of teaching it that will in fact lead to the kinds of responsible judgments we wish (advanced) composition students to make.

It is first necessary, I think, to separate argumentative writing from the idea of winning by means of persuasion. *Argumentation is the process by which people come to knowledge.* It is by putting forward ideas and attempting to find the best reasons for assenting to them that ideas are tested and adjusted. If argument were merely the process by which one belief could be made to prevail over another, then we could teach the advertiser's bag of tricks without caring whether reasons *earned* assent, so long as they succeeded in winning converts. For argument to be taught as a process of discovering the *best* reasons, student writers should not see persuasion, but inquiry, as the goal. Inquiry is a process of putting one's ideas into the context of other ideas, for the purpose of finding out whether they are supported by adequate reasons. It is by this process that one learns that what one knows is only as good as the quality of the reasons one can offer, and that this *quality* must be judged in terms of the beliefs and needs of an audience that is able to assess a writer's reasons and offer good reasons of its own. Argument can teach that ideas are flexible, contingent, and open to change and that a "good" reason is determined by communal, negotiated acts of assent. It can teach that thinking itself is a transaction, an activity involving the inquiries of all participants in a discourse community.

In trying to find a way to approach argumentative writing that enables these lessons to be learned, I have explored the advantages of the *enthymeme* (see, e.g., "An Adequate Epistemology"), and I will continue that exploration here.

The Enthymeme as a Heuristic

The enthymeme is often defined as a *truncated syllogism* or as a *rhetorical syllogism.* Whether we take rhetorical syllogism to mean a syllogism with one of its premises supplied by the audience or a syllogism based on probable premises rather than certain ones, one aspect of these definitions is shared. The enthymeme, however else it may be viewed, has always been viewed as a variation of the syllogism. As such, the enthymeme is tied to the tradition of formal logic, with all the associations that come with formal logic. Without implying, as some would, the irrelevancy of formal logic to rhetoric, I would nevertheless like to look at the enthymeme as a *rhetorical syllogism* with the emphasis on *rhetorical* and even attempt to think about the enthymeme as a construct that might be disassociated from the syllogism per se, and therefore from formal logic. Richard Fulkerson has argued that logic, either as it is defined in the technical sense by logicians or as it appears in composition textbooks, consists of "tools for criticizing arguments, not for generating them" (445). Teaching logic up front will be "unlikely to be helpful to writers because it describes products not processes and because the absolute nature of deduction ill suits the contingent nature of argumentative discourse" (450). Logic, like grammar, can be taught in the abstract, but knowledge *about* it is unlikely to result in improved practice by writers who need help becoming more logical, whatever that means.

This essay is an attempt to view the enthymeme apart from the strictly syllogistic context that generally defines it, and thereby to view it as something other than a strictly logical concept. Indeed, a general theory of the enthymeme would view it as central to rhetorical thinking, of which logic is but a part. The rhetorical syllogism is but one manifestation of rhetorical thinking. The enthymeme, in such a view, might take any form, the syllogism being only one of them. In other words, rather than seeing the enthymeme as a subcategory of the syllogism, I believe it might be more productive to try to see the syllogism as a subcategory of the enthymeme, properly understood.

Most recent interest in argumentation from a rhetorical point of view has been away from the direction of logic altogether. The works of Booth, Perelman, and Toulmin have placed rhetorical argument in philosophical contexts that do not depend on a distinction between objectivity and subjectivity, or on formal principles of validity, or on "proof" by inference from necessities. What has replaced the logical model of argumentation is something looser and more akin to psychology than to science. I do not mean by psychology the concept of persuasion promulgated in the behaviorist sense of conditioned response to stimuli or appeals to greed or image that one finds in advertising strategies. I mean a sense of rhetorical engagement as an activity bound by the conditions of appeal that exist in audiences and that are reproduced in the structures of language but not bounded by the structures of logic. For Booth, this sense of rhetorical engagement is aimed at the ways people might "meet other minds in the best possible symbolic exchange" (*Modern Dogma* 142), including all of the resources by which language enables values and attitudes to be shared. For Perelman, it is constituted by the ways in which "presence" is created by quasi-formal structures, in the absence of unambiguous ways of communicating or of demonstrating certainties. Toulmin, similarly, seeks to define it in a paradigm that accounts for "working logic" as it is actually used, as opposed to the analytic computations that play virtually no part in our performance of inference (e.g., 4). In any case, argumentation is now being seen as a negotiation conducted in a more ad hoc fashion than the *a priori* rules and fallacies of logic will permit.

For none of these rhetoricians does the syllogism per se have much relevance. A theory of rhetorical argument, recent decades have shown us, can be complete and coherent without much need for syllogisms or the baggage of inference rules and symbolic representations that comes with them from the analytic tradition of logic. In practical terms, the rhetoricizing of argument has permitted rhetoricians to get along without training in, or interest in, the logical structures that once formed the basis of theories of argumentation. This effect has been, in part, salient. It has led to more cogent, and more teachable, views of how argument functions. But it has conditioned another extreme, which is to assume what one critic has called "the tyranny of logic" and in effect to replace it with the tyranny of rhetoric, if rhetoric without logic becomes mere psychology without grounding in any theory of how the forms of assertions may account for their adequacy to generate assent. This enables rhetoricians and teachers of applied rhetoric to consider anything associated with logic to have negative connotations, connotations of scientism or of an outmoded epistemology. Thus, for some rhetoricians, if the enthymeme is a *kind* of syllogism, it is perforce part of the baggage that they wish to discard, or to repudiate (e.g., Knoblauch and Brannon 37−38). The result is that the power of the enthymeme, not as a truncated syllogism but as an architectonic rhetorical structure valuable in the invention process, can be easily ignored. If the enthymeme is a syllogism, the argument runs, and if the syllogism is no longer relevant to the study or teaching of argument, then the enthymeme is no longer relevant to the study or teaching of argument. This syllogism used against the enthymeme is implicitly invoked when the enthymeme is viewed as a mere variation on the syllogism.

How is the enthymeme an architectonic rhetorical structure? And how does the enthymeme enable students to think productively about the kinds of judgments they must make when they find themselves in real argumentative situations? To answer these questions I will describe the enthymeme in terms of its potential to function as a generative structure, not as an empty form into which ideas must be molded but as a guide for thinking about the kinds of questions that writers must somehow answer for themselves if they are to compose arguments that are responsible to their own ideas, to their knowledge of a subject, and to an audience capable of inquiring with them. "The enthymeme," as Maxine Hairston summarizes this potential, can become "an investigative tool, a stimulus to discovery, and an aid to finding rhetorical support" (65).

This function for the enthymeme derives from understanding how it may embody the conditions of any rhetorical situation. These conditions, at their most basic level, consist of:

1. a question at issue
2. a stance
3. a strategy
4. assumptions

The absence or disregard of any one of these elements will result in a rhetoric that is somehow incomplete or irresponsible.

By "question at issue," I mean the issue toward which the writer and the writer's audience direct their inquiry. It may be a question on which they disagree (as in the *stasis* questions of classical invention) or it may be one to which they both desire an answer. Something must be problematical; there must be a "crux," as Patricia Carden has recently called it (37). Inquiry and discourse are motivated by the desire to produce shared knowledge or understanding when specific differences in knowledge or understanding exist, when there is something to "unravel, solve, resolve, and interpret" (Carden 37).

By "a stance," I mean the writer's position in regard to the question at issue, whether that position is tentative or absolute, speculative or polemical. The writer is someone with something to say, with something to add to the inquiry.

By "a strategy," I mean simply a way of approaching the stance. A writer's responsibility doesn't stop with the assertion of his or her position; his or her major task is to somehow develop it, to invent and to organize the *means* that will enable the stance to be understood and shared. The need to do so is one of the responsibilities that follows from having a stance and from wishing to contribute it to the available discourse on any issue.

By "assumptions," I mean those tacit or unstated givens of a situation that are invoked whenever a particular strategy, or means, is adopted and composed. The choice to approach a subject in any particular way implies that something must be shared between the writer and the audience in order for that strategy to function. Assumptions are the conditions of appeal that are necessarily at play if the writer's chosen means are to effect a desired response.

This anatomy of the parts, or conditions, of any rhetorical situation illustrates how rhetorical invention is transactive and communal — how, in other words, the writer's choices derive from and are conditioned by that writer's presence in a situation that includes an audience. Although it is possible to reduce rhetorical invention to "the private act of an individual writer," in the phrase of Karen Burke LeFevre (1), as some pedagogies tend to do for the sake of practicing a given form, the social dimension of rhetoric is inescapable. The relationship between a writer and an audience is dialectical, even in the extreme of an adversarial relationship, insofar as the writer works with materials, issues, strategies, and procedures that are communally determined. As LeFevre puts it, "Even when the primary agent of invention is an individual, invention is pervasively affected by that individual's relationship to others through language and other socially shared symbol systems" (8). Thus, the basic conditions of the rhetorical situation may be viewed as contributions of the audience and the writer to their communal situation:

The writer's share: *The audience's share:*
                               1. a question at issue
2. a stance
3. a strategy
                               4. assumptions

What the writer chooses to say is in effect a response to a question (or crux) that would not be at issue (or problematical) were it not for the writer's presence in a situation shared by others. And how the writer chooses to develop that stance is in turn determined by what the audience makes available as potentially effective appeals. The audience determines and contributes to what the writer must think about; the writer's inquiry into what to say and how to say it is, in effect, an inquiry about the audience as much as it is an inquiry about the subject.

The enthymeme can provide a dynamic representation of these relationships and hence a focus for thinking productively about aspects of the rhetorical situation that the writer must somehow address. It can do so because if contains the same essential parts, if it is considered as a composed statement of the writer's overall purpose rather than as a local, argumentative figure. I have called this a *structural enthymeme,* the central intuitive link connecting the writer's thesis to a line of reasoning developed in response to an issue and an assumption shared with an audience (see *The Shape of Reason* 84–88). Hence the composition of such an enthymeme can facilitate a writer's attempt to make tangible and specific the elements of his or her rhetorical situation:

The enthymeme:	*The rhetorical situation:*
1. implied question	1. question at issue
2. assertion	2. stance
3. because clause	3. strategy
4. implied premise	4. assumption

Any enthymeme consisting of an assertion that represents the writer's thesis or claim and a "because clause" that represents the main reason to be offered in support of that assertion will necessarily imply, or entail, an issue to which the thesis is a response and a shared premise (or "backing") that makes the reason potentially acceptable. A thesis statement in the form of an enthymeme of this kind must result from the writer's inquiry into those aspects of the situation that are shared with the audience and those that are not. It can provide the writer with a way to make judgments about what to say and how to say it that will do justice to the writer's presence in a community of thinkers who share something, but not everything, with the writer. And the invention of such an enthymeme, which necessarily involves implicit negotiating of points of view other than the writer's—if it says precisely what the writer wishes to say, if the question it answers implicitly is in fact at issue, and if the assumption that it necessarily implies is reasonably acceptable to that same audience—enables the writer, further, to know what decisions and opportunities are implicit in the working out and further differentiating of this central enthymeme in a whole composition. The enthymeme considered in this way is not anything the writer may wish to include in the composition, in so many words; it merely stands for a threshold of thought, negotiating between those responsibilities imposed by the writer's situation on the one hand and by the further responsibilities that must be met in any composition based on that enthymeme on the other (see Gage, "Teaching the Enthymeme").

Considered as an invention technique, such a structural enthymeme, like other techniques developed for pedagogical purposes, is an artificial means of enabling writers to undergo a process of thought that is somehow implicit when writers make rhetorical decisions. Any piece of writing (limited for the sake of this discussion to nonfiction prose) can be found to have as its "deep structure" a thesis and a central line (or lines) of reasoning and these will imply that writer's sense of what the audience believes is at issue and what the audience will accept as a basis for proceeding along that line of reasoning (see Emmel, 28–44; Green 623; Hood 94–100). But this in itself does not mean that the writer either constructed such an enthymeme or was even aware of such relationships. We should not expect this any more than we would expect a writer to be conscious of all of the principles of grammar or of the kinds of sentences that are used in the writing. What the structural enthymeme represents instead is the need for writers to work with and through, tacitly, the kinds of relationships represented in the enthymeme, just as they need to work with and through grammatical and sentence patterns. A writer *may* make any dimension of the creative process a conscious one, just as a writer may become introspective, after the fact, about what kinds of decisions must somehow have been made for the prose to take the sort of shape that it did.

The literary critic R. S. Crane provided such an introspection when he mused about the issue of poetic structure from the point of view of his own writing of essays: On those occasions when the essay gathered shape and when "the sentences and paragraphs followed one another with scarcely a hitch and in an order that seemed to me the inevitable one when I came to reread the essay in cold blood," Crane attributed this success to

> a kind of intuitive glimpse of a possible subsuming form for the materials, or at least those I attached most importance to, which I had assembled in my mind and notes—a form sufficiently coherent and intelligible, as a form in my mind, so that I could know at once what I must or could do, and what I need not or ought not to do, in what order and with what emphasis in the various parts, in developing my arguments and putting them into words. I have never been able to write anything which seemed to me, in retrospect, to possess any quality of organic wholeness, however uninteresting or thin, except in response to such a synthesizing idea. It is more than a general intention, more than a "theme," and more than an outline in the usual sense of the word; it is...a shaping or directing cause, involving at the same time, and in some sort of correlation, the particular conceptual form my subject is to take in my essay, the particular mode of argument or of rhetoric I am to use in discussing it, and the particular end my discussion is to serve. (141–42)

It is this intuitive sense of the *whole,* as yet undifferentiated into a composition, that, in Crane's words, "generates consequences and problems in the detailed working out of my subject which I cannot well escape so long as I remain committed to writing the essay as I see it ought to be written" (142). The responsibilities a writer faces, in other words, are only knowable in terms of the clarity with which the "synthesizing idea" is perceived. This idea *generates* the choices that the writer confronts in the composition. Composition methodologies that assert the importance of having a thesis (and here it does not matter to me whether that thesis is discovered during the act of writing or whether it is defined in advance) are at some level attempting to enable students to have the kind of experience Crane has described. A thesis, standing somehow for the whole composition, is meant to function as a tangible, or metaphorical, substitute for the "intuitive glimpse" that Crane described, so that students can apply conscious decisions to the "problems" of its working out. Of course, to have this generative function, the thesis must first of all be an adequate response to the writer's rhetorical situation and it must in turn function as the generative principle of the essay's form.

The enthymeme has this function because of its *resemblance* to a syllogism. Without being aware of any other way to discuss the relationships implicit in the enthymeme, I have taught it as a kind of syllogism, in order for students to grasp the necessary relationship between any stated reason or strategy of support and assumptions taken for granted in the audience when such a reason or strategy is invoked (see *The Shape of Reason* 76–84). But I am becoming more aware of the disadvantages of this method of explaining the enthymeme, for at the same time that it clarifies how assumptions (implicit premises) must follow from the adoption of strategies (stated premises), it also reduces invention to a single mode—that of logic—and suggests that the enthymeme must meet the validity conditions that syllogisms (by virtue of the analytic tradition) carry with them. I do not think that an enthymeme must meet the conditions of validity that apply to syllogisms, nor do I think that rhetorical decisions are limited to the narrowly deductive. I do, however, continue to think that the enthymeme can provide a powerful formal tool for suggesting and compelling the kinds of rhetorical judgments that will make a (student) writer responsible to the central elements of his or her rhetorical situation. I think so not because the enthymeme is a kind of syllogism but because it embodies relationships that might also be present, but are not necessarily, in the syllogism when the syllogism is used rhetorically. The enthymeme may represent *rhetorical* thinking in the same way that the syllogism may represent logical thinking. And since rhetorical thinking must be understood to imply aspects of appeal that are not strictly logical, the concept of the enthymeme may be viewed apart from the logical context in which it is usually found.

The Enthymeme and Reasoning

To establish such a view, it may help to make distinctions among *logics* and to consider the classical heritage of such distinctions. Chaim Perelman distinguishes analytical and dialectical reasoning, a difference that I have already implied to support the argument in this essay: "Since truth is a property of the proposition and is independent of personal opinion, analytical reasoning is demonstrative and impersonal.

But this is not the case with dialectical reasoning. Aristotle tells us that dialectical reasoning presupposes premises which are constituted by generally acceptable opinions" (2). Perelman is not simply citing the authority of Aristotle to define dialectical reasoning; he is showing that the distinction he wishes to draw has a history and a tradition, even though that distinction must appear somewhat differently in a modern context. His aim is to show that confusion over the role of logic in argument has resulted from the subsequent merging of a distinction that was explicit in the Aristotelian canon. Because Aristotle's analytic was taken over by the tradition of logic that has come down to us, analytic and dialectical reasoning were merged, and rhetorical reasoning was reduced to trivial arts of style. "Thus with a flourish," Perelman writes, "Ramus tossed aside the Aristotelian distinction between analytical and dialectical judgments," depriving "rhetoric of its two essential elements, invention and disposition, leaving only elocution" (3). Any distinction between the kind of reasoning that applies to rhetorical knowledge, contingent and practical, and that which applies to scientific truths has, until relatively recent times, been buried by the assumption that one logic — that of the analytic tradition — suffices to account for all reasoning. So, Perelman would have us recall that dialectical-rhetorical reasoning functioned in Aristotle as alternative to analytical reasoning, applicable to situations where analytic logic was inadequate.

Perelman shows that assumptions behind analytical logic, as it developed after Ramus, are never adequate to justify its application to situations in which argumentation must take place. One such assumption is that there can be such a thing as self-evident premises separate from consensus, from which formal logical conclusions may be derived. "An argument is never capable of procuring self-evidence, and there is no way of arguing against what is self-evident" (6). Another such assumption is that the terms in which the logic is necessarily embedded will have the same meaning for all who use them. "For centuries, under the influence of rationalistic thinkers who considered mathematical language the model to be followed by ordinary language, and especially by philosophers, we have lived under the impression that messages, in principle, are clear" (43). However, Perelman says, "in natural languages, ambiguity — the possibility of multiple interpretations — would be the rule" (44). For Perelman, the realm of discourse in which propositions may be "demonstrated" on the basis of self-evident statements in unambiguous language, as opposed to the realm of discourse in which argumentative means must function, is extremely small, possibly restricted to mathematics. But the realm of rhetorical discourse, in which analytic logic does not suffice, is vast.

Rhetorical reasoning, for Aristotle and for Perelman, necessarily entails decisions made by a rhetor based on the givens of a situation;

not what is demonstrably or self-evidently true but what can be agreed upon, whether by convention or by persuasion, constitutes the basis for all rhetorical appeals. Thus, for Aristotle, the enthymeme represented a kind of negotiated logic, not one that begins in premises known to be true but in premises assumed to be shared. It is for this reason that Aristotle says that one of the premises of an enthymeme need not be stated, not because this abbreviated form is necessary to its definition but because in rhetorical situations the shared premises may go without saying. What is necessary to the definition of the enthymeme is the participation of the audience in its formulation; only premises made available by the audience may be used to form enthymemes. Thus, the kind of reasoning that is represented in the use of enthymemes in rhetorical situations entails reasoning about the audience as much as it does reasoning about the subject, for without knowledge of what the audience will accept as a basis for convincing argument, no argument can be convincing.

Aristotle does not confine this principle to the enthymeme as a kind of syllogism, one in which one of the premises is supplied by the audience. What accounts for the formation of rhetorical syllogisms is the same kind of reasoning that accounts for every other formal decision made by the rhetor. Before distinguishing enthymeme from example as two forms of rhetorical proofs (1856 b), Aristotle asserts that the enthymeme is "the body of proof" itself (1854 a), signifying two ways of understanding the concept of the enthymeme: one as a kind of appeal, or enthymemes as overt logical statememts; the other as the foundation of rhetorical thinking, the way in which the contribution of the audience functions to enable all of the rhetor's decisions (including the appeals to *ethos* and *pathos*), not only those that are overtly logical. In this second sense of the enthymeme as a process of rhetorical thinking rather than a specific form for statements to take, we find, I believe, the basis for my earlier claim that syllogisms are kinds of enthymemes, not enthymemes kinds of syllogisms. This is because the kind of reasoning that gives rise to syllogism-like statements is the same kind of reasoning that may give rise to other formal features of the argument. By calling that kind of reasoning enthymematic, we can define its qualities and also show the similarity between the process that gives rise to syllogism-like statements in an argument and that which gives rise to, say, metaphors or anecdotes. "Gives rise to" is misleading here, however. I am not proposing that there is any way to account for, or to encourage, the precise moment of creative discovery when right words instantly suggest themselves. Enthymematic reasoning is that which accounts for or encourages the *choice* of one among the potential ways in which the discourse might be shaped, however those ways might come to one's attention. This kind of reasoning involves the coming together of two essential elements: what end is desired on the part of the rhetor and what assumptions (or conditions of appeal) are available on the part of the rhetor's audience. It is a decision to speak in one way rather than another based on what the audience already knows or how it is accustomed to respond.

Aristotle himself illustrates such a process when he describes other qualities of rhetoric besides the logical. In describing epideictic narrative, for instance, he says that "it is only necessary to recall famous actions; wherefore most people have no need of narrative — for instance, if you wish to praise Achilles; for everybody knows what he did, and it is only necessary to make use of it" (1416 b). The choice of what is "necessary" for the narrator to say (from among the available things that might be said) is based on knowledge of what the audience already knows. Similarly, Aristotle considers the construction of appropriate metaphors to follow a similar process: "metaphors must not be far-fetched, but we must give names to things that have none by deriving the metaphor from what is akin and of the same kind, so that as soon as it is uttered, it is clearly seen to be akin" (1405 a–b). The metaphor that observes what Aristotle calls "due proportion" is one that manages to link the unknown term to one that is already known, so that the likeness will be clear. Of course, Aristotle is assuming that the purpose of metaphor is, as he says, to be perspicuous and appropriate. Its perspicuity results from its fidelity to the subject, but its appropriateness results from the use of terms supplied by the audience. The same principle applies to appropriate style in general: "idle chatter produces obscurity; for when words are piled upon what one already knows, it destroys perspicuity by a cloud of verbiage" (1406 a–b). Rhetorical effectiveness, in all such cases, derives from the transaction between what the rhetor wishes to do and what the audience contributes. What the rhetor chooses to say derives from a process of choice that includes the consideration of what the audience already knows, as in the construction of enthymemes.

Thus, although Aristotle clearly asserts that the "enthymeme is a kind of syllogism" (e.g., 1401 a), the *kind* of syllogism that it is entails a process of rhetorical negotiation between the aims of the speaker and the conditions for success supplied by the audience. Rhetorical forms of all kinds, then, share with the enthymeme a certain process of inquiry. Enthymemes resemble appropriate metaphors and diction, as well as appropriate narratives, as much as they resemble syllogisms. Or, to put the matter in another way, all rhetorical forms resemble the enthymeme in their manner of construction. Rhetorical forms are enthymematic insofar as they result from the decision to say a thing in one way rather than another based on what the speaker wishes to accomplish and what the audience will enable to be accomplished.

Kenneth Burke calls this process "compromise," and it is this that enables him to make a theoretical distinction, especially in *Counter-Statement,* between the "psychology of information" and the "psychology of form." The former attends to subject matter, the latter attends to "conditions of appeal" that are contributed by the reader (30−38, 49−53). Successful effects, of whatever kind, result from the use of forms that derive from "potentialities" within readers to respond in certain ways and not others. And so, for Burke, "Art is a translation, and every translation is compromise" (54). Like Aristotle, Burke regards this general process as underlying decisions that result in syllogistic as well as other kinds of form (e.g., 124).

Compromise is, of course, a loaded term, especially when taken out of the context in which Burke uses it. It may suggest something impure and dishonest, as, indeed, *rhetoric* does for many people who would rather isolate the writer from the influence of the reader than see *that influence* as among the writer's resources. The compromise at issue here, however, is a productive, enabling kind: the writer must have a way of deciding among "available means" and that way will include — at some level, no doubt tacit in significant ways — the knowledge of what the audience already knows. While this enthymematic process conditions the writer's choice of how to construct an argument, it likewise conditions the choice of what argument to make. We think, as well as compose, within the context of what our audience makes thinkable. This kind of knowledge cannot be taken for granted nor can it be inferred with certainty. It must result from exercising one's best guess, or *judgment* in the sense that I used the term earlier.

Conclusion

I am not proposing that students of advanced composition be taught rhetorical theory, as I have broached it in historical terms above. I am suggesting that students compose enthymemes (and revise them) as an invention strategy, as a response to the rhetorical situation that their class readings and discussions have created for them and as a representive statement for the whole intention of the prose essay that they desire to write in response to that situation. I am presuming a classroom in which the open discussion of problematic ideas takes place and in which a discourse community is formed by the voices available in class and in provocative readings. The enthymeme composed as a response to a class in which ideas matter will have specific functions, enabling students to perceive and control both the necessary elements of the rhetorical situation and the possible elements of a serious essay. Generated by attention to the constraints of the situation, the enthymeme may in turn generate constructive structural relationships in students' prose.

Using the enthymeme as a practical construct for focusing students' thinking can teach more, I believe, than "writing" in a technical sense. The advantage for the use of enthymemes in composition extends beyond the construction of quasi-syllogisms that derive from assumptions available to the audience. It includes the possibility of helping students to understand that any composing decision is made responsible by its faithfulness to the writer's aims and to the reader's needs. Audience should not represent for student writers an obstacle to be overcome (as in argumentation taught as persuasion) but a resource to be used and a community to be joined, because readers are assumed by the responsible writer to be equally involved in the act of inquiry that the writing enacts. One's readers provide the basis for thinking about not only what formal or linguistic or logical constructions will work but what issues and stances are available to be considered. If this is the case, the enthymeme can provide students with a dynamic and facilitating form through which to encounter the responsibilities of inquiry and composing.

To construe the enthymeme in this way, as a kind of architectonic representation of the rhetorical mode of thought, does not reduce its application to composition. Rather, it suggests that students may benefit from such an understanding if they are to view their decisions as writers as essentially rhetorical. To develop this view is to abandon, or perhaps to outgrow, other views. It is, for instance, to abandon the view that writing *contains* knowledge, or that empty forms exist into which one's ideas may be plugged unchanged. The essence of a rhetorical exchange is to construct knowledge—and form—out of the writer's contribution to what the audience already knows, or ac*know*ledges. In terms of composition, this way of thinking suggests that writing is generative rather than modeled on imitable forms, and that what generates writing is the writer's responsible inquiry into what she knows and what the audience enables to be known.

Such understandings should, it seems to me, come to students in the composition class, unless that class should mislead them about the nature of language and its function in creating community and consensus in a world where these must serve us when absolute certainty is unavailable. If some modes of teaching composition do not address such concerns, or if they teach students that knowledge is unrelated to the activity of composing, and if those modes prevail in the basic or regular composition curriculum, then certainly advanced composition, whatever else that may mean, is our next, and maybe our last, opportunity to provide students with a more adequate way to think about composing, however difficult this will prove for them and for us.

Works Cited

Aristotle. *The "Art" of Rhetoric.* Trans. John Henry Freese. Cambridge, MA: Harvard UP, 1926.

Booth, Wayne, C. *Modern Dogma and the Rhetoric of Assent.* Chicago: U of Chicago P, 1974.

——. "The Uncritical American, or, Nobody's from Missouri Any More." *Now Don't Try to Reason with Me: Essays and Ironies for a Credulous Age.* Chicago: U of Chicago P, 1970. 63–75.

Burke, Kenneth. *Counter-Statement.* 2nd ed. Chicago: U of Chicago P, 1957.

Carden, Patricia. "Designing a Course." *Teaching Prose: A Guide for Writing Instructors.* Ed. Frederic V. Bogel and Katherine K. Gottschalk. New York: Norton, 1988. 20–45.

Crane, R. S. *The Languages of Criticism and the Structure of Poetry.* Toronto: U of Toronto P, 1953.

Emmel, Barbara A. *Model Essays in the Classroom: An Organic Approach to Understanding the Epistemological Basis of Form and Argument in Composition.* Diss. U of Oregon, 1989.

Fulkerson, Richard. "Technical Logic, Comp-Logic, and the Teaching of Writing." *College Composition and Communication* 39 (1988): 436–52.

Gage, John T. *The Shape of Reason: Argumentative Writing in College.* New York: Macmillan, 1987.

——. "An Adequate Epistemology for Composition: Classical and Modern Perspectives." *Essays on Classical Rhetoric and Modern Discourse.* Ed. Robert J. Connors, Lisa S. Ede, and Andrea A. Lunsford. Carbondale: Southern Illinois UP, 1984. 152–69.

——. "Teaching the Enthymeme: Invention and Arrangememt." *Rhetoric Review* 1 (1983): 38–50.

Green, Lawrence D. "Enthymemic Invention and Structural Prediction." *College English* 41 (1980): 623–34.

Hairston, Maxine. "Bringing Aristotle's Enthymeme into the Composition Classroom." *Rhetoric and Praxis: The Contribution of Classical Rhetoric to Practical Reasoning.* Ed. Jean Dietz Moss. Washington, DC: Catholic U of America P, 1986. 59–77.

Hood, Michael D. "Aristotle's Enthymeme: Its Theory and Application to Discourse." Diss. U of Oregon, 1984.

Knoblauch, C. H., and Lil Brannon. *Rhetorical Traditions and the Teaching of Writing.* Portsmouth, NH: Boynton/Cook, 1984.

LeFevre, Karen Burke. *Invention as a Social Act.* Carbondale: Southern Illinois UP, 1987.

Perelman, Chaim. *The Realm of Rhetoric.* Trans. William Kluback. Notre Dame: U of Notre Dame P, 1982.

Toulmin, Stephen. *The Uses of Argument.* Cambridge, England: Cambridge U P, 1958.

13

Teaching Argumentation in the Junior-Level Course

Jeanne Fahnestock

A few years ago an instructor in Maryland's Junior (now called Professional) Writing Program, Dr. Temma Berg, also took on a section
of Freshman Writing in another school. For a year she served these
two different populations, and in the process of changing hats from day
to day — Monday-Wednesday-Friday in one program and Tuesday-
Thursday in another — she came to some conclusions about what it is
and is not possible to accomplish with these two different audiences.
(Like many part-timers, she turned the disadvantages of her situation
into opportunities.) Admittedly her sample was small and skewed, but
her characterization rings true to many experienced teachers.

Though two years in anyone's life might not seem like enough time
to make a significant difference, the years and experiences between the
freshman and junior year at college evidently do. Dr. Berg found her
juniors readily acquired a sense of purpose and audience, and they
willingly revised.

> They quickly see that determining audience helps them find the best
> writing strategy. Therefore, Juniors value rhetoric as a discipline and
> are willing (indeed eager) to explore such notions as emphasis,
> rhythm, diction, and style; Juniors see how revision helps them reach
> a particular audience. (H)

Paradoxically, Dr. Berg found that freshmen wrote more correctly
than juniors, perhaps because of the recency of their high school
training, but they had little to say, wrote as little as possible, and saw
"no need for revising except to correct mistakes — in grammar, spelling,
punctuation. They do not see revision as a way to reach particular

179

audiences. The audience is always oneself, one's friends, one's teacher" (5).

At Maryland we have always been interested in the connections, theoretical and practical, between lower-and upper-division writing courses (see Orgelfinger). In her article, Dr. Berg recommended turning freshman writing into a reading-based course. That solution may or may not seem cogent to some readers, but at any rate freshman writing is not the issue here. What I want to emphasize is Dr. Berg's characterization of upper-division students in an advanced composition program as ready, willing, and able for that turning to the world outside and to the communicative rather than the so-called expressive uses of language. To borrow an analogy from controversies in linguistics, advanced students show more interest in communicative rather than linguistic competence. They are less concerned with getting it right than with getting it across. In addition, with their greater maturity comes a greater willingness to take a position with public dimensions, to, in effect, argue. The social maturity of upper-division students and their chronological position, poised at entry to the workplace, make the teaching of written argument a natural in the advanced composition classroom. In fact, one might almost ask, "If you are not teaching the arts of written argumentation in the advanced composition classroom, what are you teaching?"

Breaking Down the Distinction between Informing and Persuading

In the advanced composition classroom at Maryland we teach argument not as an art of defense or debate but as the art of establishing a position or making a case. One can argue for a position, that is give reasons for holding it, though no one else has said anything on that position at all. Admittedly, students' instincts go in the other direction when they think of argumentation, toward those issues that have stalemated in our society: gun control, capital punishment, violence on TV. They think of argument as confrontation between well-established positions. Perhaps the most difficult idea we try to get across in advanced composition is that all writing is argumentation, that it is impossible to use language without selecting, and hence creating and implicitly defending, some version of reality that the author wishes the reader to share.

The presumption that prevents us from acknowledging the ubiquity of argument originates, in the ancient schism (inherited perhaps most immediately from Bain and perpetuated by others who have divided up the universe of discourses) that informing and persuading are different modes. But we can only maintain this distinction if we also maintain certain other deceptions and self-deceptions. To illustrate this point we can begin with a familiar case. We have probably all had students who have written on a much visited topic—say the dangers of nuclear power—as though only one view on that topic were possible and their purpose was to inform an audience of this correct view. In their youth and innocence, they produce a one-sided harangue; they "tell it like it is." More aware of the gross weight of words expended on such topics, we may wince at their naivete. They have adopted an informative stance not calculated to survive in any actual public forum where the issue might be addressed. They are self-deceived.

On the other hand, a particularly artful polemicist could take that one-sided performance on a many-sided issue and address it to an uninformed audience, maintaining for that naive audience the fiction that nothing much had been thought and said on the issue; the polemicist could then occupy new territory in a reader's mind through "information." This tactic can be devastatingly effective, and it is one frequently adopted by arguers. But such arguers who present arguable cases as information are deceivers.

Someone could readily protest my confounding of the distinction between exposition and argumentation by pointing out that we do sense a difference between the speech acts implied by the verbs "to inform" and "to persuade." We can examine this objection by taking a slightly more complicated if prosaic case, one that perhaps illustrates more straightforwardly this intuitive notion of the difference between informing and persuading. Imagine the much beleaguered writer of documentation who sits down with a software package and has to produce a manual; or think of the writer of instructions for ready-to-assemble whatevers. Obviously, these writers think that their task is to get it right, "to inform" potential users and builders of the correct sequence of steps required to make use of the product. They don't imagine themselves actually engaged in persuading an audience to do things their way. Yet how many readers of software manuals or assembly instructions actually do follow the steps outlined in detail? Readers' needs are usually more pressing, and unless instructions are highly persuasive indeed, their attempt to control the sequence of steps will be ignored. Rare is the person who actually reads through a manual before booting the program or putting some pieces together.

The same mismatch between intent and effect hampers bureaucrats "informing" the public of how they may file their taxes, apply for a school lunch program, or avoid AIDS. Again, our hypothetical bureaucrats may imagine, in all good faith, that they are engaged in the speech act of informing, but since the effect of their texts will be the willingness or unwillingness of their readers to file, apply, or avoid, they are actually persuading.

Overall, then, we think we are engaged in the speech act of informing when we can imagine no alternative content for our message and our sense of ends is limited to "transportation," carting data from x to y. But once again, that transportation is part of larger processes—ends and means—dictated by human needs and desires. It is all persuasion.

We can take an even harder example, one that, unlike the school lunch notice, does seem removed from human motives. Imagine the writer for the U.S. Department of Agriculture who sits down to write a pamphlet describing the life cycle of a particularly annoying agricultural pest. (The government produces such "information bulletins" by the ton.) It would seem that this writer's sole motive is to "get it right," to inform an audience of certain facts. But there is no end to the "facts" that can be generated about any natural phenomenon. Someone must select among those facts, and since one person might do the selecting differently, any particular selection of the facts is an argument. It implicitly attempts to persuade an audience that it is the best or only true version. Its objective voice and graphic embellishments are among its rhetorical tactics to serve that end. (This constructionist view by no means implies that verifiable facts do not exist.) Furthermore the agricultural pamphleteer will inevitably feel constrained to describe the pest's life cycle in a way that suggests possible moments of intervention, places in the cycle from egg to egg layer where the pest would be vulnerable to the removal of a host or a large dose of diazonon—even if such interventions were never mentioned in the pamphlet. Similarly, an entomologist writing up the discovery of a new insect species would be under several constraints in selecting and presenting "information" in order to be persuasively convincing in the chosen format. The life cycle facts would have to resemble those of insects in whatever taxonomic niche the new species belonged; but some of the details would also have to be "new" to justify the claim of "new species."

Despite these counter examples, our belief in sanitized, objectified information is probably increasing. We have a new ruling image of information as bits of binary-encoded data exchanged at the speed of light in our "information society." Facts whiz along in "information networks," facts like the monthly payment record on a credit card balance, the sales performance of a certain model car in far western states, the purchase price of skiing equipment to be checked against available credit. But this information is all meaningless unless it is part of a larger "network" of human goals.

Theoretical Base for an Argument Course

While we may be quite convinced what ultimate perceptions and abilities about language and argumentation we want our students to learn, our wish list does not generate a curriculum or syllabus. Furthermore, when we turn to recent tradition for help, we find almost too many alternatives and textbooks. We could go the "critical thinking" route, an area growing once again, fueled by the informal logic movement in philosophy. Here our teaching emphasis — to go by texts like Freeman's *Thinking Logically* — would be on small-scale arguments, several sentences or paragraphs in length, and on so-called fallacies. Or we could model ourselves on a general speech course using texts like Rieke and Sillars's *Argumentation and the Decision Making Process* or Sproule's *Argument: Language and Its Influence.* Here the debate model would be strong, as would an emphasis on the various social contexts or argument fields that arguers find themselves in.

In the last five years composition teachers have offered texts that take various approaches, but in composition, as well as in critical thinking and speech, the Toulmin model has gained favor as an analytical heuristic. The familiar upside down triangles linking data, claim, and warrant appear frequently in the pages of texts devoted to argumentation. However, while the Toulmin model may be a powerful analytical device (one can force the unpacking of enthymemes with it), the gulf is prodigious between a Toulmin diagram and a fully written argument. Students cannot readily build up discursive arguments from little Toulmin diagrams.

Still other approaches would have students of argument start at the other end, first studying an issue or controversy and then writing, in effect, position papers. The problem with this approach is that it is not easily generalized; students may come away from such a course thoroughly aware of various positions on nuclear waste disposal but entirely ignorant about any general tactics for approaching and writing on other issues. No wonder English departments often like to punt the whole problem to *other* departments in some WAC programs.

Marie Secor and I have written elsewhere on our preferred approach to teaching argument, an approach derived from the classical doctrine of the *stases* (Fahnestock and Secor, *A Rhetoric of Argument* and "Toward a Modern Version").

Briefly, this approach divides arguments into types according to the four kinds of question addressed: What is it?, What caused it?, Is it good or bad?, and What should we do about it? Each question in turn provokes a certain type of argument with predictable structural features, so students can move more easily from a theoretical awareness of the kind of argument they are producing to a flesh and blood text.

Working through the stases, a student who is arguing in the first stasis on the nature or existence of a phenomenon, for example, "Most homeless people are mentally disturbed," identifies (1) problems with a definition of the term "mentally disturbed"; (2) obstacles in obtaining representative samples of the homeless; and (3) appropriate judgments of the published and anecdotal or first-hand evidence obtainable. The art of the arguer, in this case, begins in defining "mentally disturbed" in such a way that it fits the available evidence and is at the same time plausible to an audience. As teacher and student work through this problem, the assault on the information/argument dichotomy begins. The case that is eventually made for the sample claim about the homeless may look "informative," but it is an argumentative construction that could be made quite differently.

The Stases and Process

In describing the structural problems of an argument to support the sample first-stasis thesis on homelessness, I have distorted the actual process the student works through. Obviously the student does not begin with a fully formed thesis springing from her forehead, let alone one which is qualified with a "most." Rather she begins with a topic that interests her and an awareness, in part from classroom discussions, of the difficulties of supporting claims/characterizations about large, imperfectly accessible subjects. She also should have learned the dangers in amorphous labels like "mentally disturbed." Instruction in techniques of definition will suggest that in *her* situation an operational definition might be most useful. Only the actual quality and quantity of the evidence she obtains will tell her how she can finally qualify her thesis—with a few, some, many, most, or whatever. The final thesis may evolve to something like "Many of D.C.'s street people have histories of treatment for four mental disorders."

Nevertheless, the provisional thesis statement serves as a heuristic throughout the process of constructing the argument. The student knows she must bring the two ends of the thesis together, making the accessible evidence about the homeless overlap with a plausible, supportable definition of mental disorder by observable symptoms or treatment histories. Furthermore, on this first paper we hold the student to a standard of explicitness unlike the standard she will find in most journalistic writing. We ask that she indicate all her sources of evidence and assess their relative trustworthiness, imagining an audience with a serious interest in the verifiability of her claims. And we ask that at some point she formulate the definition of her key predicate term explicitly, though later that definition may well be dispersed throughout her argument. In making these demands for early drafts, we in effect give the student a standard of comparison against which she can judge the claims about the existence and nature of things as she is bombarded with them in the media. It is the beginning, we hope, of a healthy skepticism about the purposes and motives that inevitably shape "information."

It is also, we hope, the end of reliance on sources accessible through the *Reader's Guide,* such as *Time, Newsweek,* and *U.S. News and World Report.* We appreciate that students begin with their presumptions formed by such publications, but we do not want them to stop at these sources. We suggest that they consult specialist publications (for the example on the homeless, e.g., the newsletters of social workers and mental health workers and journals in sociology). And we nudge them to conduct interviews, ask questions, and engage in as much seeing and doing as possible. We do not, however, ask them to engage in any lengthy or involved original research. We can not teach the research methodology of the different disciplines; we simply hope that, as upper-division students, they come to the advanced composition classroom familiar with some of that methodology.

Staying with the Same Topic

In our current curriculum we strongly urge students to stay with the same topic throughout the semester and through the four stases. We can illustrate this process by following our hypothetical student through the stases. The student who wrote her first paper characterizing the mental health of a segment of the homeless population, will undertake in her second paper to give a convincing argument about causes. The argument on the causes for the presence of significant numbers of mentally disturbed individuals among the homeless may look back to the dramatic changes in treating the mentally ill in the sixties and seventies. Again, the classroom will provide models and descriptions of the structure and techniques of causal argument.

Next comes evaluation — Is it good or bad? On the face of it, the student working on homelessness cannot imagine the need to convince any audience of the moral horrors and social cost of the problem. Again, presumption already favors a negative evaluation. But this student can argue about the *degree* of the problem; that is, in *The New Rhetoric*'s (Perelman and Olbrechts-Tyteca), terms, she can seek not to form or change opinion but rather to increase the adherence she finds in a particular audience. She may argue for the *seriousness* of the problem. In doing so she will learn the two basic resources of evaluative argument: the appeal to an ethical standard and the appeal to consequences, tactics that reprise the techniques of the first two arguments she has written.

At this point it is also possible that the student will change gears slightly, depending on what has evolved from her work on arguments in the first two stases. The student who believes she has identified a significant cause of homelessness in the "extramural" and supposedly community-based treatment of the mentally ill may turn her evaluation argument into a criticism of such practices in her area. Now the work she has done on the earlier arguments—trying to substantiate the proportion of mentally ill among the homeless—becomes the fuel for the consequence portion of her evaluation. The moral and ethical component of an evaluation argument is another, and usually more difficult, matter to teach, but it becomes somewhat less so if the student has been committed to a topic through several papers and has gradually built up an acquaintance with its complexities through interviews and discussions with classmates, potential audiences, and the instructor as devil's advocate.

Finally, the student is ready for the highest stakes argument—the proposal. This last argument in the stasis series asks the student to recommend a specific course of action to alleviate or correct the problem that has emerged in the work of the first three papers. This proposed solution must be specific and doable, not some pie-in-the-sky exhortation to go and fix things up. We want students to practice the complete form of the proposal argument, which begins by demonstrating a situation and evaluating it as a problem and ends by arguing for the feasibility of a particular course of action, including, if necessary, its cost in time, money, and effort and the identification of whatever first step would bring it about. Obviously this last paper recapitulates the series: it opens with reworked versions of the first and third papers and includes causal argument if it is germane to the proposal (i.e., if the recommended action will remove one of the original causes of the problem). To ask students to write such a proposal *without* the preparation of the earlier, smaller scale arguments and many weeks of research is to invite disaster.

The Stases and the Toulmin Model

The stases, then, give us a method of teaching argument that is logically compelling in itself and transferable. Students can apply this model to any argument they read as well as any argument they construct, no matter what the discipline. Furthermore, the stases can readily be combined with the Toulmin model as a way of schematizing arguments in order to analyze them and, in particular, to uncover implicit warrants. In fact, the stases clarify the Toulimin model because arguments in each stasis require unique kinds of warrants. Arguments in the first stasis, for example, which characterize or identify a situation, require a definition as a warrant. Part of our sample argument about the homeless could be diagrammed as follows:

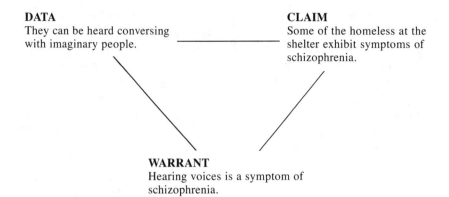

The full Toulmin model (with slots for claim, data, warrant, backing, modality, and rebuttal) draws attention to the need to qualify a claim carefully according to the degree of the evidence and, particularly useful in arguments hinging on definition, it leaves a gaping hole demanding substantiation or backing of the warrant. The student working on the homeless argument must cite authorities supporting each portion of the definition of a mental disorder such as that used in the example above; she cannot conjure up the definition herself and assume her audience will find it convincing.

Causal arguments require another unique kind of warrant — not definition, but agency. An agency is a basic belief in what can cause what; heat causes ice to melt and the human impulse to imitate can motivate a whole range of behaviors. Agencies are often invisible in their simplicity or may even seem tautological, but the verbalization of these causal warrants required by the Toulmin model can be enlightening.

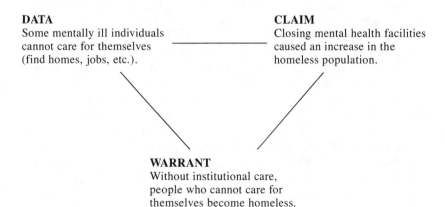

Evaluations use the basic structural tactics that the first two types of argument required. An ethical argument is a form of definition argument, and a consequence argument is causal. Formulating the warrant in an ethical argument makes clear the arguer's belief and can help the student appreciate an audience's likely response.

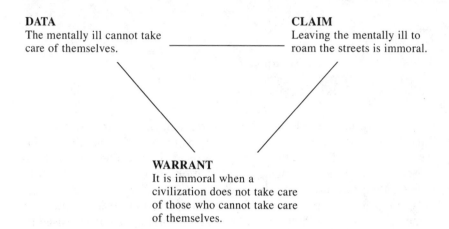

DATA
The mentally ill cannot take care of themselves.

CLAIM
Leaving the mentally ill to roam the streets is immoral.

WARRANT
It is immoral when a civilization does not take care of those who cannot take care of themselves.

The final proposal argument, as pointed out above, combines all three earlier types. It is a composite argument and, like all extended written arguments, would pose a significant challenge to the person intent on reducing it to diagrams. Nevertheless, the key feature of the proposal argument — what distinguishes it from the earlier arguments — is its feasibility section, which aims to convince a particular audience that it has the power (time, money, skill), authority, responsibility, and/or moral right to take the recommended action. As such, a feasibility argument must build on a warrant that expresses what an audience should believe about itself. This move in the proposal argument sometimes requires that the arguer identify or even create a group the audience can belong to. Individual readers are assumed or invited to belong to this group. By the time she reaches the proposal argument, the student working on the homeless issue will craft her proposal argument with a very particular audience in mind. She learns that feasibility, in the sense of authority, will be less of an issue if she addresses a group that has come into being *because* it has been invested with a particular responsibility: for example, the governing board of the local mental health facility or the committee of the county council or state legislature that oversees such services. (Thus, writing a proposal argument is often a crash course in local politics.) For such audiences feasibility is more a question of finances and trade-offs; authority and responsibility can be assumed and built on.

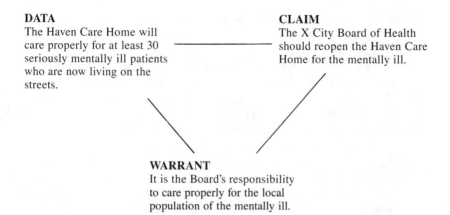

DATA
The Haven Care Home will care properly for at least 30 seriously mentally ill patients who are now living on the streets.

CLAIM
The X City Board of Health should reopen the Haven Care Home for the mentally ill.

WARRANT
It is the Board's responsibility to care properly for the local population of the mentally ill.

Analogy is a particularly strong resource in proposal arguments, since people often gain the impulse to act in a certain way when they are convinced that others in a similar situation have so acted. If our advocate for the homeless can find a parallel case, a Board of Health in a similar city that reopened a facility, she will have a strong argument for the feasibility of her proposal.

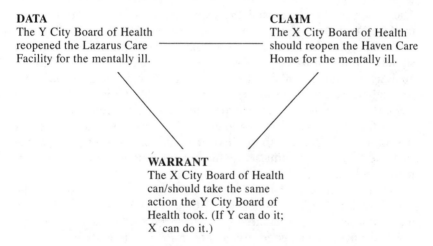

DATA
The Y City Board of Health reopened the Lazarus Care Facility for the mentally ill.

CLAIM
The X City Board of Health should reopen the Haven Care Home for the mentally ill.

WARRANT
The X City Board of Health can/should take the same action the Y City Board of Health took. (If Y can do it; X can do it.)

The Toulmin model helps the arguer formulate the warrants that any single part of her argument may be building on, and it draws attention to the potential need for backing those warrants. Other explicators of the Toulmin model have pointed out that the data can require the support of verification too, just as the warrant requires backing (Brockriede and Ehinger). But while the Toulmin model may help a student expand on a given data-claim (or premise-conclusion) pair, it does not have the generative power of stasis theory. Distinguishing the type of argument according to stasis theory directs the student to the relevant tactics of support and comes closer to suggesting a possible arrangement of the final argument.

Furthermore, an awareness of the stasis of an argument clarifies some advice often given haphazardly in argument texts. Take examples, for example. Students may be taught the distinction between real and hypothetical examples without being taught where hypothetical examples can be used and where they should not be. A hypothetical example, one that the arguer fabricates, can certainly be used in causal argument to illustrate the working mechanics of a causal process. It can also be used in a proposal argument to give an audience a glimpse of how the recommended solution would work or what a situation would be like free of the problem under attack. But arguers should not use hypothetical examples when they draft first stasis arguments whose purpose is to define or characterize reality. Though examples are inevitably shaped and patted to fit a thesis, they must not be fabricated in such arguments. General advice about tactics of argument, then, can be precisely the wrong advice for certain kinds of argument.

"The Rhetorical Stance"

The order of the stases and the explanatory power of the Toulmin model provide the student with powerful invention heuristics for constructing arguments. But anyone who has actually taught argument to students in a writing course (as opposed to a course that emphasizes analysis or critical thinking) knows that something is still missing. We remember the example (presumably real!) of Wayne Booth's graduate student who wrote execrable papers until he had a genuine exigence for writing and a perceivable audience. Those were provided when he passionately disagreed with Booth over a point of interpretation. Before that, he had been writing academic exercises addressed to the void, merely rehearsing, as a neophyte in a discipline, the conventions of academic discourse in that discipline. Writing to the void is already the student's situation in most college writing assignments; it is a situation we do not want to perpetuate in the advanced composition classroom. We will not get very good arguments from our students if their sole purpose is to practice certain disciplinary formulas.

What we would prefer is the student's genuine engagement in a topic for which there is real, external exigence — that is, a real audience (Bitzer). To work toward this ideal we allow our students to choose their own topics, encouraging them to settle on topics that overlap with their majors. The process of working through to a topic that will yield a series of four arguments is, frankly, the trickiest part of the advanced composition course; teaching the Toulmin model and the stases is easy by comparison. Finding a viable topic requires individual conferences, sometimes exchanges of memos, and workshop consultations. There is, not surprisingly, a tendency for students to select certain old chestnuts that have been moldering around composition classrooms for decades: violence on television, use of solar energy, gun control, and, perhaps soon to join the rolls, the illustrative example used in this article, the problem of the homeless. If students want to work on these trampled topics, we encourage them to find a new slant or local application. But fresh new topics are to be found everywhere, in the pages of local newspapers and in the lives of Maryland students, most of whom are commuters working part- or full-time jobs in a chaotic urban area as well as "citizens" of ever larger polities. Students have written on economic exchange with Ecuador, copyrights on clothing design, scholarships for students of Japanese culture, desertification in the Sahel, the problems of county hot-line operators, vandalism at local archaeology sites, the advisory system in the psychology department, the retention of minority students at the university, and the army's use of reconnaissance drones. Eventually, student and teacher find a unique topic, one the student is already interested in and familiar with, one for which a rich variety of sources is accessible.

As if these topic demands were not enough, we have another, one that is most crucial in our quest for a genuine rhetorical stance. We require our students to address their final proposal argument to a real audience — and to send it to that audience with an appropriate cover letter. The desertification proposal went to a U.N. subcommittee; the recommendations for the psychology department's advising system went to the chair of that department (prompting his angry phone call to the program's director claiming that the student's characterization of the problem was inaccurate); the proposal to computerize a local county hot-line referral system was adopted; the recommendation that the army use reconnaissance drones went to a U.S. Senator and through him to an army research facility, which corresponded with the student; the recommendation on minority retention went to the Chancellor (and received his personal thanks). Nothing replaces a real audience as a stimulus to good writing and arguing. A student was once discussing with his teacher what seemed a very promising topic. He was going to look at some recent changes in the rules of chess competition, assess their consequences, and recommend some alterations. "Excellent," said the teacher. "You can send your final proposal to the U.S. Chess Federation." "Oh," said the crestfallen student, "then I really have to do it."

Pedagogical Means

To achieve our philosophical goal of giving students a skeptical respect for language and our practical goal of giving them confidence in their ability to present a case, we have evolved certain pedagogical practices in the advanced composition classroom at Maryland. Since these may differ from those outlined in other essays in this collection, they are perhaps worth mentioning to provide readers with a sense of options.

In the first place, we value the classroom, or rather the class as a whole, as a pedagogical setting, though not of course to the exclusion of individual conferences with the instructor or of small-group workshops. But the class itself (usually with about 20 students) offers the best forum for the discussion of rhetorical issues, simply because it is a larger social unit representing a greater diversity of viewpoints. Even if most members of the class adopt the same stance toward an issue, one individual is still more likely to raise an opposing view or a unique reconfiguration of a problem in the larger group. Discussions of potential topics, approaches, and rhetorical strategies thrive in this exchange. And so does mutual help. In the course of a semester devoted primarily to one project, the students come to know each other's topics, and they share sources and leads. They also acquire a kind of pride of identity in their own topics.

Maryland's advanced composition course also has, as does every composition class, the corollary goal of improving students' language skills. Our main method of nudging students toward greater stylistic confidence is the ancient one of variation for *copia* (Erasmus). How many other ways are there, we ask, to express a point or phrase a passage, and which way is probably best to achieve the writer's purpose in a particular rhetorical situation? In the process of in-class language fiddling, students should learn, for example, the distinction between loose and periodic sentences, the virtues of variety in sentence length, the whys and wherefores of combining and decombining, and—for chunks or passages—the logic of transitions expressed or implied and of topic/comment connections. Some instructors adopt an extra text on style to reinforce and organize the language skills component of the curriculum.

Finally, we do not use literary texts or belletristic essays as models or as points of departure for class assignments. Though works in these categories are definitely rhetorical, it is not the work of the writing classroom to rediscover their original rhetorical context. We prefer contemporary pieces on contemporary issues, complete with warts, and, of course, front and center, the students' own writing.

Our purpose in the advanced composition classroom is not to indoctrinate students into the genteel tradition or to brainwash them into any one ideologic perspective but to prepare them for survival in the world's war of words. To that end we want to teach them that the stance of informing is a rhetorical choice, that the challenges and complexities of making a case can at least be approached by the order of the stases and the analytical insight provided by the Toulmin model, and that arguing is an intentional, social act requiring a genuine exigence and audience.

Works Cited

Bain, Alexander. *English Composition and Rhetoric*. 2nd American ed. New York: Appleton, 1867.

Berg, Temma. "Marking the Differences: Teaching Freshman and Junior Comp." *Maryland Composition Review* 4.2 (1984):2–9.

Bitzer, Lloyd. "The Rhetorical Situation." *Contemporary Theories of Rhetoric: Selected Readings*. Ed. Richard L. Johannesen. New York: Harper, 1971. 381–93.

Booth, Wayne C. "The Rhetorical Stance." *The Writing Teacher's Sourcebook*. Ed. Gary Tate and Edward P. J. Corbett. New York: Oxford UP, 1981. 108–16.

Brockriede, Wayne E., and Douglas Ehninger. "Toulmin on Argument: An Interpretation and Application." *Contemporary Theories of Rhetoric: Selected Readings*. New York: Harper, 1971.

Erasmus, Desiderius. *On Copia of Words and Ideas*. Trans. D. B. King and H. D. Rix. Milwaukee: Marquette UP, 1963.

Fahnestock, Jeanne, and Marie Secor. *A Rhetoric of Argument*. New York: Random, 1982.

——"Toward a Modern Version of Stasis Theory." *Oldspeak/Newspeak: Rhetorical Transformations*. Arlington, TX: NCTE, 1985. 217–26.

Freeman, J. *Thinking Logically: Basic Concepts for Reasoning*. Englewood Cliffs, NJ: Prentice, 1988.

Orgelfinger, G. "Differences between Teaching Freshman and Junior Level Composition." *Maryland Composition Review* 4.1 (1983): 12–17.

Perelman, Chaim, and L. Olbrechts-Tyteca. *The New Rhetoric: A Treatise on Argument*. Notre Dame: U of Notre Dame P, 1969.

Rieke, R. D., and Sillars, M. O. *Argumentation and the Decision Making Process*. 2nd ed. Glenview, IL: Scott, 1984.

Sproule, J. M. *Argument: Language and Its Influence*. New York: McGraw, 1980.

14

From Artifact to Utterance: Toward a Revised Conception of Critical Thinking in Advanced Composition

Gary A. Olson
Evelyn Ashton-Jones

While there certainly isn't consensus in composition studies on the aims and objectives of advanced composition, many compositionists argue that the advanced course should focus on critical thinking. We, too, believe that the advanced composition course should help students become critical thinkers; however, we take issue with the way a good many theorists and practitioners approach critical thinking. In this essay we will examine the current conception of critical thinking, discuss its limitations, and propose a revised conception of critical thinking more consistent with the goals and methods of advanced composition.

Current Approaches to Critical Thinking

Many instructors integrate critical thinking into their advanced composition classes by asking students to read, analyze, respond to, and write about published essays. Such analysis and response can benefit students, but many instructors unwittingly present a rather limited approach to analysis, one informed by New Critical assumptions about meaning and text: the text is an artifact *containing* meaning; the critical enterprise is one of close reading; and close analysis of the words on the page leads to an accurate conception of the artifact's meaning. Thus, the New Critical method is pseudo-scientific: the subject is laid upon the table, dissected, interpreted, and evaluated. Implicit in this endeavor is the assumption that this process leads to meaning, to truth. And although poststructuralist critical theory offers several satisfying alternatives to this kind of reading — alternatives that perhaps are more appropriate for advanced composition courses — such New Critical assumptions still underlie the kind of critical thinking practices proposed, and even promulgated, by compositionists. And even many of the compositionists who employ reader-response and other epistemic approaches in their advanced composition classrooms tacitly revert to the kinds of procedures valorized by the New Critics when they turn to the activity called "critical thinking."

In the context of critical thinking, the New Critical examination of texts for balance, unity, coherence, and irony translates into what Anthony Petrosky calls "strip-mining selections for verifiable information and facts," an enterprise that directs students to glean sentences and paragraphs in search of "such things as main ideas, subordinate ideas, and author's purposes" (3). Textbooks on critical thinking and chapters of composition texts typically lead students systematically through this process of locating the thesis, main points, supporting evidence, unqualified assertions, and so on. The objective of this process is to help students "understand" the "meaning" of the work under examination. Unfortunately, what students really learn is to see meaning, in Petrosky's words as "something external, something contained in a text (the way a can of peas contains peas) or something that exists in the world" (3).

In fact, the language of critical thinking textbooks illustrates this emphasis on external meaning, on verifiable truth. One such text is named, quite appropriately, *Asking the Right Questions*. Presumably, the authors know the "right" questions that will lead to the "right" answers — that is, to truth. Similarly, in the prototypical critical reading textbook, *Preface to Critical Reading*, Richard Altick writes that the "critical spirit" is a "determination to see everything for what it *really is*" (xi). Another text, Vincent Ryan Ruggiero's *The Art of Thinking*, has this to say about the concept of truth:

> It is ironic that so much confusion exists about truth. Even otherwise intelligent people can be heard saying things like "Everyone makes his own truth," "One person's truth is another person's error," "Truth is relative," and "Truth is constantly changing." All of these ideas undermine thinking. (18)

Truth, Ruggiero contends, is "something separate from and unaffected by individual perspectives" (19). Clearly, Ruggiero assumes that truth is objective, universal, and, above all, unchanging. Attempts to create truth or meaning, attempts to change truth, are subversive: they "undermine thinking."

Such discussions of critical thinking also establish "proper" strategies for finding truth. For example, in "How Rational Thinking Affects Student Success," Foster E. Tait writes repeatedly that "being rational means being able to reason correctly" (75). The headings peppering Tait's article are permeated by this idea of "correct" reasoning: "The Need for Correct Reasoning" "Reasoning: Correct and Incorrect"; "The Logic of Correct Writing"; "Correct Reasoning and How to Accomplish It." Throughout his essay Tait talks about "the rules of reasoning," "making proper connections," and "correct thinking and arguing." And, as we have implied, this particular method of critical thinking mimics the scientific method: students learn to become "objective" and "detached" analysts, incisively examining the specimen — the artifact — before them; ostensibly, such "professional detachment" helps students better find truth and meaning. Thus, as advanced composition instructors we teach *detachment* rather than *engagement, uninvolvement* rather than *involvement, inaction* rather than *action.* We teach students to treat discourse as puzzles to be solved through detached calculation, not as human utterances that provide a basis for interaction between reader and writer who, together, create meaning.

Definitions of critical thinking, expressed in the first chapter of just about any book on the subject or in the critical thinking component of any composition text, provide an even clearer picture of how pervasive these notions of correctness, logical thought, and unchanging meaning are. Vincent E. Barry writes that critical thinking "emphasizes a rational basis for beliefs and provides procedures for analyzing, testing, and evaluating them" (9). Ruggiero calls it "a searching for answers, a reaching for meaning" (2). The editors of an essay anthology for composition classes define a critical thinker as a person who is able to "discern fact from fiction" (Ray, Olson, and DeGeorge 2). Neil Browne and Stuart Keeley define critical reading as "reacting to what you read through systematic evaluation" (1). And the California State University system, in defining the objectives of critical thinking instruction, mandates that students learn to "reach factual or judgmental conclusions based on sound inferences drawn from unambiguous statements of knowledge and belief" (qtd. in Benderson 4). Notice that these definitions reveal a proclivity for specifying rightness and correctness, for discerning fact from fiction, for systematically analyzing and evaluating. They presume that the entire endeavor called critical thinking is systematic, rule-bound, and designed to reveal immutable truth. Critical thinking thus becomes a simple matter of following prescribed procedures that derive their validity from a single criterion: the rules of logical reasoning. Such notions of meaning inhering in texts, and correct and systematic ways of locating and thinking about it, seem almost like parodies in light of poststructuralist critical theory.

Strangely enough, the current influence of critical methodologies that encourage multiple perspectives and of liberatory pedagogies that attempt to break down authoritarian hierarchies does not seem to have extended to critical thinking pedagogies. In advanced composition classrooms, in the name of teaching "more sophisticated thinking skills," we may in fact be teaching students to follow directions unquestioningly, to follow steps that lead to the "truth" that others (that is, "we") possess. Thus, in offering students procedures designed to help them discover meanings that we have already decided are appropriate, we establish an opposition between knower and known and, of course, between those of us who know and those who do not — oppositions that work to the advantage of those of us who are the knowers, that is, those who *establish* what is to be known, what is worth knowing.

This epistemlogical hierarchy is furthered and sustained by curricula designed to teach critical thinking. Much of the instructional literature indicates that critical thinking proponents see themselves as helping students reach "higher stages" of cognitive development. Thus, they have identified numerous discrete thinking "skills" and devised various sets of instructional exercises to teach those skills. They have attempted to specify which are the "most sophisticated" thinking skills and have subdivided these skills further into subskills, producing lists of "thinking skills" and corresponding instructional methods. For instance, a document circulated at the Seventh Annual and Fifth International Conference on Critical on Thinking and Educational Reform, entitled "Goals for a Critical-Thinking/Reasoning Curriculum," outlines in great detail the "dispositions and abilities" involved in critical thinking (Ennis). In a traditional outline format, including not only primary and secondary levels but a bewildering *six* levels, Ennis specifies 13 "dispositions" and 12 "abilities" of critical thinking. These abilities are further divided into 62 subabilities, which are further divided into 45 sub-subabilities, which are further divided into 18 sub-sub-subabilities, which are divided into four sub-sub-sub-subabilities.

While this list is perhaps more intricate than other such lists, it nonetheless represents a general tendency to divide and isolate thinking skills. In fact, an entire industry seems to have developed for the specific purpose of specifying these skills, studying them, devising instructional procedures to teach them, and promulgating the entire package to other educators. Collett Dilworth writes that we should "find discomfort in the urgency with which agency after agency is compiling lists of 'thinking skills' (CEEB, NIE, The New Jersey Task Force Taxonomy of Thinking Skills)." She goes on to lament that critical thinking has become "a sub-discipline spawning such facilities as the Center for Critical Thinking and Moral Critique at Sonoma State University" (18). Dilworth's concern seems legitimate. Not only are Allan Bloom, E. D. Hirsch, and William Bennett determining what content students should learn, but now critical thinking specialists and entire institutions are specifying *how* students should think, by giving them an array of thinking strategies and by valorizing certain strategies as "skills" while disregarding others.

The Limitations of Current Conceptions of Critical Thinking

The present conception of critical thinking is limiting for several reasons. First, the present preoccupation with discrete thinking skills is reductive, in much the same way that the current/traditional paradigm's concentration on grammar skills is reductive. Composition theory and research have shown quite conclusively that direct instruction in grammar not only is ineffective but may even be harmful, because it consumes valuable class time that can be used more productively and because it leads students to believe that effective writing is simply a matter of avoiding error. Yet critical thinking specialists seem to employ the very same kind of skills orientation that compositionists now consider so unproductive. In "Grammar, Grammars, and the Teaching of Grammar," Patrick Hartwell jokes that if knowledge of the rules of grammar—that is, grammatical skill—led directly to good writing, "then linguists would be our best writers" (115). By analogy, then, if a command of discrete thinking skills necessarily led to sophisticated thinking, then cognitive psychologists or curriculum specialists would be our finest thinkers. Hartwell has difficulty envisioning linguists as our best writers; it's even more difficult to envision cognitive psychologists and curriculum specialists as our best thinkers.

Similarly, compositionists who base their classroom activities on theory and research long ago gave up drills-skills workbooks and a writing pedagogy that leads students from words to sentences to paragraphs to essays. This atomistic approach is ineffective in part because it is arhetorical; that is, it asks students to write in a vacuum—without context, without purpose, without audience. In the same way, teaching students discrete thinking strategies and then asking them to apply those strategies is acontextual. Asking students to memorize lists of logical fallacies, for example, and then to hunt for fallacies in a published essay or to avoid them in their own writing is no different from asking students to memorize various sentence types and to use them consciously in their papers. Just as learning various sentence types doesn't necessarily make a student a good writer, learning to indentify fallacies—or a thesis statement or any other purely textual feature—doesn't necessarily make a student a good thinker. As James L. Kinneavy writes, "There are seventy years of research which demonstrate overwhelmingly that the isolated teaching of grammatical skills has little or no transfer to use in actual composition. . . .I suspect that the same can be said of the insulated teaching of logical skills" (292).

Second, the tacit assumption that truth is absolute, universal, and verifiable according to the rules of logic and reason limits students' perspective of the complexities involved in "coming to know." We agree with Kenneth A. Bruffee:

> We are mistaken when we tie our study and teaching of the humanities to a notion of "truth as something which exists and endures apart from" human beings. Abstract thought, archetypal figures, mythology, notions of Reason with a capital "R" and Truth with a capital "T," notions of established order, universals of sound reasoning. . .are all forms "of what Nietzsche called 'the longest lie'—the lie that there is something beyond mankind to which it is [our] duty to be faithful." (787–88)

Clearly, the current conception of critical thinking—emphasizing logic as the means to an absolute truth—mystifies and distorts students' roles in creating and maintaining knowledge. Along with Richard Rorty, we argue that critical thinking has little to do with such notions of Truth and Reason; rather, it involves "playing off alternatives against one another, rather than playing them off against criteria of rationality, much less against eternal verities" (11).

Third, these univeralist assumptions downplay the role of context in critical thinking. Such an approach may help students see the trees but certainly not the forest. It's rather ironic that anyone should need to argue that critical thinking should emphasize context. Historically, the critical thinking movement itself has been an attempt to introduce context to instruction in logical reasoning. When courses in formal symbolic logic did not seem to be helping students become better thinkers, educators in various disciplines hypothesized that these courses were ineffective because students found it difficult to apply abstract, fomulaic rules to real-life situations. Thus, as Meredith Marble explains, critical thinking was born "out of a practical need to reason, that is, to make decisions, in real-life contexts involving values and standards" (67). Ralph Johnson and J. A. Blair describe it as "a turn in the direction of actual (i.e., real-life, ordinary, everyday) arguments in their native habitat of public discourse and persuasion, together with an attempt to deal with the problems that occur as the result of that focus" (5).

Yet it is exactly this criticism—that they are not sufficiently contextual — that we have of current methods of teaching critical thinking. While informal logic is a substantial improvement over symbolic logic in that it frames questions of logic within descriptive scenarios, current critical thinking pedagogy has not gone nearly far enough. Students may very well have a contextualized scenario from which to work, but very little attention seems to be paid to how the context itself contributes to meaning. For example, in "A Critical Thinking Heuristic for the Argumentative Composition," Marble includes an appendix in which she uses "standard argument form" to analyze a short argument by Jerry Falwell. Marble dissects the argument, identifies its parts ("major premises," "rhetorical questions," and so on), labels each part (P1, P2, RQ, and so on), and arranges these labeled parts in a neat schematic. Here is her conclusion:

> This is a deductive argument (the conclusion is entailed by the premises) with the addition of unstated premises. However, because so many of the premises are problematic, it is not a valid argument. (76)

Such an analysis, perhaps, is a beginning; but it's not an end. Despite the contextual frame of such scenarios, the main focus remains the "rules" of logical reasoning and the search for a "truth," a right answer. Thus, the current critical thinking model is like a sugar-coated pill; the medicine (that is, the cure for poor thinking) remains the rules of logic, while the sugar coating is the realistic scenario that makes the whole process more palatable to students.

It's ironic, too, that critical thinking proponents advocate "active" reading and thinking over the passive. For example, the editors of *The Process Reader* write, "Good readers ask questions, look for answers, demand support. When you read in this active way your are a critical reader and a critical thinker" (Ray, Olson, and DeGeorge 2). Undoubtedly, such pedagogies help students become active in the sense that they learn not to wait for a teacher or other authority figure to *give* them knowledge, to tell them *what* to think. Students learn instead to *search* for knowledge elsewhere, usually in a text, and the teacher explains how to go about finding it. Such active reading and thinking certainly are preferable to the passive mode they replace, but they are not active enough. Substituting a pedagogy that tells students how to think for one that tells them what to think continues to position students as *recipients* of knowledge; they are receivers of meaning, not makers of it. Thus, one kind of passive pedagogy substitutes for another.

Active learning is perhaps best defined as a process in which students themselves are empowered to become encoders, makers of meaning. As Kathleen Welch suggests, instructors teach students to become passive readers, *de*coders of texts, rather than active writers, *en*coders of their own texts. The answers still are predetermined; only now students are made to feel that they actually are active participants in the knowledge game when, in reality, their participation is just as restricted as it ever has been. Students are made to feel as if they are more free than they are, free to make choices, free to make meaning. Welch writes.

> The potentially dangerous activity of writing is bypassed by construct-
> ing many — perhaps most — writing classes as passive reading classes. . .
> a point that process compositionists such as Peter Elbow and James
> Moffett have been making forcefully and persuasively for a genera-
> tion. Writing textbooks appear in most writing classes partly because
> they are comforting to the teachers and partly because they allow
> passive reading, as opposed to critical reading, to dominate the class.
> (253)

Even compositionists who incorporate reader-response techniques into their critical thinking pedagogies must be wary of *how* they teach students to "respond" to what they read. Response itself can be just as passive as absorbing facts in a lecture. This concern over how we treat response is echoed by a panel of distinguished scholars who met at the seminar of the International Federation for the Teaching of English in order to formulate recommendations about teaching practices. Al-though the following note of caution from those recommendations principally concerns response to *literature,* it is equally appropriate to response to any text (or to any verbal argument, for that matter):

> We need to achieve a better understanding of the notion of reader
> "response." Response theory does not stop with mere response.
> Unexplored, the word "response" may too readily suggest reaction to
> a text almost on a stimulus-response model. This tends to distract us
> from a full apprehension of how literature [or any text] is socially and
> ideologically constructed in the first place and then re-made in the act
> of reading. It also tends to lead to a pedagogy where mere *response* is
> validated. We need to consider the personal and societal uses of. . .
> discourse. We need to develop constructive social criticism in going
> beyond response *to consider action* . (Tchudi 174)

This emphasis on *action* is important. True critical thinking is neces-sarily tied to the action of making meaning. In an advanced composition course, such action should necessarily translate into writing — not writing that simply communicates "truth" but writing in which students take on the power and responsibility of *creating* meaning.

Contributing to the problematics of critical thinking pedagogy are problems with *how* we introduce texts to our students, what these texts represent, and how students are likely to perceive them. Many of us who teach advanced composition use essay anthologies, readers. Most readers are collections of articles or book excerpts that are constantly reanthologized from reader to reader. When a new work is introduced to the canon of anthologized essays, it often is an article by one of several authors — Joan Didion, Carl Sagan, and Lewis Thomas, for example — whose works are continually republished, regardless of topic or, it seems, even quality. Thus, we have established a canon of acceptable works by acceptable authors on acceptable subjects. And how students perceive these works is important. In his well-known *Ways of Seeing*, John Berger argues that "when an image is presented as a work of art, the way people look at it is affected by a whole series of learnt assumptions about art" (11). That is, once a painting is hung in a museum, *how* we perceive that work immediately and forever changes; once the work is validated by its admittance into the elect of the museum collection, we see the work with new eyes, and we bring to the work an entire network of preconceptions about what such works should and should not be and what it *means* to be "a work of art." No doubt, a similar change in perception occurs when an article is published in an essay reader. The anthology, like the museum, functions as a locus of display, publicly validating the work's worth. Even though students learn that it is acceptable to critique and even criticize these works, the very fact that they are published in a special collection of essays must immediately affect students' attitude toward and perception of the works. Welch writes,

> Reading a "perfectly" produced textbook can be a tidy, organized, lovely, and passive experience. ...Both issues — the beauty of the professionally-printed page and the attitude of reverence toward sanctified writers — lead to deemphasizing student activity. (254)

Not only can such anthologizing and sanctifying lead to passivity but they can contribute to the decontextualization that we have already suggested is a problem. A work in a reader is wrenched from its context, detached from the place and time in which it originally appeared, thrust, sometimes rather violently, into the company of other works. No wonder it is so difficult to perceive the important role context plays in a work's "meaning."

Critical Thinking in Action: A Revisionist Approach

The critique just outlined suggests that a reconceptualization of critical thinking is needed. Specifically, it suggests an expanded conception of critical thinking based on the following premises:

- that both texts and readings of texts are situated in significant contexts;
- that meaning does not exist somewhere "out there" but is negotiated through social process and, thus, that learning to make meaning is more than mastering a series of discrete cognitive skills;

- that the student's role is an active one, involving more than passively decoding texts *or* contexts; and
- that truth, reason, and knowledge are concepts to be problematized.

A first step in realizing such a conception of critical thinking requires that texts be approached not as artifacts but as human utterances emanating from ongoing conversations. In other words, instructors should teach advanced composition students that texts are not artifacts that stand alone, detached from human beings and human motives; rather, texts are manifestations of ongoing conversations on various subjects. The critical enterprise, then, necessarily involves examining how a particular text—that is, one voice—fits into the larger conversation.

Such a process leads to *active* reading, in that students transcend strip-mining and treasure hunting and become genuine creators and participants. Approaching a text as part of a conversation situates it in a social context and situates the student in a social context as well. Karen Burke LeFevre recommends that we look at writers as "part of a community, a socioculture, a sphere of overlapping (and sometimes conflicting) collectives," that we draw "our attention to social contexts, discourse communities, political aims," and that we remember that writers compose "not only in the study but also in the smoke-filled chamber" (93). The same can be said of all critical thinkers/readers/ writers. Because people and their texts are inseparable from their sociocultural contexts, students must be able to recognize that every text is situated in a larger conversation; they must be able to reconstruct that larger conversation; and they must be able to establish their own place in it. Only when students are encouraged to explore the political and social contexts will they be able to join in the conversation as full participants. This is how critical thinking connects with action: students not only learn the various aspects of the ongoing conversation but are able to take part in that conversation as active participants, making meaning and *creating* a voice of their own.

As an example of how we see the role of context, consider an essay—a speech, really—that perhaps should win an award for being the work reprinted most frequently in essay readers: Martin Luther King's "I Have a Dream." Disregarding, first of all, the fact that many of us seem tacitly, if not overtly, to valorize logical appeals over the emotional, consider how we are likely to treat the article in class. Undoubtedly, we would examine how King employs metaphors to construct an emotional appeal that builds to a climax in a rising, emotional crescendo. Besides analyzing King's metaphors and other figures of speech, we would also examine the surface-level features of the article's context: that the piece was originally a speech; that it is a major statement of the civil rights movement of the sixties; that it marks a historical event, the 100th anniversary of the Emancipation Proclamation; that the celebration itself was a historic event in that a quarter of a million civil rights proponents met at the nation's capital to hear King and others. And, in an attempt to encourage students to connect the piece with the present, we might even ask, "Have things changed since King's time?"

Such an approach is an excellent beginning, but it treats King's speech as an artifact, as a static entity, a "masterful" use of language for a particular purpose. The little context that is discussed is done so only in relation to the work's supposed effectiveness or ineffectiveness. But this is not enough. If we consider the full context, if we view the text not as an artifact but as an utterance in an ongoing conversation that began long before King and that continues to the present, several perspectives become possible. By viewing the text as an utterance, we add an important dimension to the analysis: temporality. An utterance occurs in time as part of that larger conversation that is also happening in time. Opening up this dimension allows students to view an essay not as a *thing* (an artifact only occupies space) but as part of a *drama*, an action, and it encourages students to imagine the scene and other players in this drama and to speculate about what the other players have had to say. For example, it allows students to see King's work on the context of racial segregation, public lynchings, segregated schools and workplaces; it allows them to imagine other voices, such as Ku Klux Klan pronouncements about white supremacy and black militants' cries for revolution. And, perhaps most importantly, it helps them begin to position themselves in that unfolding drama as readers and as writers, as people who have something to add to the conversation.

Other perspectives are suggested by another very important context: the social and political milieu that informs the student's response. Is the student reader predisposed to share in King's ideals? Is the student's own background so different from that of poor blacks that King's message is foreign? Or is the opposite true? What stake might the reader have (or not have) in what the author has to say?

Still other perspectives are suggested when we consider another context: the anthology in which the essay itself appears. Why is it, for example, that King's speech has been anthologized in literally hundreds of readers? Who publishes these anthologies? Could it be the white power structure? What other important essays by blacks appear (or don't appear) in the reader? Are there other, perhaps even more important, civil rights statements that were omitted in place of King's speech? Does this anthology, for example, contain a work or works by black "militants" such as Angela Davis or Malcom X? Could it be that the white power structure perceives "I Have a Dream" as a safe utterance because it speaks of hope and not of defiance; of peace, not war?

Once the student has explored contexts as well as the textual and logical features traditionally analyzed in a critical analysis, the student is much better prepared to respond as a meaning-maker. The shift from artifact to utterance better enables the student to respond; an *artifact* isn't something that suggests the possibility of response, but an *utterance,* in the other hand, a human voice, elicits such response. Viewing the essay as an utterance, in other words, positions the student reader in such a way as to allow him or her not simply to *de*code the reading but to *en*code, to join the conversation in which the author participates and the student seeks to join. This approach locates the text in that dynamic ongoing conversation and, thus, illuminates the possibility of joining, of connecting with it in an empowering way. And this, after all, is the goal of an advanced composition course—not simply thinking, however "critical" that thinking may be.

This emphasis on active participation is essential to true critical literacy and, in fact, is close to how Paulo Freire defines the term. According to Ira Shor, Freire defines critical literacy as that which "provokes critical awareness and desocialization" and transcends "basic competency":

> Critical literacy invites teachers and students to *problematize* all subjects of study, that is, to understand existing knowledge as a historical product deeply invested with the values of those who developed such knowledge. A critically literate person does not stay at the empirical level of memorizing data, or at the impressionistic level of opinion, or at the level of dominant myths in society, but goes beneath the surface to understand the origin, structure, and consequences of any body of knowledge, technical process, or object under study. (24)

Thus, critical thinking reaches far beyond the rules of logic to situate texts and utterances in a social milieu.

This approach, as we practice it in the scholarship of the field (it's not usually applied to pedagogy), is increasingly becoming known as *cultural criticism.* According to Patricia Bizzell,

> To do cultural criticism means to regard all human activity as subject to a particular kind of interpretation, a kind of reading that draws out the ideological assumptions or world view enabling the activity to take place. Cultural criticism foregrounds ideologies that may be not only taken for granted but also actively suppressed from the consciousness of people acting on them; cultural criticism calls attention to the ways that important value systems can be erased or suppressed, especially the political motives that may lead one social group to try to impose such concealment upon another. No absolute standards of truth or morality are available which would uncover concealed

ideologies. The cultural critic's own interpretive activities are informed by ideological predilections. (225)

To a cultural critic, then, meaning divorced from social context is meaning-*less*. Preoccupation with textual factors is a form of misdirection, a way to distract students from considering factors that may very well be more important than any matters of logic or proper reasoning.

To illustrate what we mean, consider a cultural critic, Richard Ohmann, in action. In *Politics of Letters,* Ohmann spends some time discussing former education secretary William Bennett's call (in "To Reclaim a Legacy") for a return to the Great Books tradition. Ohmann asks, "Where is this discourse coming from? Why is anyone listening?" (13). He then proceeds to show where Bennett *is* coming from, demonstrating just how such contextual information is essential to a sophisticated understanding of the report:

> Bennett made the case for the political disinterestedness of culture, in "To Reclaim a Legacy," from his political post at the National Endowment for the Humanities. In preparation for his report, he assembled a conference of mainly right-wing educators whose ideas have gained credence only within the ambience of the Reagan administration, and who gain further legitimacy from their association with Bennett's report. The power of those ideas grows with his political appointment as secretary of education, from which position he can exercise a more direct influence on federal legislation and on state bodies that control public schools. His agenda for the humanities is deeply etched with the New Right's design for our future. (16)

The kind of analysis Ohmann engages in here is essential to a genuine *critical* reading. Critical thinkers constrained by simple factors of text, be they logical fallacies, unqualified assertions, or grievious omissions, necessarily arrive at a purely textual analysis — an analysis that is one-dimensional in that it is oblivious to the fact that real texts written in the real world are composed for real purposes by real people who have real motives, ideologies, political agendas, and entire networks of sociocultural assumptions and preconceptions. Rarely does simple textual/logical analysis lead to the kind of rich analysis that Ohmann achieves in this excerpt.

And, as Bizzell suggests, critical thinkers ought to go even further, coming to terms with their own ideological predilections as readers. For instance, Ohmann should also deconstruct his own context as a reader of Bennett's report, if not in his article at least personally for his own benefit. We all view texts — and everything, for that matter — from our own social, ideological perspective. Ohmann is no exception. As a Marxist intellectual, a member of what is often referred to as the New Left, he will view any text according to certain preconceptions;

most Marxists, for example, are interested in determining how authority figures (like Bennett) consciously or unconsciously use their power and how institutional power structures operate to provide or deny social justice. Clearly, these are considerations of Ohmann's as he analyzes Bennett's report. As a critical thinker, Ohmann should (and probably does) keep in mind that these are specific priorities of his own intellectual framework so that he can continually monitor how his own assumptions and perspectives come into play as he reads and interprets a text. Similarly, we must teach students to monitor their own intellectual frameworks as they engage in critical analysis, just as we, as teachers, must monitor our own.

Don't get us wrong. We are not recommending that classroom instructors discard the traditional concerns and methodologies typically associated with critical thinking. The ability to spot logical fallacies and unsupported assertions, for example, is just as important to good thinking as the ability to use correct grammar and punctuation is to good writing. What we *are* recommending is that teachers of advanced composition extend the critical process to include the kind of contextual, cultural criticism that we have been discussing. And it is important that *context* not become yet another artifact to be examined, another "text" to be strip-mined. That is, we are not simply broadening the scope of a search for "truth." In effect, we are removing critical thinking from what James Berlin calls the realm of cognitive rhetoric, for which "the real is the rational," and we are situating it in the realm of social-epistemic rhetoric, for which "the real is located in a relationship that involves the dialectical interaction of the observer, the discourse community (social group) in which the observer is functioning, and the material conditions of existence." Thus, knowledge, as Berlin continues, "is never found in any one of these but can only be posited as a product of the dialectic in which all three come together" (488). Such an approach is in line with William Covino's definition of advanced composition as an attempt to "enfranchise dialogic writing" and the "open intellectual play of multiple perspectives" so that students learn not to seek the emotional security of closure and certainty (120, 114).

Whether the approach presented here, which encompasses concerns not typically associated with current conceptions of critical thinking, can still be called *critical thinking* is an open question. However, if we sincerely propose to teach critical thinking to "advanced" students in advanced composition, it seems unwise to ignore the overwhelming body of work in modern critical theory, epistemology, and rhetoric.

Works Cited

Altick, Richard D. *Preface to Critical Reading*. New York: Holt, 1969.

Barry, Vincent E. *Invitation to Critical Thinking*. New York: Holt, 1984.

Benderson, Albert. *Critical Thinking*. Princeton: Educational Testing Service, 1984.

Berlin, James. "Rhetoric and Ideology in the Writing Class." *College English* 50 (1988): 477–94.

Berger, John. *Ways of Seeing*. London: BBC; Penguin, 1972.

Bizzell, Patricia. "'Cultural Criticism': A Social Approach to Studying Writing." *Rhetoric Review* 7 (1989): 224–30.

Browne, M. Neil, and Stuart M. Keeley. *Asking the Right Questions*. Englewood Cliffs, NJ: Prentice, 1981.

Bruffee, Kenneth A. "Social Construction, Language, and the Authority of Knowledge: A Bibliographical Essay." *College English* 48 (1986): 773–90.

Covino, William A. "Defining Advanced Composition: Contributions from the History of Rhetoric." *Journal of Advanced Composition* 8 (1988): 113–22.

Dilworth, Collett B. "Critical Thinking and the Experience of Literature." *English Record* (1986): 18–20.

Ennis, Robert H. "Goals for a Critical-Thinking/Reasoning Curriculum." Unpublished document, Illinois Critical Thinking Project, 1985.

Hartwell, Patrick. "Grammar, Grammars, and the Teaching of Grammar." *College English* 47 (1985): 105–27.

Johnson, Ralph, and J. A. Blair. *Informal Logic, The First International Symposium*. Inverness, CA: Edge P, 1980.

Kinneavy, James L. "The Relation of the Whole to the Part in Interpretation Theory and in the Composing Process." *The Territory of Language: Linguistics, Stylistics, and the Teaching of Composition*. Ed. Donald A. McQuade. Carbondale: Southern Illinois UP, 1986. 292–312.

LeFevre, Karen Burke. *Invention as a Social Act*. Carbondale: Southern Illinois UP, 1987.

Marble, Meredith. "A Critical Thinking Heuristic for the Argumentative Composition." *Rhetoric Society Quarterly* 16 (1986): 67–78.

Ohmann, Richard. *Politics of Letters*. Middletown: Wesleyan UP, 1987.

Petrosky, Anthony. "Critical Thinking: Qu'est-ce que c'est?" *English Record* (1986): 2–5.

Ray, Richard, Gary A. Olson, and James DeGeorge. *The Process Reader*. Englewood Cliffs, NJ: Prentice, 1986.

Rorty, Richard. "Hermeneutics, General Studies, and Teaching." *Synergos: Selected Papers from the Synergos Seminars*. Vol. 2. Fairfax, VA: George Mason UP, 1982. 1–15.

Ruggiero, Vincent Ryan. *The Art of Thinking: A Guide to Critical and Creative Thought*. New York: Harper, 1988.

Shor, Ira, ed. *Freire for the Classroom: A Sourcebook for Liberatory Teaching*. Portsmouth, NH: Boynton/Cook, 1987.

Tait, Foster E. "How Rational Thinking Affects Student Success." *College Is Only the Beginning: A Student Guide to Higher Education*. Ed. John N. Gardner and A. Jerome Jewler. Belmont, CA: Wadsworth, 1985: 75–86.

Tchudi, Stephen N. *Language, Schooling, and Society*. Portsmouth, NH: Boynton/Cook, 1985.

Welch, Kathleen. *The Contemporary Reception of Classical Rhetoric: Appropriations of Ancient Discourse*. Hillsdale, NJ: Lawrence Erlbaum, forthcoming.

15

"Real World" Research: Writing Beyond the Curriculum

Timothy R. Donovan
Janet Carr

> In your work and in your research there must always be
> passion.
>
> Pavlov

In "University Days," a chapter from *My Life and Hard Times*, James Thurber recalls that "all botany students had to spend several hours a week in a laboratory looking through a microscope at plant cells, and I could never see through a microscope. I never once saw a cell through a microscope." Thurber recalls, too, the frustration of his instructor, who vowed to make him see those cells — or leave teaching. But Thurber could see only "milk," until the day something finally appeared through his lens, and he quickly took pen in hand to sketch this specimen for his instructor. It turned out to be the reflection of his own eye. Eventually the young Thurber gave up. (It is not clear whether his instructor gave up teaching.)

Many a frustrated instructor of writing has also taught students unable (or perhaps unwilling) to focus on the nature of their world. Some students, like Thurber, admit to not seeing it, and perhaps others sketch whatever they imagine they are supposed to see. Research writing in particular, even for those students who know their way around a laboratory, or a library, is not always a tool for learning. The word *research* itself may conjure up for them images of white-coated scientists or dust-coated archives. They certainly don't consider research central to their lives, much less develop any "passion" for it. They may even regard it as competition for their professors' time and attention. No, the microscope belongs in the lab, or on the shelf—except when the call is issued specifically for a research paper.

When the papers are turned in, professors often despair that so many are just a rehash, cut 'n paste jobs, virtually plagiarized. The students, on the other hand, may seem relieved just to be done with what they consider an academic exercise and a rite of passage in the course. This dissatisfaction is shared by Richard Larson, who has concluded that the generic research paper, at least as commonly assigned in writing courses, is "not defensible" (812). With such a poor track record in the university, the research paper would seem a bad bet as the basis of an advanced composition program.

Indeed it is, yet research writing has a place in courses purporting to be "advanced." This is not to say that other forms of nonfiction (e.g., the memoir, familiar essay) are not as valid or as advanced; nor is it to say that all writing doesn't involve some research, even if it means just remembering a remark from a few days ago or an incident from a few years ago. Still, much of the university community, of which students are members, considers research writing as specifically related to its interests and values. The earnest researcher investigates a problem, discovers new information, interprets its meaning, derives some solution, and, with any justice, sees the whole business into print. This is the time-honored method that has always generated knowledge—and status—in higher education. Thus, if one considers a good writing program, as David Bartholomae has asserted, to be the "local expression of a generally agreed upon attitude toward writing— what it is good for" (6), research writing probably comes about as close as anything a faculty might agree upon as appropriate for advanced composition.

Most students, however, have little sustained practice with research writing. Their only direct instruction from the English department, for example, may have been as freshmen through a single (and more aptly named) "term paper" or "library paper," often on some literary work or author.[1] Nor are students routinely assigned much research writing in other departments, save in a vigorous program for writing across the curriculum. By the time students have committed to a major and possibly a career, some sort of further instruction in research writing is usually needed. At this stage, too, they should be able to handle more formidable and complex tasks.[2] They also *know* a great deal more, and so should be positioned to expand their knowledge in the way that research allows.

Yet, as the traditional vehicle for doing just that, why isn't the research paper a more successful assignment? Why, for example, does the exploratory nature of research lose out to the exhortatory nagging of the instructor to make the thing look right? So often the paper appears to be a montage of index cards, an imitation of surface form and convention. Of course, one might argue that a dedicated, savvy instructor endeavors to avoid that sort of product by showing students how to develop a thesis, critique sources, blend in their own ideas, and so on. One might say, too, that even with modest results the assignment at least forces students to engage the scholarship, to learn something of the issues of a discipline, and to write it all up in a way that looks like the coin of the realm.

Problems with the research paper, however, are not just the result of lame teaching or limited aims. They arise from the "rhetorical stance" itself, in Wayne Booth's phrase, from which the paper is often written. Just what, we might ask, is the authority of the student in relationship to library sources that usually bulk up most of the paper? Indeed, what is the authority of the student toward the specialist who is the direct or indirect audience for the paper in most cases? Finally, what authority is to be found in the voice or persona of such a paper?

A "theory of verbal practice" proposed by Paul Hernadi may be helpful here if the research paper is considered as a form of discourse and not just a student assignment. Briefly summarized, Hernadi's theory focuses on the role of *act, creation*, and *signification*. In all discourse, whether spoken, written, or mental, he asserts, we are "doing" something, that is, causing something to happen, as when a lawyer defends a client before a judge and jury. We are also clearly "making" something that has form and content, whether a Wordsworth poem or a "Help Wanted" sign. Such discourse, finally, "means" something is conveyed to others and is construed by them. These three functions of discourse, he continues, are interconnected and simultaneous: "Whenever we 'say' something — whether in speech, in writing, or in silent deliberation — we thereby do, make, and mean something at the same time" (749).

The research paper would seem potentially the single most extended instance of doing, making, and meaning in an educational setting. Yet as an *act*, it is not likely to persuade students that what they are *doing* is solving a problem of importance within a particular field, say, the definitive authorship of the Shakespeare plays. Neither are they capturing the attention of their peers in the field, and thereby winning acclaim and recognition. In truth, most anything produced will be news only to the student and acknowledged only by the instructor — a rather abbreviated loop for the results of one's "research."

Thus, as something *made*, a student research paper in college might be regarded like a reproduction in a museum: not out of place exactly, but not the real thing either. It harks back to the five-hundred word theme, an in-house exercise that students came to think of as an actual form of writing. Similarly, a review of the literature, typically a starting point for scholars, may become an end in itself for students, blurring the distinction between research and a report. Their paper devolves, as Susan Wall has put it, into "language about language" (1). It has the veneer of scholarship but not much of its deeper grain.

The extent to which the research paper can ultimately be "an event of meaning and a thing meant" (Hernadi 750) is thus problematic at best. What does the paper really *mean* to students if they have not established some real relationship with their subject, sources, and language? They are unlikely to labor under the illusion that their instructor is now about to be instructed by their paper (though we sometimes are). Their difficulty here is summed up by Bartholomae and Petrosky in discussing one of the challenges of learning to write and read academic prose: "The student has to appropriate or be appropriated by a specialized discourse, and he has to do it as though he were easily and comfortably at one with his audience, as though he were a member of the academy. And, of course, he is not" (8). What does, or could, the research paper *mean* , then, to the academician in such a reader-writer relationship? If students must play the role of would-be scholars, the instructor as intended audience must suspend disbelief and view their papers as would-be scholarship. Yet it doesn't wash because the instructor remains that audience with which students are most familiar: the teacher as evaluator (Martin et al.). They continue to guess at the instructor's ideal text, while perhaps second-guessing the assignment itself.

As discourse, then, the research paper usually doesn't live up to its name, and as a genre it is decidedly limited. Its shortcomings suggest that an instructor or department might reconsider the role of research, and perhaps thereby reconceive the research paper itself. What, it might be asked, should students research, how should they go about it, for what reason and what audience? The answers to these questions will produce no surefire, foolproof formula. But they might lead to a rhetorical stance that puts students on solid ground, that stands a chance of producing authentic, vital discourse.

A Context for Research

Advanced composition at Northeastern University stresses research writing in courses, under various rubrics, that are taught by instructors from the English department. We don't pretend that we are experts in the discourse of all disciplines. We are part of a larger effort at writing across the curriculum that includes tandem or team teaching, inter-disciplinary faculty seminars, writing in "content areas," and so forth. The charge we take up in these courses, therefore, is not to turn out better writers of history or biology or engineering but just to turn out better writers. Our students are not, then, necessarily writing *in* their discipline, although some in fact do so, particularly if they are in specialized sections (e.g., technical or business writing). They are nevertheless encouraged to write in some way that *concerns* their discipline. We assume there are enough similarities in the composing processes of all disciplines, regardless of their methodology, that English faculty can be helpful to most undergraduates.

A good deal of the teaching and learning in our courses is under-pinned by a dialectical view of knowledge. This is not necessarily a profound epistemology nowadays, nor is it one we always profoundly enact. It is, however, one we try to promote in research writing through the concepts of *self*, *society*, and *world*. As fleshed out in our classrooms, this dialectic takes into account writers who are, first, individuals of different backgrounds, ambitions, interests, experiences, and opinions; they are also students who are grappling with new ideas encountered in a wide variety of lectures and texts; and, finally, they are workers who hold jobs at newspapers, courts, hospitals, engineering firms, computer companies. These "selves" interact with others in society who may influence them: professors, students, friends, bosses, co-workers, clergy, and family. Further, they intersect with a physical world of classrooms, libraries, offices, businesses, dormitories, homes, and so forth.

Set in dialectical relationship, these concepts allow us to imagine assignments that, in turn, allow our students to imagine genuine op-portunities for research writing. We encourage students to undertake projects involving something of what they already know (*self*), as well as someone else who can lend insight (*society*), and some place where their subject may occur (*world*). We are also aware of the dangers of adhering too strictly to any abstract scheme of mental or creative processes; project proposals that don't conform are not rejected out of hand. Yet this dialectic seems particularly apropos at Northeastern, a large, comprehensive university in Boston. Most of our students par-ticipate in the Cooperative Education plan, alternating one or two terms of study with a career-related job. Their education is considered one in which learning is a partnership with business, government, and the professions. Knowledge is advertised as being put to use.

We find ourselves not uncomfortable with this philosophy; in fact, to some degree we play to it. Yet neither is ours just an ad hoc approach, applicable only at Northeastern or universities like it. As

Toby Fulwiler observes, "in the true spirit of research, our whole social, physical and cultural environment is both library and laboratory" (88). We agree. A beeline to the stacks, in other words, is not necessarily the first move for our students in tackling the research assignment.

Julie, a physical therapy major, had dropped out of Northeastern because of a job-related injury: while transporting a wheelchair patient she had severely wrenched her back. She was required to undergo physical therapy and to wear a brace. Upon returning to school and enrolling in an advanced composition course, Julie researched the history of her own back injury, including diagnosis and treatment. She then placed her findings within a larger framework of medical knowledge about back injuries, using health professionals and medical books as additional resources. Her final paper was both an informative work and a personal catharsis.

It seems to us that Julie was successful as a writer because of the way her research permitted her to arrive at knowledge. In starting with an obvious individual interest, then on through association with various people and places, she took a global approach to a topic that had occurred to her literally by accident. She came to understand how that back injury constitutes both a subject of scientific discourse and a societal concern for health professionals who may be Julie's co-workers after graduation. Her knowledge even encompassed a new appreciation for the chronically ill or disabled. In a sense, her relationship to the world of patients, hospitals, and medicine was changed by her research. The way she sees herself, as both learner and researcher, may also have changed.

Students need not, then, be content with scanning texts somewhat passively when the whole world, as anthropologist Clifford Geertz has it, can be a text (30). Students such as Julie can go at their research with an authentic curiosity, *authentic* perhaps with a meaning close to that of an *author* as an originator. Their topic originates with them as individuals, as students, as workers; their papers are ones that they author and in which they have a personal stake.

A Rhetoric of Research

In many of their papers our students are not addressing the specialist in a field but a more general audience. As the inevitable reader, an English instructor is well suited and competent to act as such an audience. By training and temperament, he or she is usually the university generalist anyway. And while it is possible for an instructor to be occasionally baffled, even hoodwinked, by some of the more obscure material in a paper, the trade-off seems well worth the risk (and there are usually alternatives in dealing with such cases). The student now has a reader who may be genuinely informed by the paper. True, their positions are not totally reversed; the instructor is still more erudite and perceptive, still the expert on composition. Yet even this situation can be turned to advantage if he or she is regarded as a guide to wisdom rather than the source of it all, becoming, in effect, the student's research partner.

Students stand to gain by writing for a general audience when they want to focus and sharpen their more technical papers, too. Such was the case with Jim, a respiratory therapy major on a co-op assignment to the Massachusetts General Hospital, in Boston. In addition to working at the hospital, he was fortunate to be invited to present a paper at a national conference for health care workers. He decided an advanced writing class would give him an opportunity to formulate his ideas. Since no other students in the class were of the same major, Jim tailored some rather technical information for a more general audience. His final paper contained an overview of respirators, a summary of current research, and a proposal to compare six respiratory machines presently in use at MGH.

Jim sought to develop a paper that was sophisticated enough for his professional group but also one that his class could understand. He succeeded in both these goals. As he tested out information on his immediate classroom audience, Jim enhanced his own understanding of it as well. (He also became less intimidated by his eventual audience.) In growing more comfortable with his knowledge, he grew more confident in his role as a professional and a maker of knowledge for others. E. D. Hirsch has posited the "abnormality" of an unseen and unknown audience as the greatest difficulty in the act of writing (58). With other students as well as the instructor comprising both an abstract and physical audience, a good deal of that difficulty may be overcome. But this audience serves other purposes beyond just helping out with some composing problems. In this case they evidenced to Jim a respect for his work as a therapist and the importance of his professional development. His sense of himself as a writer-researcher was thus reinforced.

An audience comprised of learners, rather than the learned, may benefit the students' writing style as well. Certainly there is an increased burden to present concepts clearly, to define jargon precisely, and to write engagingly. Authors such as Dillard, Eiseley, Tuchman, Gould, Clark, Gombrich, Thomas, Galbraith, and Mead have demonstrated this burden for many students. And presenting technical information to nonspecialists is practice for later, "real world" occasions when they often do just that—as colleagues in other departments, particularly engineering and business administration, have often impressed upon us.

Whatever the audience, researchers should believe they are contributing a body of knowledge *to* a body of knowledge. It can be no less true for students. That contribution may be to journals, magazines, and newspapers, but also to any other interested parties, such as classmates, professors, businesses, organizations, and the writing instructor. That is why the rhetorical stance in our program is insured somewhat by requiring students to publish one of their papers in a course booklet. Everyone in the class gets a copy. Everyone sees his or her paper in print, as it were, collected with those of the rest of the class, which has become in many respects the student's "interpretive community." Their course booklet is emblematic of a collective effort to make research matter, and to make it good.

A Pedagogy of Research

A curriculum dependent upon a dialectical philosophy leans naturally toward a pedagogy that might be termed *dialogic*. Ann Berthoff has made this connection quite splendidly, observing that speaking and hearing, reading and writing are all dialectical because of their reflexive character, and, further, that all language is ultimately dialogue. *Dialectic* and *dialogue*, she notes, are cognate, with the *dia* signaling reflexiveness (119). The interaction of self, society, and world gears our students for such dialogue. Our classes bring together writers and readers, speakers and listeners.

As an initial foray into research, primary sources are especially valuable in promoting dialogue. Students are forced to regard phenomena — visual, spoken, printed — unmediated by the crutches of secondary sources usually relied upon. From the outset they are obliged to compose a language, or dialogue, largely on their own. That language may be conceived of as "internal dialogue" (I. A. Richards), "inner speech" (Lev Vygotsky), or oral "psychodynamics" (Walter Ong). What is most important, we think, is that students at this stage trust themselves to start with primary research and then transform data into new knowledge as they move along into their subject.

One form of primary research that encourages individual interpretation of this sort is *direct observation*. Though writers, both of fiction and nonfiction, have always watched the world around them to find material, within academia it has been the natural sciences that have relied most upon direct observation.[3] We don't routinely send our students off to conduct experiments, but some sort of field observation is usually feasible. Often they just need an assignment requiring them to "be there," wherever *there* is, in order to decide for themselves how things look, sound, smell, and feel.

One of our students, a mechanical engineering major named Bob, was asked by his uncle to look into some structural weaknesses at a condominium complex. This was in preparation for a possible suit by the owners against a general contractor. Using his engineering expertise and some direct observation, Bob uncovered several areas of faulty construction. From his field notes he prepared a report that identified the flaws and offered several recommendations for correcting them.

The activity of research for Bob was a dialogue, in effect, involving what he had known before, what his own eyes told him, and what other parties at the condominium needed to know. That the paper turned out well was important to him, and so was the hands-on experience he gained while dealing with a serious engineering problem. Perhaps what was most clearly demonstrated to Bob was that he could trust himself to fashion a discourse of significance and value to others.

Another traditional form of primary research that engenders, indeed depends upon, dialogue is the *interview*. (Here, too, it seems we are again borrowing, this time from the social sciences, though many writers — journalists and biographers particularly — have always relied upon the interview.) We routinely encourage students to contact others who have experience with the topic of their research.[4] Possible informants can range from the professor down the hallway to the developer across town to the bureaucrat across the country. The dialogue can be oral or by correspondence, over the telephone or in person. An interview with experts reinforces for students the living and applied nature of knowledge. It also spurs them on, keeping the excitement, perhaps even the suspense, of the research alive. And while the meaning of, say, a published text might be disputed by different readers, an interview offers the opportunity through questioning to eliminate misunderstanding. Experts may also recommend to students the texts that they have found influential, which may in turn point to other people who might be interviewed.

A criminal justice major, Gary, had been concerned about homeless people in Boston. Deciding to write a paper on that topic, he began his research by heading downtown to find out for himself about their situation. He took the extraordinary step of donning clothes that gave him the appearance of being homeless. He then spent a day talking with the homeless, exchanging comments and seeking opinions that added up to some interesting ethnographic material. With this background material in hand, Gary subsequently interviewed (in more conventional garb) a city official familiar with the homeless situation.

As a result of his dialogue and some follow-up at the library for relevant statistics and commentary, Gary developed a personal angle on the problem of the homeless. He felt close to his topic throughout the project, perhaps remembering the people he had met during his research. Possibly he wanted to do them justice in his paper. In any case, his research allowed him to enter the public conversation about this issue with great conviction, and his writing showed it.

A related form of primary research common in the social sciences is the *survey* or *questionnaire*, though students need not work with the scope of the Gallup organization. While some level of validity and reliability is important, a very manageable sort of survey can provide useful insights for students.

As a marketing major, Barbara was interested in a career in retail management. She began working on a paper about a supermarket in the area and the factors that influence the purchasing decisions of its customers. She developed a survey that would elicit information about pricing, quality, displays, service, anything she needed to know in order to draw some conclusions about effective management. With the permission of the store owner, Barbara then surveyed customers in the store. Supported by her own reading and knowledge of marketing, she produced helpful insights for the storeowner, for other students — and consumers — in the class, and, of course, for her paper.

What we particularly appreciate here is that Barbara was able to use her prior knowledge to fashion a tool that would harvest further knowledge, which in turn was passed on to others. That is the way a library also works: knowledge, not just books, circulating. The library is indeed an important resource for our students, a repository of "the best that is known and thought," in Arnold's classic phrase. Here, too, we encourage primary research when appropriate, especially for papers in the humanities. Primary texts may include literature, letters, diaries, government data, historical records, and various other kinds of raw material. A colleague of ours has been successful assigning students to describe the world as it was on the day of their birth, as inferred through the newspapers published on that date. But a library is perhaps most useful when students are primed somewhat for their reading. Those who arrive with questions needing answers stand a better chance of benefiting from a library than those who are just fishing around for a topic.

Another business major, Maureen, was about to leave her studies at Northeastern to take a co-op position in a Central American country. She was concerned about the cultural differences she might encounter there. In particular she wanted to know more about the local business customs so as to avoid the possibilty of offending her future colleagues. Maureen was encouraged to write a paper on that topic. A good deal of her research started at, and in a way added to, the library. Her final draft proved so useful that the Cooperative Education Department requested that it be loaned to other students assigned to that country.

Research writing as we have portrayed it here is not intended to replace thoughtful and coordinated assignments from professors in various disciplines. In fact, we support and advise on such matters elsewhere in the university. Yet we do intend our own courses to be more than editorial assistance, another so-called service, advanced or otherwise. Students do get all the help we can provide with formal matters, including a session or three on documentation and bibliography. Not surprisingly, these concerns seem more important to them when their papers seem important as well.

Research writing can indeed motivate students, often in ways that more extemporaneous composition cannot. In each of the cases we've described here, students were given much the same chance, however brief, that their instructors have been given: the opportunity to cultivate the life of the mind in ways that seem to them constructive, creative, and meaningful. "The various disciplines and quasi-disciplines that make up the arts and sciences," Geertz reminds us, "are, for those caught up in them, far more than a set of technical tasks and vocational obligations; they are cultural frames in terms of which attitudes are formed and lives conducted" (14). Research is one crucial way that our cultural frames are defined. Students can also attempt such definition as they form their attitudes and conduct their lives in college. When they are looking through the microscope, their options are not just to see what is expected, to see only their own reflection, or to see nothing at all.

Notes

1. The goal of the course may also be modest, simply to get incoming students to write the "decent sentence" one hears so much about. But for more positive, philosophical arguments on not stressing research at the freshman level, see Rutter.

2. Given the range of abilities called for, and potentially sharpened, in completing a successful research paper, it is a wonder that some turn out as well as they do. Toby Fulwiler reminds us of just how challenging the research assignment can be. It calls upon students "(1) to think through their interests and concerns in a given area, (2) to formulate a problem or question of a particular interest, (3) to discuss the question with the teacher, which calls for personal interaction, (4) to look in places, both familiar and arcane, for answers and solutions, (5) to use information indices and catalysts, (6) to practice the art of skimming to glean pertinent information, (7) to master taking and organizing condensed notes, (8) to refine and reconceptualize the original problem as new information leads, perhaps, to new questions, (9) to integrate disparate pieces of information in some coherent conceptual framework, and (10) to compose the whole into a report that provides some solution or answer to the questions posed" (87).

3. Berthoff on the uses of scientific observation: "I have always advised English majors to minor in biology, if only because they need an understanding of organic structure as a way of understanding organic imagery" (116).

4. Some students are apt to be reticent about interviewing, and they may need a fair amount of guidance on techniques. Ken Macrorie, in *Searching Writing* (now, in revised form, titled *The I-Search Paper*) offers particularly insightful advice about interviewing as well as other techniques for teaching the research paper.

Works Cited

Bartholomae, David. "Words from Afar." *The Teaching of Writing: Eighty-fifth Yearbook of the National Society for the Study of Education.* Part II. Ed. Anthony Petrosky and David Bartholomae. *NSSE*, Chicago: Chicago UP: 1986, 1−8.

Bartholomae, David, and Anthony Petrosky, eds. *Facts, Artifacts and Counterfacts: Theory and Method for a Reading and Writing Course.* Portsmouth, NH: Boynton/Cook, 1986.

Berthoff, Ann E. *The Making of Meaning: Metaphors, Models, and Maxims for Writing Teachers.* Portsmouth, NH: Boynton/Cook, 1981.

Booth, Wayne. "The Rhetorical Stance." *College Composition and Communication* 14 (1963): 139−45.

Fulwiler, Toby. *Teaching With Writing.* Portsmouth, NH: Boynton/Cook, 1987.

Geertz, Clifford. *Local Knowledge: Further Essays in Interpretive Anthropology.* New York: Basic, 1983.

Hernadi, Paul. "Doing, Making, Meaning: Toward a Theory of Verbal Practice." *PMLA* 103 (1988): 749−58.

Hirsch, E. D. *The Philosophy of Composition.* Chicago: U of Chicago P, 1977.

Larson, Richard. "The 'Research Paper' in the Writing Course: A Non-Form of Writing." *College English* 44 (1982): 811−16.

Macrorie, Ken. *The I-Search Paper.* Portsmouth, NH: Boynton/Cook, 1988.

Martin, Nancy, et al. *Writing and Learning Across the Curriculum 11−16.* London: Ward Lock, 1976. Available in the U.S. from Boynton/Cook, Portsmouth, NH.

Ong, Walter. "Literacy and Orality in Our Times." *ADE Bulletin* 58 (1978): 1−7.

Richards, I. A. *How to Read a Page.* New York: Norton, 1942.

Rutter, Russell. "Research Writing in Advanced Composition: An Essay in Definition." *Journal of Advanced Composition* 6 (1985−86): 131−38.

Thurber, James. *My Life and Hard Times.* New York: Harper, 1933.

Vygotsky, Lev. *Thought and Language.* Cambridge: MIT Press, 1978.

Wall, Susan. "The Case in Question: Participant Observation as an Alternative Approach to Research Writing." Paper presented at Conference on College Composition and Communication, Dallas, TX, 1981.

16

Coming into the Country...
and Living There:
Literary Nonfiction and
Discourse Communities

Charles Anderson

On a dusty spring day in West Texas in 1972, my friend Colt introduces me to a blond-haired, blue-eyed veteran of the Vietnam War he
calls Weird Russ. We talk and drink Southern Comfort and smoke
cigarettes long into the night. Later, I hang around Russ's table in the
student union, listening to the war stories he and his friends tell. At
night we drink more whiskey, smoke more cigarettes. I hear that
Weird Russ carries two guns and a knife, that the yard around his
trailer is mined with radio-controlled explosive charges, that he carries
homemade grenades in his car, and that he sent some "very heavy
shit" stateside near the end of his first tour of duty.

One morning, after a long night of Southern Comfort and stories,
we are in Colt's truck flying north and low toward Lubbock, Texas. I
am driving—drunk, dead-tired, half-asleep—when Weird Russ fires
his .32 automatic pistol one, two, three times across the cab in front of
my nose, just to see if I'm paying attention. I am, and I almost lose it
before I can bring us to a stop on the left shoulder of the two-lane
road. I climb into the back, wrap myself in an old blanket, and hear
Colt and Russ howling with laughter as we pick up speed.

The next week I see Weird Russ just before our history midterm
test, and he tells me that he will not fail because he has his gun
beneath his coat where he can get to it quickly. He unzips the field
jacket so I can see that he isn't lying. I tell him not to sweat it, that the

223

test doesn't mean anything, to be cool, cool. I move to the other side of the room and do not look up until I am almost done with the test. Russ is gone. I never see him again.

Years later I open Michael Herr's *Dispatches*, scan the text and hear his voice and the voices of his colleagues, see the staring eyes of the dead, the photographs, and the souvenirs. I feel the quick intake of breath at the scream of an incoming round, and share a filthy, dangerous hole with the terrible, beautiful marines whose lives have been forever changed by the fear and the death and the exultation they experience in the pages of this Vietnam book. I absorb their stories, share their wonder, smell the stench of decay. I learn their language. As I do so I enter the world Herr's text offers. And, with no more and no less insistence than from Weird Russ's mined front yard, his three bullets, and his history midterm is my world again penetrated and my sense of reality again altered.

Still another spring day, this one damp and cold, and I am standing before the Vietnam War Memorial in Washington, D.C., that deep, black granite gash in my nation's heart. I hold my daughter's tiny hand as we descend deeper and deeper into the war. I swallow hard. My vision blurs. My wife touches my shoulder and we draw together, pressing our child close between us. I see an old woman kneeling, praying, stroking a place near the bottom of one of the longest columns of names. I smell the flowers she has brought. I hear a family talking in low tones, mourning the man whose name they study so intently. I think of Russ and Colt, of Gary and Day Tripper and Mayhew, and of others I have known, the ones who came home again, the ones whose names are not on this wall. I wonder whose name is here, whose name I know but do not know that I know. I reach out at last and touch the smooth, dark stone, run my fingertips across the roughened names of the dead, and remember.

I begin with my stories because they help me to demonstrate that the intensity and urgency readers experience as they read quality literary nonfiction is directly related to the intensity and urgency with which human beings create and maintain the various communities of which they are a part. When we approach a new community, we become engaged in telling and hearing stories, in puzzling out routines and rituals. Our chief means of making sense of the group is our ability to understand how its members use language and to grasp the significance they attach to the stories they tell. As we make sense of the group, we increase our chances of becoming a full participant in the community. In our conversations, in the time we shared, and in the stories we made, I became a part of Colt and Russ's Vietnam War, a war in which I did not fight, a war that penetrated my world in a powerfully symbolic way, a war about which I now have stories to tell.

Literary nonfiction brings us into the communities its texts present in exactly the same symbolic manner.

Literary nonfiction, because it is factual material focused and shaped by the lenses of fictional technique and persona, argues vehemently that it can be believed, that the symbolic world it presents is as real as the one we experience every day. We trust its facticity, respond to its power as we do to the power of all compelling literary discourse, and are drawn into its events (Weber 2; Hellman 139). As I became a veteran of the aftermath of the Vietnam War and as my participation in its values and stories was renewed and strengthened by *Dispatches* and my visit to Washington, D.C., so were my readers invited to participate in the representation I offered in my opening narrative. If they accepted my invitation, we formed a small community sharing a symbolic reality, a reality powerful enough to shape our attitudes and responses to events in the outside world, powerful enough, perhaps, to compel us to vote against political candidates who would engage in Vietnam-type military adventures, to push us to support veteran's relief legislation, or to help us understand something of the difficulty many veterans of the war itself still face.

But the work of literary nonfiction is not limited to its effect upon the reader. As I composed and revised the opening paragraphs of this chapter, I consolidated the pieces of my post-Vietnam experience, shaped them, made sense of them, and discovered connections and implications of which I had not been aware. I learned that I am, in a very real and curious way, a veteran of that time, a survivor of a war in which I did not fight, part of a community of which I had never considered myself a member. Thus the psychological, symbolic, and rhetorical energies of literary nonfiction flow both directions. What readers *and* writers gain from this flow is an intensification and extension of their natural inclinations and abilities to engage in the communal transformation of raw, factual experience into the word-saturated, socially constructed realities within which we all dwell.

To understand how and why this intensification takes place, we will first need to look closely at the relationship between language and community, a relationship that provides the very foundation upon which all human communities are erected. When we have this foundation, we will be able to see:

1. how symbolic and linguistic processes essential to successful literary nonfiction are congruent to those necessary to the formation and maintenance of human communities,

2. how particular writers and their personae reflect and exemplify particular individual/community relationships and stances, and

3. how we can create advanced writing courses designed to take

advantage of the interactions among writer, reader, text, persona, and community.

Language and Community

In "Science and Linguistics," reprinted in *Language, Thought, and Reality*, Benjamin Lee Whorf describes the interaction between language and experience in the following way:

> We dissect nature along lines laid down by our native languages. The categories and types that we isolate from the world of phenomena we do not find there because they stare every observer in the face; on the contrary, the world is presented in a kaleidoscopic flux of impressions which has to be organized by our minds — and this means largely by the linguistic systems in our minds. We cut nature up, organize it into concepts, and ascribe significances as we do, largely because we are parties to an agreement to organize it in this way — an agreement that holds throughout our speech community and is codified in the patterns of our language. (213)

Within the macrocosm of each natural language speech community there is a virtually endless array of smaller, specialized microcosms comprising groups of persons sharing particular values, interests, knowledge, dialects, expertise, occupations, geographical locations, personal histories, and so on. Literary critics, cowboys, Alaskans, medical doctors, members of Alcoholics Anonymous, street people, and auto mechanics, because they share a common interest and speak a common "language" with their peers, constitute equally potent and equally important communities. Members of such groups are drawn together through rhetorical processes that Kenneth Burke, in *A Rhetoric of Motives*, calls "identification" and "consubstantiality" (20–23). These processes urge each individual to see and to understand herself, through language and other symbolics, in relation to others. In response to this fundamental human urge, group members gather, talk, and act together, upon one another, and upon others to achieve a state of cooperation (43).

While there are no hard and fast rules for the ways such groups interact, sociologist Robert Bales, in *Personality and Interpersonal Behavior*, provides a useful description of the general contours many groups follow. When groups form or when a person seeks membership in a new group, there is usually an explicit or an implicit entry routine to go through. If the group is an established one, the routine will have to do with acclimating the new member to the group's established or normal workings. Medical school is a good example of the lengths to which a very complex and well-established community will go to incorporate new members. In new communities, a Bible study group or a support group for instance, initial time is devoted to "water treading," or negotiating manuevers designed to allow members to discover common ground upon which the group can work. Members may spend weeks, months, or even years getting comfortable enough to begin their corporate work. Prior to this beginning, interaction within the group focuses upon what Bales calls "fantasy themes," which are stories, anecdotes, explanations, and observations shared by members of the group as they talk their way toward community.

If the group can create for itself a dramatic or narrative representation — a fantasy — in which it achieves an identity and fulfills an important or necessary function, then members of the group may begin to align with the roles of specific characters or types in the fantasy and to behave and believe as those roles suggest. As particular episodes or symbolic possibilities capture the group's collective imagination, members undergo a process called *chaining*, in which those possibilities become elaborated and tightly related to the central concerns of the group. Chaining engages individuals in the collective verbal drama of the group, calibrates their values and assumptions, and provides a situation or group-specific "idiolect" that all members share. "As the individual person creates and maintains a system of symbols with other persons in a group," says Bales, "he enters a realm of reality, which he knows does or can surpass him, survive him; which may inspire or organize him, and which may threaten to dominate him as well. He 'comes alive' in the specifically human sense as a person in communication with others, in the symbolic reality which they create together, in the drama of their action" (151–52).

As the bonds of community strengthen, groups begin to develop their own specific cultures, *culture* being a term for the more or less stable sum of the group's collective experience over time. In Bales's words, "the culture of the interacting group stimulates in each of its members a feeling that he has entered into a new realm of reality — a world of heroes, villains, saints, and enemies — a drama, a work of art. ...In such moments, ...one is 'transported' to a world that seems somehow even more real than the everyday world" (152). Thus, if Bales is accurate in his portrayal of group processes, literary and linguistic experience are absolutely essential to the formation and maintenance of community at all levels. They are also, as I have argued above, essential to successful literary nonfiction.

Discourse Communities and Literary Nonfiction

When members of our professional community convene to talk about the symbolic and linguistic phenomena that bring and bind people together, we generally say we are talking about *discourse communities*: groups of people who do just what we are doing—gathering, examining, and languaging their world. I have not successfully traced that specific phrase to its source, but the concept behind it is dealt with in Kenneth A. Bruffee's *College English* article, "Collaborative Learning and the 'Conversation of Mankind.'" In this article, Bruffee describes the importance of "knowledge communities" in the learning process and argues for greater peer involvement in writing classrooms. Following Stanley Fish's insistence upon the determinative role of his "interpretive communities," Bruffee constructs a theory of social interaction and knowledge that resembles the strong form of the Sapir/Whorf Hypothesis (see the Whorf quotation above for a weaker version) in linguistics, which holds that the rules of speech communities are absolutely determinative. We can do what our community allows us to do and little more. If we depart from our community, we do so occasionally and briefly.

While Bruffee's theory is compelling and has been quite influential, I think it goes too far in discounting individual experience and valorizing the community. It loses sight of the crucial, dialogic role played by the interaction of individual experience and community knowledge. This leads Bruffee to conclude that the main purpose of expository writing classes (perhaps of all classes) is to demonstrate "to students that they know something only when they can explain it in writing to the satisfaction of the community of their knowledgeable peers" (652). Because his intention is to more effectively educate students in the normal rules of academic discourse, Bruffee never seriously deals with the process of negotiating individual knowledge with that of the community, despite the fact that this negotiating is the most important and persistent tension within any discourse community and is precisely the process by which knowledge is enlarged and change brought about over time.

Because literary nonfiction is driven by the same psychological, symbolic, and rhetorical energies as human discourse communities, it provides excellent and abundant opportunities for students to study, to experience, and to experiment with many different registers and rhetorics in an infinitely varied succession of human conversations. Literary nonfiction provides students a place in the negotiations. It shows them that the role any individual plays in the discourse of a given group is shaped not by a single factor (the normal discourse of the group) or by a single process (induction into the group) but by a complicated and highly individual set of experiences with this and other communities, by expectations and assumptions arising from those experiences, and most of all, by the degree to which the individual is conscious of his or her stance toward the community. Literary nonfiction can help them learn ways of negotiating their membership in different communities and of using the knowledge and insights of one community to enrich their experience and heighten their understanding of others. And finally, focusing the writing class on reading and writing literary nonfiction can put students in touch with some of the very best contemporary writing and can empower them to participate in the community organized around that writing, a community that includes such writers as John McPhee, Joan Didion, Richard Selzer, Maxine Hong Kingston, Tom Wolfe, Annie Dillard, Tracy Kidder, Sue Hubbell, Loren Eiseley, John Steinbeck, Jane Kramer, Gretel Ehrlich, Bill Barich, N. Scott Momaday, Alice Walker, and many others.

While I do not intend to suggest that literary nonfiction and discourse communities function in exactly the same way in every particular, I do want to draw upon the theoretical perspective I have presented to point out crucial similarities, whose exploration can provide a rich and powerful paradigm out of which the writing and the writers in an advanced composition course may grow. Important and useful parallels between the workings of literary nonfiction and those of discourse communities exist on three planes, which I have represented in Figure 16-1.

At the most obvious level, there is a subject, or "manifest content," around which a given discourse community gathers and organizes

Figure 16-1
Parallels Between Discourse Communities and Literary Nonfiction

Discourse Communities		Literary Nonfiction
Background and expectations of individual participants enter the group's verbal drama as it talks its way through its concerns.	**Past and Future**	Writer-community relationship determines the nature of the final text. Reader background and expectations determine meaning.
Stories and fantasies define and sustain communities as members interact.	**Here and Now**	Reader, community, text, and persona interact in present-time reading transaction.
Manifest content provides the impetus for individuals to gather.	**Content**	Nominal subject embedded in the discourse of the community centers the text.

itself—the Vietnam War, birdwatching, alcoholism. In literary non-fiction, the equivalent is the nominal subject that centers the text—the idea of conservation, time spent at a California racetrack, a back-packing trip across a glacier, the building of a new computer. In communities, "manifest content" leads to a second plane, which Bales calls the "here and now" interaction of the group—the community engaged in creating and maintaining the stories and fantasies that define and sustain it. The literary nonfiction parallel is the four-way interaction taking place here and now in reading time—among the reader, the discourse community surrounding the nominal subject, the text, and the persona the writer creates. Simultaneously, on a third plane, the backgrounds and expectations of discourse community par-ticipants are brought to bear upon the drama of the community as it talks through its concerns, extending the here and now into the past and the future. In literary nonfiction, the interaction is a complex interplay of the writer's background, expectations, and community alignments with the symbolic reality or sense of the world offered by the community about which the writer writes as she researches and composes her text. The sense of the community the writer will offer in the text depends upon the nature and quality of this interaction. During composition, audience functions are fulfilled by the writer's imagination, by critical and peer reviewers, and by editors. Once the text is published, expectations and experiences of actual readers enter the process, where they serve to determine the total meaning of the text (Bales 136ff).

While literary nonfiction almost always has a nominal subject at its center, it is the community surrounding the subject and the writer's representation of that community that comprise the main event and the primary interest for both reader and writer. Richard Selzer does not write about surgery; he writes about surgeons and about patients. Tom Wolfe does not write about LSD; he writes about people who drop acid. Tracy Kidder does not write about a computer; he writes about a group of people who build a computer. The reader's chief access to the main event of such texts is through the writer's persona (see Figure 16–2).

What the reader knows of the community, how she is likely to feel, and whether she is likely to act or not depend very much upon the attitude of the persona through whose language and perspective she experiences the text. Although the writer and the persona are almost never identical, the relationship between writer and subject community (Figure 16–1, Past and Future Interactions) and the nonfictive obligation of the text exert a significant influence upon the nature of the persona and its subsequent stance toward the community as represented in the text. While enormous variation is possible, writer-community relation-

Figure 16–2
Nominal Subject and Discourse Community Are Viewed Through the Literary
Nonfiction Text and Its Persona

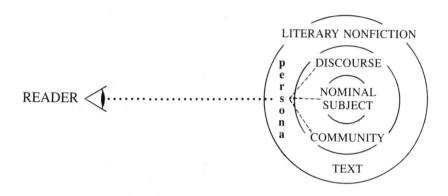

ships and persona-community stances can be generalized into a relatively simple taxonomy that constitutes a natural and highly productive organizing structure for advanced writing courses. In Figure 16–3, I have drawn out a taxonomy of writer-community relationships and persona-community stances with representative authors. Specific titles and appropriate bibliographical information are included in the list of works cited at the end of this chapter.

Writer-Community Relationships

I see four basic persona-community stances arising from two distinct writer-community relationships, which have to do with whether the writer begins as a member of the discourse community at the center of the piece or whether the writer begins as an outsider to that community. Writers who begin as outsiders can become members of the communities about which they write. Or they can maintain their outsider status and their allegiance to other discourse communities. In the first case, the resulting nonfiction texts present subject communities to the reader through the experiences of personae engaged in becoming members of them and afford readers an opportunity to experience the ways in which new discourse community alignmemts are made. The crucial characteristic of this stance is the change in perspective and understanding that occurs as the persona in the text becomes a member of the discourse community and learns that community's normal discourse. Such personae model the processes by which outsiders learn the normal discourse of a given community.

When writers maintain their allegiance to communities other than

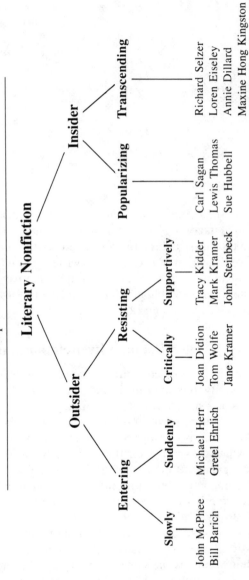

Figure 16–3
Writer-Community Relationships, Persona-Community Stances, and
Representative Authors

the one about which they write, their personae often assume stances that lead to the critical and argumentative processes that arise from contact between discourse communities with differing values. Writers in this relationship interpose a certain aesthetic, political, professional, or personal distance between themselves and the communities about which they write. The experience suggested by these writer's texts is not one of entrance, but of resistance. In some cases the result is parody, rejection, or exposé. In others, when the writer is a sympathetic or a "neutral" outsider, the result can be a favorable rendering of the community and its concerns or a journalistic exploration. In texts composed by such outsiders, the primary focus is upon the sensibilities and thoughts of the persona as it encounters and responds to the presence of a community of which it will not or cannot become a member. The persona analyzes, evaluates, and argues for and against. Such texts afford readers an opportunity to study the means by which members of specific discourse communities negotiate their own knowledge with that represented by other communities.

When writers begin as members of the communities about which they write, there are two general directions in which their texts develop: one affirms the discourse of the community and works to make the knowledge arising from that discourse accessible to outsiders; the other works through literary processes toward a new understanding of the knowledge arising from the discourse of the community. In the first instance, the reader is introduced to a popularized version of the community's normal discourse through the perspective of a persona that adopts a helpful, teacherly stance. The result is that the reader takes the first steps toward becoming a member of the community by learning a simplified version of its discourse.

In the second instance, the reader is introduced to a situation in which the knowledge and the discourse of a community become insufficient or unable to fulfill the needs of one of its members. When this happens, the member either resigns from the community or engages in the process of creating new knowledge through the introduction of a radical new perspective, an "abnormal discourse" (Rorty 320–22). In most communities, abnormal discourse is distinctly literary, drawing upon the "rules" of metaphor, analogy, and symbol to shift, to refocus, and to expand the vision, the language, and the knowledge of the community. Bruffee says this process cannot be directly taught, and perhaps he is right, but literary nonfiction in which the persona adopts this stance allows the reader opportunity after opportunity to witness the creation of fundamentally new knowledge from the discourse of an established community. It teaches the reader how to push the outside of the envelope.

Persona-Community Stances: Outsiders

John McPhee's *Coming into the Country* provides one of the very best examples of a persona slowly, consciously, and thoughtfully working to become a part of the subject community. From the opening pages, McPhee's persona is deeply engaged in the process of becoming as nearly a member of the Alaskan community, especially the subcommunity of the bush, as he can. A key element in this movement is the persona's attitude toward grizzly bears, which changes from fear of being eaten to a kind of holy communion in which he accepts that the concept of eating and being eaten is simply a part of being in the country, a concept that comprises a fundamental term in the discourse of Alaskans. A second movement is his evolving sense of the vastness and implications of the wilderness and his understanding that he must discover new terms for wilderness if his experience in Alaska, the nominal subject of the book, is to make any sense. By studying the specific shifts in McPhee's representations of these and other elements of his experience, readers and writers study precisely how one enters any new discourse community, whether it be populated by Alaskans, trout fisherman, street people, in-laws, or literary critics.

Michael Herr represents the outsider whose entry into the subject community is not a gradual, conscious building up of knowledge and experience. In *Dispatches,* Herr writes to make sense of his participation in the Vietnam War, a war he became a part of suddenly and brutally: "I went to cover the war," he writes, "and the war covered me" (27). His text, composed within the symbolic space of a single, fearful, held breath, literally explodes with facts and images, language and stories and myths that convey the horror, the fear, the ugliness, and the beauty of Vietnam. Herr circles around and around two central issues: (1) why he was there, an issue that astonishes the marines who learn that he could go home any day; and (2) what he finally has to say about the war, what sense he can generate from his experience to pass along to those who will read the book he composes years later.

Herr's response to both questions is to create a text and a persona that symbolically duplicate his own experience, a text and a persona that immerse his readers in the events, the stories, the values, and most of all the languages of the war in the same sudden, breathtaking, brutal way he was immersed in its actuality. Herr's readers, like Herr's persona, do not have to participate, but if the text works, they are drawn so deeply into the community of soldiers and correspondents it represents that they become symbolic participants, experiencing the fragmentation, the fear, and the contradictions of Vietnam through the literary discourse of the text. And when they reach the end, the assertion that whatever else can be said, the war was also wonderful makes a terrible kind of sense to them because it is true to their own literary experience as it was true to Herr's actual experience: "Vietnam, Vietnam, Vietnam, we've all been there" (Herr 224).

Much of Joan Didion's work, especially her first collection of essays, *Slouching Toward Bethlehem*, provides examples of the resisting outside writer who maintains her allegiance to the values of her own community as she writes about others. In this collection, Didion's prose is a highly crafted artistic vehicle for her persona's very particular political and social views, a vehicle through which her readers experience the perpetual, often heated conflict arising from contact between a member of a community with extremely conservative tendencies and members of communities with more radical or less coherent ones. Didion's persona resists entering into the subject community as strongly as McPhee's works to join it. The point of Didion's collection is to reveal the persona's values through encounters with other communities in such a way that the reader is persuaded to affirm those values.

In the essay "Slouching Toward Bethlehem," for instance, the reader is constantly aware of the ways in which Didion's persona sets herself apart from the community of flower children about which she writes — her age, her refusal to participate in the drug experience, and the presence of her photographer. On a thematic or argumentative level, this distance feeds a strong — though mostly implicit and inferential — criticism of the group's way of life, especially present in Didion's attention to the flower children's inability to articulate their values in a language compatible with that of her own much more conservative discourse community. Even the title, an allusion to W. B. Yeat's poem "The Second Coming," suggests an inflexible attitude and argumentative stance toward the subject community. When Didion's persona looks at the flower children, she sees disaster, a "rough beast" creeping inexorably toward her culture.

On the other side of Didion's argumentative relationship lies that of resisting writers such as Tracy Kidder, who write to examine and describe communities they cannot join but that they greatly admire. In *The Soul of a New Machine*, Kidder describes the process by which a group of young computer engineers and their superiors design and build a new computer. The computer, though it is at the center of the book, is not the center of the book. The soul of the new machine is the group that builds it. Kidder is not only aware of the importance of this community; his text is a virtual handbook for representing the normal actions and discourse of any community from the perspective of an outsider who admires and respects the work and the people he observes. The opening chapter, for example, contains a story about

Tom West, the group's leader, weathering a storm at sea that puts most of the crew below deck, a story that becomes emblematic of the personality and drive necessary to overcome the obstacles to the new machine, traits Kidder finds admirable and problematic.

As West and his lieutenants recruit the design team, Kidder focuses upon the rhetorical and linguistic devices employed to bring them into the community via a ritual West calls "signing up." In subsequent chapters, Kidder describes both the evolution of the machine itself and of the community that builds it, focusing again and again upon the symbolic and linguistic factors that energize the process and hold the community together. And finally, in the last chapters, he deals with the dissolution of the team. But even in the sections in which Kidder's persona plays the same computer games that members of the team play and comes close to becoming hooked on these games, as members of the team are hooked, he maintains critical detachment, realizing and helping the reader to realize that while Kidder is a sympathetic outsider, he is an outsider. This detachment enables him to tell the truth, and to acknowledge that it is a truth affected by his sympathetic relationship with the team.

Persona-Community Stances: Insiders

The writer who is a member of the subject community and who works to make the discourse of the community more intelligible to the outsider is the popularizer. Such writing deals with the knowledge the writer shares with other members of the community, with the "normal discourse" of the group (Rorty Chapter 7). These writers create personae that function as intermediaries or translators, working to clarify and simplify so that less-informed readers may understand the community's concerns, accept its actions, or share its motives. Their prose draws upon the literary in order to inform and to clarify in the way a simile develops an explicit comparison in order to explain. They seek to bring life to the facts of their fields. The difference between these writers and writers like Kidder is simply that they are not coming to the community from the outside. In some ways this is an advantage, but it can also blind the writer to aspects of the community and to needs of the reader that are obvious to the outsider. Writers who seem to me to participate in this relationship include Carl Sagan (*Cosmos*), Lewis Thomas (*The Youngest Science: Notes of A Medicine Watcher*), Sue Hubbell (*A Country Year: Living the Questions*), and in some cases, Loren Eiseley (the middle essays of *The Immense Journey*).

But Eiseley (in the first two and the final three essays in *The Immense Journey*) and Thomas (in many essays in *The Lives of a Cell: Notes of a Biology Watcher*) also participate in the other dimension of this persona-community stance, the dimension in which the writer emerges from the discourse of his own community seeking a new sense of what that community means. These writers become aware that their normal discourses are inadequate to fully express the implications of the knowledge those discourses have led them to perceive. They become literary nonfiction writers because it is the literary mode of language, with its naming, story-telling, and poetic activities, that empowers people to posit new understandings of the events, values, and vocabularies central to their lives. While each of the other relationships produces knowledge for the writer and for the reader, this perspective has the potential to create new knowledge for the members of the community as well, asserting in the tensive, interactive way a metaphor does, that *A*, a fact or a story everyone in the community understands in a particular way, is not *A* at all, but is instead *B*, something quite different.

For this group of writers, the literary elements of literary nonfiction allow a transcendence of "ordinary" experience. Their texts are often revolutionary in the sense that Thomas Kuhn used the term to signify the result of a building up of inconsistencies leading to a reconceptualization of the central values of the community. They provide excellent examples of abnormal discourse working to create new forms of normal discourse. Often, after such writers begin writing they are perceived by their peers to have violated the rules of the community, are ostracized, and then, after an appropriate exile, are readmitted to the community as its members come to see the value of the new discourse the writers have created.

Although I did not list him with the writers above, I see Richard Selzer as one of the clearest and most potent representatives of this group, especially in the first three essays of *Mortal Lessons: Notes on the Art of Surgery*. In these essays, Selzer describes the anomolies within the workings of his surgical community, which built to a point that he could no longer participate fully or with confidence in the shared, assumed values of that community. Becoming a writer allowed him to reconceptualize and to rearticulate the experience of being a surgeon through the voices of his various surgical personae and their patients in such a way that his particular symbolic representations of medical and surgical realities could include both the normal discourse of the community and his own more radical insights. The result, for his readers, is a textual experience that challenges and alters expectations, an experience that argues a fresh and startling awareness of crucial issues at the heart of both medicine and the mortal condition.

When Selzer began to write, he was rejected by his colleagues for suggesting that surgeons might be less certain of themselves, less in control of their procedures, and more in need of an alternative to the rhetoric of power, which lies at the center of surgical practice, than they were able to admit. But once Selzer revealed the surgeon "in his darkened office, sweating and afraid" (18), thoughtful colleagues began to affirm that indeed there are elements of fearfulness and uncertainty in their practice and that Selzer's representation contained elements not readily accessible through the normal discourse of medicine. As their acceptance became an affirmation, though never a universal one, of Selzer's vision, his perspective became a possibility or a "term" in surgical discourse, which is where it remains.

An Advanced Writing Course

The goal of an advanced writing class centered on reading and writing literary nonfiction ought to be to enable writers to explore each of the writer-community relationships and several of the persona-community stances. If this is to happen, I think the advanced writing class must focus upon the formation and implications of community from the very beginning. That is, the class itself must demonstrate what the writing assignments are asking the students to learn, which is that knowledge and understanding are human events arising from human interaction through the telling of stories and the sharing of information among potential peers. Students need to become members of a community of writers. They need to become conscious of the dynamics of this community. They need to learn to "see" their own communities in writerly ways. And then they need to move away from their own communities toward others about which they may write, returning to their writing community for criticism and support as they compose their actual and symbolic relationships with other communities in the texts they create. In the remainder of this chapter, I will describe an advanced writing class designed to achieve all five of these objectives.

In my undergraduate expository writing class I run two parallel strands throughout the semester (see Figure 16−4). The first is made up of assignments I give and the second of writings generated in response to the reading each student does. The first strand has three parts: (1) two sequences of assignments designed to explore the particular talents, interests, expertise, and writing abilities of the members of the class (forming community); (2) a sequence focused on the relationships among story, storyteller, and context within one of their own communities (exploring community from the inside); and (3) an opportunity to move into the world of another community and to write about it (composing community from the outside).

Forming Community

The first sequence begins with exercises designed to break the ice and to get members of the class ready to work with each other. These

Figure 16−4

Chart Showing Two Strands of Advanced Writing Course with Assignments on "Community" and Reading

STRAND ONE

Sequence One	Sequence Two	Sequence Three
Forming Community	**Exploring Community**	**Composing Community**
Category Sheets	Workable Story,	
"Where I Stand"	Interesting Character	
Interviews	Group Criteria	
Introductions	Find a Storyteller	Introduce Final Writing Project
Revisions	Record a Story	
Profiles	Share Stories	
Group Profiles	Re-tell as Literary Events	
Writers on Writing	Re-contextualize	List Possible Groups to Join
"How I Write"		or Study
Writing Groups Form		Quick Write
Writing Autobiography		Folklorist or Anthropologist
		Workshop

STRAND TWO

Reading and Responding

- *Introduce journal*
- *Respond to writers on writing*
- *Read for stories and characters*
- *Compare told stories to literary stories*
- *Consider larger purposes of literary stories*
- *Examine role of time and place in stories*
- *Immersion in a group*
- *Point of view*
- *Time*
- *Sentences and style*
- *Implications*
- *Making meaning*

include sheets of categories, or characteristics, that each student finds others in the room to fill — same number of children in your family, same musical interests, same hobbies, etc. These sheets plus the first writing assignment — a self-introduction entitled "Where I Stand" — lead to interviews and oral introductions of classmates. When the introductions are completed, I ask for a revision of the self-introduction that focuses on one aspect of each student's interests or experience that has not been covered at all or has not been adequately covered in the opening days of the class, a piece telling the group about something important that the writer is now willing to share.

Meanwhile, I ask each student for a quick freewrite focused on creating a profile of the class, based on what he or she has learned over the first few days. In groups of three, the students negotiate individual profiles into a collaboratively written one directed toward a particular audience, designed to fulfill a specific purpose, and aimed at a place of publication (a brochure for exchange students, a radio promotion for the university, a set of legislative hearings on higher education at the state capitol), which they will present to the class. By the end of this sequence, the class begins to see itself as a community of people who can work together. When the revisions of the introductory pieces come in, we shift the focus to writing by doing a whole-class workshop of three or four of the essays. This enables the students to direct their energies toward helping writers become better writers. Not only can they work together, they can also work together as writers.

The second sequence in the opening part of the first strand contains two assignments. The first is to compose a piece entitled "How I Write." We read essays by writers on writing to support this assignment — Joan Didion, E. B. White, George Orwell, and students from former classes. Mostly I am concerned with getting the students to take a close look at their own processes because, until they know those processes, they are not likely to be able to alter them in productive ways. When these pieces come in, I ask the students to represent their processes graphically and to talk to the class about the pictures they draw. While each student is talking, I ask the others to locate one writer in the class who does something they need or want to learn to do. For example, some writers do not revise. Some do. Some have a very hard time starting. The people they select (there are almost always clusters of three or four) become the writing groups they will work with over the course of the semester.

The second assignment in this sequence is to recontextualize the writing-process descriptions by expanding them into writing autobiographies. These pieces are the first ones the groups work with as groups. By this point, students see themselves as members of a writing, reading, responding community and understand that their job in the class is to help each other get better at all three tasks. They have engaged in the process of creating a significant working community.

Reading and Responding

The second strand I mentioned above is a reading and responding strand. When students read the pieces by writers on their writing, I introduce them to the constraints and to some of the possibilities of the reading and responding strand, which is essentially a reading journal. Usually we have a collection of essays or excerpts from professional writers that we work on together, but I also ask that they read a long work by a single author. I suggest writers and titles they might want to look at. Many of them choose books by the literary nonfiction writers I listed earlier in this chapter, though I am open to new writers as well. If they read other writing or want to write about their classmate's writing, I am open to that. What I want to accomplish in this strand is to get them to read like writers, looking at technique and point of view and at the issues of community I described above, issues we talk about in class. Many journal entries serve as starting points for class sessions on the more technical aspects of writing—introductions, conclusions, structural possibilities, stylistic issues. I read the journals occasionally and respond to them as fully as possible, working to shape and direct in productive ways. Figure 16–4 shows more clearly some typical relations between the reading journal—the strand of reading and responding—and the other assignment sequences in the course. There are, of course, many, many other possibilities.

Exploring Community

The second part of the first strand is a sequence of assignments designed to help students begin to understand what writers do as they shape knowledge to meet the needs and demands of readers who are not members of the communities about which the writers write or to which the writers belong. Because I want them to learn the ways literary nonfiction writers shape what they know, this part of the course focuses upon technical and substantive issues that help students effectively represent both the knowledge they have as members of their own communities and the knowledge they will gain later in the course as they explore communities of which they are not a part. By focusing on these issues, students begin to deal with knowledge in "writerly" ways, not merely dumping what they know onto the page, but shaping it into texts that will appeal to and inform the outside reader. They begin the process of moving from one community and discourse to another.

The first assignment in this part is to look through the reading they have done for descriptions of people and for stories that seem particularly interesting or worth reading. I ask them to copy those stories and descriptions and to compose a short piece on what makes them workable, interesting stories or character descriptions. They discuss their pieces and excerpts in small groups and arrive at a consensus on what constitutes successful character descriptions and stories in a literary nonfiction text. I ask them to sift through all the people they know with an interesting story to tell and to decide upon the person most likely to have a story or two that fulfills their own criteria. I ask them to write a short description of the person, a description that meets their interesting character criteria. Then I ask them to contact the person and to simply record the story or stories he tells, on tape or in longhand, verbatim.

In class, we listen to their verbatim stories and focus on the differences between the verbatim stories and the more literary ones they copied earlier from their reading. The differences almost always provide striking evidence of the shifts in language, form, and even content that happen when told stories become literary representations, even literary representations claiming to be nonfiction. I then ask the students to retell their verbatim stories as literary stories, not changing the truth of what was said, but changing the presentation to meet the criteria for workable stories that they developed in groups.

In a third, more extended writing assignment, I ask the students to contextualize the person and her story by mapping the story into its particular time and place through library research, additional interviews, or expansion of the specific situation within which the story was told. We look at the way most literary nonfiction writers use characters and stories to point to something larger than simply the story itself. The opening chapter of *The Soul of a New Machine*, for instance, is the story of a storm at sea, but it also points to personality traits necessary for sustaining a project the size of a new computer and sets the tone for the rest of the book. N. Scott Momaday's description of his grandmother near the end of the introduction to *The Way to Rainy Mountain* gives us his grandmother, but also points to Momaday's and the Kiowa Nation's devastating sense of loss at the passing away of their mythic world, at the deicide they had witnessed, and it sets the stage for the stories, meditations, and comments that comprise the remainder of Momaday's book.

The assignments in the Exploring Community sequence are designed to provide writers with the tools necessary to move away from their own communities toward new ones. Even if the storyteller is the writer's father or mother and if the story has been repeated so many times that teller and listener know it by heart, the literary shaping necessary to complete the three writing assignments invites the writer to push past the everyday and to see the teller and the story from a fresh, more comprehensive perspective. It invites the writer to reassess the knowledge that he or she has as a member of a given community in the act of making that knowledge available to outside readers. In terms of the taxonomy represented in Figure 16–2, students either popularize their community's knowledge or, occasionally, they see new implications in old stories and engage in the act of creating new knowledge for themselves, for their own community, and for their readers. In either case, students begin to develop the exploratory and analytical abilities necessary to complete the final sequence of the course, abilities that enable them to decenter themselves now and later, to understand, perhaps to enter, new communities.

Composing Community

The final sequence in the first strand pushes the writer out of his or her normal communities into a new one. I pave the way for this assignment much earlier by explaining exactly what the students will do so they can begin early, since time can become a crucial factor. To kick off this writing, I ask my students to list a number of things they have always wanted to do, groups they have always wanted to join, or organizations about which they are curious. They cannot already be participants, but they can have some knowledge to begin with, certainly some interest. In class we do a series of writings designed to eliminate some of the groups—listing, focused freewriting, clustering, looping. We share ideas and possibilities. If students have already begun their work, I ask that they quickly draft a description of what they have done and what they have learned.

The actual assignment is to study the group for the rest of the semester and to write about it as an outsider "coming into the country" or as an outsider researching the group. We spend class time talking about the kinds of communities they might enter and issues of responsibility, trust, deception, and honesty. We eliminate certain groups as being too dangerous (prisoners in the county jail) or too private (a church) or too rhetorically loaded (an abortion clinic). I advise them to find someone they know who is already a member of the group so they will have a mentor who can help them gain access to the group experience. I warn them that a single trip into the group—attending one meeting of the local Star Trek Society—will not do.

The class at this point becomes more of a workshop than anything else because different writers will be at different points in the process and will need different kinds of help. The central text we work with is the introduction to Norman Sims's *The Literary Journalists,* which describes how writers such as McPhee and Kidder go about investigating and writing their books and essays. We focus most of our time on the idea of immersion in the community as an enabling constraint leading to understanding. We always have either a folklorist or an anthropologist or both come to the class to talk with us about this kind of research, in particular about the implications of being an outsider and how this will affect our understanding of the events we observe. Our aim is not to get at the group's "absolute" truth, but to make meaning of experience as we move from our own value systems toward that of the subject community by composing in the outsider writer-audience relationship. Some writers wind up being very critical of their communities and some become very sympathetic, but in both cases, issues of language and of story and of meaning are at the heart of the experience and the texts.

Communities my students have explored in the past include those organized around weight reduction clinics, body building, flea markets, plastic surgery, funeral homes, guns, military reserves, psychiatric wards, alcoholism, law enforcement, bingo, department store security at holiday time, and a public basketball court. While I do not have room to quote extensively from essays I have gotten in response to this assignment, I do want to end this chapter with sections from two of the very best essays I have received. The first is from a writer named Deborah Russell, who had lived in Arkansas among male raccoon hunters all her life without ever going on a hunt or understanding the allure of the sport. The assignment gave her an opportunity to do both and to read extensively in such publications as *American Cooner,* where she encountered a story about a cemetery for hunting dogs, a story that amused and puzzled her. Her concluding paragraphs show exactly the kind of sense-making to which a course centered upon literary nonfiction can lead. After two unsuccessful hunts, Deborah writes,

> There were only a couple of weeks left in the coon season, and we were going to go hunting with Rex again. Unfortunately, flu season came first. Up until the last minute, we tried to arrange a hunt, but it just wasn't to be. The season ended, and I had only been twice. And I never got a coon.
>
> But I did get something else. I got the answer to my question. Why do coon hunters have a cemetery for their dogs? Because the dogs *are* the hunt. They are what makes coon hunting possible. Most of the men who coon hunt are almost fanatical about it, and they spend hours out in the woods, often by themselves. A good dog's enthusiasm and determination are the only things that make the hunt possible. I can see why the owners of those dogs value them so highly, and I caught that feeling myself. That's why I'll be calling Rex

and Craig in the middle of November next fall. The season starts November 20, and I plan to be there. I *will* get my coon.

The second excerpt is from an essay by Cindy Schmiedeskamp who chose, against my advice, to explore the biker subculture of Little Rock, Arkansas. Though the community seemed a little more dangerous than I could send a student out to face, Cindy insisted. She was fortunate enough to have a fine mentor who steered her through the community beautifully. The section below comes from near the middle of her piece, written about the day she rode with the bikers on their annual Toys for Tots parade, up Twelfth Street to the Arkansas State Capitol. It describes the significance of the Harley Davidson motorcycles that are the standard of the group.

> There were all types of motorcycles—Hondas, BMW's, Suzukis, Yamahas, and of course, Harley-Davidsons. Harley is the *creme de la creme* of motorcycles in the world of bikers. It symbolizes the counterculture, hard-core individualism that being a biker is all about. Not only is it a mean looking machine and the best made motorcycle in the world, but in a strange expression of patriotism, it is most valued because it is American made. Almost every Harley there displayed an American flag, from the small, toy-sized ones fastened between handlebars to the large, impressive, full-sized stars and stripes on mounted poles flowing out behind the seats. Interspersed with the American flags were several black flags showing support for Vietnam's casualties, POW's, and MIA's, which said in white lettering, "To our 50,000 brothers who never came back, you are not forgotten."

Writers who achieve the levels of commitment and the degree of understanding that these two writers achieved cannot help becoming better, more thoughtful writers. And this is certainly what an advanced writing course ought to accomplish. But even more than that, I think such a course ought to make writers very, very conscious of where they stand in relation to the communities about which they write, conscious that the roles they choose in the dramas they represent will have an enormous effect upon the texts they create and the experiences their readers will have as they read those texts. And most importantly, I think an advanced writing course ought to break free of the merely academic classroom entirely by helping writers discover that the language of the nonfiction they write is the very same everyday, literary language in which each of us "'comes alive' in the specifically human sense as a person in communication with others, in the symbolic reality...[we] create together, in the drama of [our] action" (Bales 151–52). Focusing the advanced writing course on reading and creating quality literary nonfiction can help students learn that there are many, many ways to participate in the conversations through which human beings conduct the business of being human. And it can make them participants.

Works Cited

Bales, Robert Freed. *Personality and Interpersonal Behavior*. New York: Holt, 1970.

Barich, Bill. *Laughing in the Hills*. New York: Viking, 1980.

Bruffee, Kenneth A. "Collaborative Learning and the 'Conversation of Mankind.'" *College English* 46 (1984): 635–652.

Burke, Kenneth. *A Rhetoric of Motives*. 1950. Berkeley: U of California P, 1969.

Didion, Joan. *Slouching Toward Bethlehem*. New York: Touchstone, 1979.

Dillard, Annie. *Pilgrim at Tinker Creek*. New York: Harper, 1985.

Ehrlich, Gretel. *The Solace of Open Spaces*. New York: Penguin, 1985.

Eiseley, Loren. *The Immense Journey*. New York: Vintage, 1957.

Hellman, John. *Fables of Fact: The New Journalism as New Fiction*. Urbana: U of Illinois P, 1981.

Herr, Michael. *Dispatches*. New York: Knopf, 1968.

Hubbell, Sue. *A Country Year: Living the Questions*. New York: Random, 1986.

Kidder, Tracy. *The Soul of a New Machine*. New York: Avon, 1981.

Kingston, Maxine Hong. *The Woman Warrior: Memoirs of a Girlhood Among Ghosts*. New York: Vintage, 1977.

Kramer, Jane. *The Last Cowboy*. New York: Pocket, 1977.

Kramer, Mark. *Invasive Procedures: A Year in the World of Two Surgeons*. 1983. New York: Penguin, 1984.

Kuhn, Thomas. *The Structure of Scientific Revolutions*. 2nd ed. Chicago: U of Chicago P, 1970.

McPhee, John. *Coming into the Country*. 1977. New York: Bantam, 1979.

Momaday, N. Scott. *The Way to Rainy Mountain*. Albuquerque: U of New Mexico P, 1969.

Rorty, Richard. *Philosophy and the Mirror of Nature*. 1979. Princeton: Princeton U P, 1980.

Sagan, Carl. *Cosmos*. New York: Random, 1980.

Selzer, Richard. *Mortal Lessons: Notes on the Art of Surgery*. 1974. New York: Simon, 1976.

Sims, Norman, ed. *The Literary Journalists*. New York: Ballantine, 1984.

Steinbeck, John. *Once There Was a War*. New York: Penguin, 1985.

Thomas, Lewis. *The Lives of a Cell: Notes of a Biology Watcher*. 1974. New York: Penguin, 1978.

———. *The Youngest Science: Notes of a Medicine Watcher.* New York: Bantam, 1983.

Weber, Ronald. *The Literature of Fact: Literary Nonfiction in American Writing.* Athens, OH: Ohio U P, 1980.

Whorf, Benjamin Lee. "Science and Linguistics." *Language, Thought, and Reality.* Ed. John B. Carroll. 1956. Cambridge, MA: M. I. T Press, 1972.

Wolfe, Tom. *The Electric Kool-Aid Acid Test.* New York: Bantam, 1968.

Walker, Alice. *In Search of Our Mothers' Gardens.* New York: Harcourt, 1983.

17

Creative Nonfiction,
Is There Any Other Kind?

Lynn Z. Bloom

"Works of nonfiction can be coherent and crafted works of literature," observes Annie Dillard, in explaining her own work in this "misunderstood genre, literary nonfiction":

> It's not simply that they're carefully written, or vivid and serious and pleasing, like Boswell's *Life of Johnson* or St. Exupéry's wonderful memoir of early aviation, *Wind, Sand, and Stars*. It's not even that they may contain elements of fiction, that their action reveals itself in scenes that use visual descriptions and that often use dialogue....It's that nonfiction accounts may be literary insofar as the parts of their structures cohere internally, insofar as the things are in them for the sake of the work itself, and insofar as the work itself exists in the service of idea ("To Fashion" 72–73).

Yet Dillard's "literary nonfiction," what I am calling here "creative nonfiction," in the view of far too many critics and teachers is an oxymoron. As Jim Corder observes, this opinion holds that essays, "reports, propositions, evidences, reminiscences" are "chunks of actuality": "They are not *fictions*; hence, they are not created." As a consequence, such nonfiction modes "never made it into any hierachy of literary types. They are outside and otherwise" (237).

In this exclusive, excluding definition, "creative" is equivalent to "fictive." Any mode of writing that purports to be true, or to have a basis in fact, not only cannot be considered "creative" but is excluded from the literary canon and consequently from serious consideration as a work of literature (Rygiel, 393–97; Tabachnick). Thus such nonfiction modes as autobigraphy, biography, diaries, letters, history, philosophy, social and political commentary, the literature of travel and

249

place, nature writing, science writing, and much humor are rarely central to conventional literary curricula, if they are included at all, either as works to be studied as literature, or as literary models for "creative writing."

Burton Hatlen astutely observes in "Why is *The Education of Henry Adams* 'Literature,' While *The Theory of the Leisure Class* Is Not?" that as long as such writings are perceived to "tell the [literal] truth," as long as they remain "live options," they will not be read as literature. In this view, only when such works, for instance Emerson's *Nature* or Henry Adams's *Education,* are no longer seen as presenting "truth about the [actual] world" can they metamorphose into literature. In this altered status they can then be read "not as a description of the 'real world,' but rather as a coherent presentation of a 'possible world' — a world which we do not inhabit, but which we find it profitable to visit from time to time" (672). Yet the texts to which Hatlen refers have not changed at all when they make the transition from the vast, vague, amorphous realm of nonfiction to the intimate province of literature — only the way of reading them has changed.

In a careful, thoughtfully reasoned argument, Hatlen proposes expanding the canon and the curriculum to include lively examples of these living modes of nonfiction — a view articulately argued as well by Phyllis Frus McCord in "Reading Nonfiction in Composition Courses: From Theory to Practice." Thus Hatlen's proposed course on "The Innocent Abroad: Travel Writings from Marco Polo to the Present" would include writers as diverse as William Byrd, Margaret Fuller, Darwin, Melville, Twain, Lawrence (T. E. and D. H.), Rebecca West, and Margaret Mead. A course in nature writing might range from Izaak Walton, Jonathan Edwards, and William Bartram to Thoreau and Darwin, to Henry Beston, Rachel Carson, Loren Eiseley, Stephen Jay Gould, Annie Dillard, Barry Lopez, and John McPhee.

To expand the literary canon by treating such nonfiction authors as the serious and distinguished stylists (as well as thinkers) that they are has a number of advantages both critical and pedagogical. An expanded canon provides subjects and literary models that are accessible to a wide variety of students' majors and interests (scientists, engineers, business majors). It furnishes expanded options for a lifetime of reading and perhaps writing that these students are likely to encounter in the real world after graduation. And it realistically reflects the dominant nature(s) and types of contemporary writing of quality — a phenomenon acknowledged by the "nonfiction" category recently added to the annual Associated Writing Programs' contest.

The view of these scholars/teachers is eminently reasonable — in my opinion, incontrovertible. Indeed, I will argue here that although different premises govern the essential transaction between writers and readers of nonfiction, as opposed to writers and readers of fiction, many forms of both creative nonfiction and fiction use the same literary techniques. Although my most detailed examples here involve published autobiographies and student essays, the points I make apply as well to many other types of nonfiction writing.

For instance, S. Michael Halloran insightfully analyzes a 900-word scientific essay, "A Structure for Deoxyribose Nucleic Acid," James Watson and Francis Crick's understated proprietary claim to the double helix (*Nature*, 25 April 1953). Halloran shows how the article's "'stylistic proclivities and the qualities of mental life of which those proclivities are tokens,'" (Edwin Black, qtd. in Halloran 71), carefully, perhaps insidiously, establish a distinctive *ethos*. With laconic economy, these scientists "dramatize themselves as intellectual beings in a particular style," articulating through their argument, genteel language, and ironic understatement "a recognizable public persona"—that of *"the scientist speaking"*—in deliberate contrast to their actual mode of behavior; "in the flesh they were obstreperous and irreverent" (74–5). In this brief report, as in their later publications, Watson and Crick employ a "confident, personal, rhetorically adept *ethos*" (79)—in contrast to another, quite different, yet equally contrived scientific *ethos* found in many other technical writings, that of the cautious, depersonalized transmitter of masses of data, carefully and conservatively interpreted. Halloran argues that Watson and Crick's style and ethos greatly enhanced their claim for rapid admission of their theory "to the canon of established knowledge in biology" (78), while comparable claims couched in more cautious rhetoric were treated far more skeptically.

Halloran's analysis of the rhetorical strategies of Watson and Crick, in a nonfiction mode erroneously considered by many to be objective and straightforward, even inartistic, reinforces my claim—and I overstate the case only slightly, to emphasize the point—there is no other kind of nonfiction except creative nonfiction.[1] It follows then that all advanced composition courses, no matter how general or how specialized, should reflect that premise and an awareness of these literary techniques, as do the courses that I describe in the concluding section of this paper.

Reader-Writer Transactions in Fiction and Nonfiction

Fiction, poetry, and drama—"creative writing"—are by definition fictive, "drawn from the imagination of the author rather than from history or fact."[2] Readers understand, respect, and accept this as a fundamental quality of the work; they do not believe that what they are reading is literally true, and they do not hold the author accountable for presenting verifiable fact. This is the case even with fictive works in which there is an extraordinary concern for verisimilitude, such as *Robinson Cursoe*, which in their biographical particulars, even on the title page, are indistinguishable from bona fide autobiographies.[3]

Indeed, in *Autobiographical Acts*, Elizabeth W. Bruss explores the proposition that the major difference between fiction and nonfiction is not necessarily dependent on structural or stylistic features of a given text but on the way readers respond to that text. Bruss offers three criteria for defining autobiography and distinguishing it from fiction, derived from John R. Searle's speech act theory. What she says about autobiography applies to other forms of nonfiction as well.

1. Nonfiction works are assumed to represent and to be derived from facts that, independent of the text itself, are assumed to be publicly verifiable.

2. These works purport to be true, whether they are concerned with private experiences or publicly observable occasions. Readers are expected to accept the author's truth, although they are free to try either to verify or discredit it.

3. The writers of these works purport to believe what they assert, "whether or not what is reported can be discredited, whether or not it can be reformulated in some more generally acceptable way from another point of view" (10–11).

In short, irrespective of formal characteristics or mode, different premises govern the transaction between readers and writers of fiction and nonfiction. Readers of nonfiction assume, with reason, that writers are telling the truth, usually verifiable. Writers of nonfiction agree, implying or claiming that they are telling the truth even as they are shaping, interpreting, and recreating their subject. They do not do this to mislead their readers or to deny the truth but to get at the essential truth that lies beneath, or within, the mass of details that occur in the course of everyday existence. Thus for writers of nonfiction, as for writers of fiction, the significant or essential truth may at times be most accurately conveyed by altering features of the existential truth. While all serious writers know this, the literalists among their readers may not and, innocent of the "felt truth," may erroneously expect total external verifiability as the basis for a faithful rendition.

In commenting on how he wrote *Growing Up,* his autobiography, Russell Baker answers the question "How much of your book is truthful and how much is good writing?":[4]

> Well, all the incidents are truthful. A book like that has certain
> things in common with fiction. Anything that is autobiographical is
> the opposite of biography. The biographer's problem is that he never
> knows enough. The autobiographer's problem is that he knows much

too much. He knows absolutely everything; he knows the whole iceberg, not just the tip....So when you're writing about yourself, the problem is what to leave out. And I left out almost everything [that didn't contribute psychologically, artistically to "the story line"] —there's only about half a percent in that book. You wouldn't want everything; it would be like reading the *Congressional Record*. ("Life" 49—50)

Reading and Writing Creative Nonfiction

Readers of fiction do not make the same assumption as readers of nonfiction: they expect writers to shape, interpret, and even invent their subject. Thus although many of the processes and techniques of fiction are common to both, fictive works command a different response than nonfiction does.

College teachers whose courses include both fiction and autobiography have doubtless seen this generalization verified. In my own experience students, ranging from innocent freshmen to sophisticated graduates, invariably read autobigraphy as the true story of an actual life, irrespective of its fictive qualities. Yet they never treat fiction (except autobiographical bildungsroman, such as Sylvia Plath's *The Bell Jar*) as if its characters existed outside the books. Thus they respond, intimately and sympathetically, to Richard Wright's *Black Boy* as the angry, searing account of an actual life of deprivation and prejudice; but treat with far greater detachment Wright's equally angry, searing account of Bigger Thomas's life of deprivation and prejudice in the fictional *Native Son* because they do not believe it really happened.

Yet, as McCord wisely contends in "Reading Nonfiction in Composition Courses," it is not only possible but appropriate to encourage students to read nonfiction and fiction alike with attention to the way "their form embodies their message," that is, with attention to their "literary elements" rather than with regard to whether or not they are true.[5] In this way of reading, "fictionality turns out to be a rhetorical category, rather than a definition which requires us to read by disregarding a work's truth claims and viewing it simply as an 'as-if' construction" (750—50; Hatlen 672—74). What is an appropriate rationale for reading, I contend, is an equally appropriate rationale for writing truly creative nonfiction and especially germane to courses in advanced composition.

Neither students nor anyone else should have difficulty in conceiving of nonfiction as creative, because both fiction and nonfiction have so many formal elements in common. As Halloran's analysis of Watson and Crick's scientific prose illustrates, writers of nonfiction establish, as do all writers, persona and voice. They interpret their subject, adapt style and structure to that interpretation, employ themes and motifs, repetition and variation. In many cases they use monologue, dialogue, scenes, characterizations, and other features associated with fiction but that are nearly as common in nonfiction. It is consequently not surprising that many of the best autobiographies are written by novelists accustomed to using fictive models and techniques (indicated in brackets in the examples below). They know how to tell a good story to get at, as Yeats says, the truth that is at "the deep heart's core."

In the first volume of her autobiography, *Memories of a Catholic Girlhood*, Mary McCarthy employs the unusual technique of providing an afterword to each chapter, in which she tries to sort out memory from imagination, sometimes questioning her own fidelity to fact, while continuing to assert the truth of the heart. McCarthy's parents died when she was six, leaving her and her three younger brothers under the guardianship of an ill-assorted Dickensian couple — dull-witted, abusive Uncle (by marriage) Myers and his unimaginative but doting middle-aged wife, Aunt Margaret [characterization, character types]. In the "Tin Butterfly" chapter, McCarthy anatomizes her searing memory of a prolonged conflict with Myers, a test of wills and stamina of body and character [dramatic conflict]. When a tin butterfly from a Cracker Jack box [symbolic object], Mary's infant brother's prized (and virtually only) possession, disappeared, Margaret and her scrawny wards tore apart the house in a frenzied search. To no avail. The search continued, amidst escalating emotion as Myers accused Mary of taking the butterfly and she protested her innocence [rising action; conflict of good and evil]. When, in perverted triumph, Myers flung back the tablecloth to reveal the butterfly pinned to the silence cloth under Mary's plate [dramatic gesture], she continued to deny his accusation [escalation of emotional intensity]. The "terrible whipping" that ensued could not make her confess to a crime that she hadn't committed, despite the pleas of her terrified aunt for Mary to lie and stop the torture [this conflict is expressed through dialogue and action]. That is the incident as McCarthy recalls it, memorialized in an architectonically elegant account.

But did the incident really happen that way? From a retrospective adult view, 30 years after the fact and enhanced by a self-righteously — and self-servingly — moralistic memory, McCarthy wonders. Did Myers actually perpetrate this malevolent plot? Or did Mary "fuse two [separate] memories," the butterfly episode and the whipping (which her brothers can verify) and "the idea that Uncle Myers put the butterfly at my place," which may have been suggested by her college playwriting teacher? She can't remember; she acknowledges the alternatives; she apologizes (*"mea culpa"*); but nevertheless leaves in this chilling evidence of Myers's "capricious brutality" (82–83).

In writing his autobiography, *Growing Up*, journalist Russell Baker had to contend with the opposite problem, too much information but no central characters. The book's first version consisted of 450 pages of careful "newspaper reportage" of Baker's aged relatives "talking about what life was like long ago." "Being the good journalist, I kept myself out of it" ("Life;" 41). Being the dutiful son, he kept his domineering mother out, too. Finally, during a candid lunch with his unhappy editor, Baker realized that he had to rewrite the whole book, which "was about the tension between a child and his mother, and everything had to hinge on that. . . . I had been dishonest about my mother. What I had written, though it was accurate to the extent that the reporting was there, was dishonest because of what I had left out. . . . And that dishonesty left a great hollow in the center of the original book" ("Life;" 43–44).

The totally rewritten version restored the central charaters, focused on their taut relationship, and so became an honest book, compellingly endearing. Baker's mother, Lucy, widowed young during the Depression, nagged, prodded, poked, and harangued him to "make something of yourself" [characterization]. Lucy insisted that her son, an unusually shy, timid, bookish nine-year-old, sell *The Saturday Evening Post* to passing motorists [introduction of primary conflict] – a task his younger sister performed with aplomb while Baker cowered [characterization, secondary conflict]. Predictably, the tension escalated as Baker grew older and sought to escape her control. As a college student and Navy veteran, Baker stayed out late (and didn't tell her where he was going, or with whom) [development of new dramatic conflict]. Then, as a fledgling reporter he took up with Mimi, exactly the kind of woman he knew his mother would disapprove of. Mimi, the antithesis of the "wholesome," dull girls Baker's mother liked, smoked, drank, and wore bright lipstick and sexy clothes. She had a job, lived in an apartment (rather than safe at home), and dated men she met on business trips [symbolic as well as literal manifestations of character]. Baker waged his ultimate struggle to attain maturity and independence over his right to marry Mimi [major conflict established through a succession of scenes], and thus successfully opposed his mother even while fulfilling her prime tenet: as a writer, to "make something of yourself."

Literary Techniques in Contemporary Nonfiction

The literary techniques discussed here pervade distinguished twentieth-century nonfiction, attaining their most conspicuous concentration in such works as Tom Wolfe's *Radical Chic and Mau-Mauing the Flak Catchers* and Truman Capote's "nonfiction novel," *In Cold Blood.*

Though these techniques are not new, they appear in greater abundance and in more combinations in contemporary nonfiction than in comparable writings of previous centuries. Nevertheless, examples may be found in some types of medieval and Elizabethan works, such as the partly fictive *Travels of Sir John Mandeville* (first published in 1366) and the more reliable compilation *Hakluyt's Voyages* (1600), notably in accounts by Anthony Jenkinson and Sir John Hawkins.

Many contemporary nonfiction authors, for instance, make their points through carefully designed compositions of scenes: Jan Morris interprets the native customs and haunts of "Manhattan" and *Venice*; George Orwell demonstrates the political antagonism between colonists and natives in Moulmein and "Marrakech"; Jonathan Kozol pleads for decent family housing by introducing us to *Rachel and Her Children* and a host of other *Homeless Families in America*.

Each nonfiction author of distinction has a recognizable style, an identifiable persona. Investigative reporter Jessica Mitford, grand dame of contemporary muckrakers, appraises famous writers with ironic self-righteousness. Nature writers, unassuming loners like Thoreau and Annie Dillard, are self-reliant, resourceful optimists, confident that careful observation will be rewarding: "I wake expectant," says Annie Dillard, "There are lots of things to see, unwrapped gifts and free surprises" (*Pilgrim* 2, 16). Scientists (except for the schemers like James Watson racing for the Nobel Prize) are generally cool and competent, even when, like Rachel Carson, they are passionately committed to preserving the sea around us.

Yet even scientific writers such as physicians Oliver Sacks (*The Man Who Mistook His Wife for a Hat*), Richard Selzer (*Mortal Lessons*), and Lewis Thomas (*The Lives of a Cell*) use dialogue to clarify the nature of disease, the functioning of the human body, or the way scientific phenomena work. Thomas even has the audacity (or *joie de vivre*, if you will) to personify moths under the irresistible influence of pheromones: "'At home, 4 p.m. today,' says the female moth, and releases a brief explosion of bombykol, a single molecule of which will tremble the hairs of any male within miles and send him driving upwind in a confusion of ardor" (18).

Other writers also employ these techniques in diverse nonfiction modes: E. B. White's benevolently incisive interpretations of city and country life. Maxine Hong Kingston's autobiographical writings, mingling "dream and memory, myth and desire" — techniques also found in the autobiographies of Eudora Welty, Vladimir Nabokov, Alfred Kazin, Frank Conroy, and a host of others. Robert Coles's interviews, portraits, and sociological analyses. Jonathan Raban's worldwide travel writings — "there is a *there* there"; and Paul Theroux's long railway journeys. M. F. K. Fisher's and Calvin Trillin's deliciously vigorous discussions of food and places. John McPhee's accounts of geology, country doctors, oranges, Alaska, Berton Rouéche's "Medical Detectives," a decades-long *New Yorker* series on public health investigators in action. Stephen Jay Gould's careful scientific analyses that become arguments for current social policy, as in *The Mismeasure of Man*; and William Warner's evocative natural history, *Beautiful Swimmers*, that does likewise. Carl Sagan's analyses of physical phenomena that range from the height of the heavens to the end of the world.

None of these writings is objective; all of them are true, and their authors are utterly reliable. These works epitomize creative nonfiction; there is no other kind.

Teaching Students to Write Creative Nonfiction

If there were a single ideal advanced composition course, especially one guaranteed to produce truly advanced (if not distinguished) writers, there might be some consensus on what it should be, in theory or in practice. But alas, college teachers appear to be no closer to agreement now than they have been during the past thirty years (see Dicks, Tate).[6] Nevertheless, it is possible for any advanced composition course to incorporate instruction in the techniques of creative nonfiction, as long it concentrates on actually writing rather than on studying grammar, linguistics, the history of the language, rhetorical theory, or other material learned primarily through reading rather than writing (see Dicks 182–84). This is true no matter whether the course emphasizes the conventional material of freshman composition, tightened up a notch; critical or argumentative writing; narrative or descriptive writing; journalistic feature writing; legal, business, technical, or scientific writing; or writing in the student's major field, perhaps even including the writing of grant proposals, since the results must be projected in advance of conducting the research—truly an imaginative act.

The rest of this essay will demonstrate ways in which the advanced writing courses I taught at Virginia Commonwealth University (1982–88) encouraged the writing of creative nonfiction. One of the courses is Advanced Composition, an upper-level undergraduate course in belletristic and/or feature writing, variations of which I have also taught over the past 20 years at Case Western Reserve and Butler universities, the College of William and Mary, and the University of New Mexico. This course attracts undergraduates in diverse majors wanting to improve their writing, journalism students seeking extra practice in supervised feature writing, and others aspiring to professional publication, including some faculty in science and medicine. The other course is Writing Nonfiction, a graduate workshop in professional nonfiction writing offered for the past four years as part of VCU'S MFA program in creative writing, but open to MA students in English as well. The common features of these courses include philosophy, aims, approach, and subject matter.

Philosophy

These courses affirm a self-fulfilling prophecy, that every student who takes an advanced writing course of any kind can learn to write with a fair amount of sophistication and a great amount of enjoyment. Writing and rewriting, with constant feedback on works-in-progress from peers and an instructor who also writes and rewrites and publishes, are the heart and soul of each course.

These courses assume a continuum of writing ability extending from innocence on the freshman level to considerable experience on the graduate level; each course on the continuum represents a distinct *advance* over its predecessors in knowledge of and expectations about writing. No advanced course should duplicate and preferably not even review material covered in freshman composition, unless this is done in individual conferences. Although the techniques of creative nonfiction are not off-limits to beginning writers, advanced composition courses are better suited to the development of more sophisticated writing, which involves setting scenes, presenting carefully contrived and perhaps diverse authorial personae and voices, experimenting with alternative and sometimes dramatic organizational structures, creating or recreating characters and scenes, and employing dialogue and figurative language.

Aims

These advanced composition courses aim to enable students to write very well, in a diversity of nonfiction modes, for a real audience (or audiences) of the student's choosing, and to attain clarity, grace, and an individual style in the process; to develop some measure of ease and efficiency in their writing process(es); and to publish. Even those students who take the undergraduate course primarily to fill a requirement are soon won over when they see that it is possible for their peers to accomplish these aims. My students do publish — in student, suburban, and metropolitan newspapers; in trade publications, house organs, and state agency newsletters and pamphlets; in little magazines, professional journals, and with small and major trade presses. Students who publish invariably inspire those who don't, or who haven't yet done so, for peer success brings the seemingly impossible within reach.

Emphasis on writing for an audience other than one's classmates —
perhaps the amorphous one acknowledged by Gertrude Stein's "I write
for myself and strangers" — is the best incentive I know for encouraging
students to use the techniques of creative nonfiction. For instance, they
can ask of their own or others' writings such questions as the following:

- What kind of authorial persona does this piece present? Does the
  author come across as knowledgeable, honest, engaging, or in
  other ways that either reinforce or undermine the message?

- Does the author consciously play or create any roles (expert,
  advocate, humorous character, innocent)? In what voice(s) does
  the author speak? Have any other attributes of an authorial persona
  crept in unintentionally to indicate an author incompetent, ram-
  bling, or insensitive to the audience? If so, what can be done to
  alter these negative elements? (See Bloom 35–36)

- Does the form of the writing (such as narrative, argument, technical report, how-to) fulfill an audience's expectations of the typical
  mode? (For instance, does a scientific paper sound like and and
  follow the format of a typical scientific paper? Does a travel piece
  transport its readers happily to an unfamiliar locale, specifically
  described?) If so, what saves the writing from being humdrum and
  thoroughly predictable? If not, do its unique features enhance its
  content?

- What is the writing's structure (e.g., straightforward chronological
  narrative, step-by-step account of a process, give-and-take of an
  argument or a developing relationship)? Are there other arrange-
  ments of the same or alternative materials, such as flashbacks or
  sequences of scenes, that would make the point more convincing,
  memorable?

- If the material were dramatized (through scenes, characters, dialogue), would it come alive in appropriate ways?

- In what ways, if any, would more colorful language enhance the
  presentation? Could the same point(s) be made through a higher
  proportion of figurative language, such as similes or extended
  metaphors, than is currently or customarily used?

The Way It Works

Students will not grow and develop as writers unless they are both
rigorous thinkers and risk-takers — willing to experiment with subject,
form, style. As Eudora Welty says, "All serious daring starts from
within." The two central questions, always asked in tandem, that
govern class discussion of both student and professional writing are

more daring than they seem, because they imply that the text (and therefore the writer) is never static and always susceptible to change: What's right about this piece? What could be done to make it better? These positively oriented questions encourage students to become discriminating listeners to prose (especially their own), as well as discriminating readers and writers. These make it easy to both imagine and try out some of the possibilities suggested by the techniques of creative nonfiction identified above, and more.

A low-key way to encourage such experimentation is to use what I call the eye-doctor approach, reiterating my eye doctor's perpetual question in selecting the right lenses: "Is it better *this* way? Or [inserting a different lens into the viewing machine] *this* way?" And again, with different lenses, "Is it better *this* way? Or *this* way?" "*This* way? Or *this* way?" After trying (or even imagining) a myriad of possibilities, you know you've found the best way when the blurry universe suddenly snaps into sharp focus, etching even minute details with sharp precision. The sharper the vision, the more effective the criticism, whether of one's own writing, a peer's, or a professional's—and the students are on their way to becoming tough-minded and, ultimately, independent judges of writing. Their learning (and one hopes, their writing) must last a lifetime, not just a semester.

Subject Matter

Anything, everything should be included, most of it written in modes common to belletristic nonfiction, which are discussed in detail in my book, *Fact and Artifact: Writing Nonfiction*. These include writings about people, places, performances (including music, theater, books, restaurants, sports), controversy, science, how-to, and humor (including parody, satire, and humorous narrative). Four examples of typical student writing illustrate the possibilities (the techniques of creative nonfiction are indicated after each passage):

> **Writing about people:** autobiographical narratives, interviews, character sketches, individual or group portraits, delineation of a significant relationship, partial biography, family history.

> "Red Eubanks, Foreman," by Steve O'Connor. *Just then a huge, jacked-up green Chevy pick-up roared in through the mud tracks left by the derrick-tractor. I could see a Confederate flag decal on the back window and a fat, freckled hand grabbing the can of Skoal off the dashboard....*

> *Red seemed glad to see me when I introduced myself, and he smothered my hand as I shook his beefy paw. I surveyed my new boss and saw that he was a short man, but built like a tank, with forearms as thick as telephone poles. With his fiery orange hair and sharp, inspecting eyes*

riveting on me over his barrel chest, I hoped that I would never be the object of this man's anger....Opening a can of Skoal and, to my shock, shoving the entire contents into his fat cheek, Red called the attention of the crew. "Men, this here's Steve. He's a college boy from New Mexico State, the Aggies, and he's gonna be with us for the summer." Bits of the powdered tobacco were flying out of his mouth. "Now I want you all to go easy on this boy for the first couple days, so's we can show him we got nuthin' against Yankees."

Persona: Refined college student. *Tone:* Red—energetic, robust, confident; student—somewhat timid. *Scene:* construction site. *Symbolic details:* jacked-up pickup truck, Confederate flag, chewing tobacco. *Figurative language:* built like a tank, forearms as thick as telephone poles. *Dialogue and dialect:* This here's Steve....we got nuthin' against Yankees. *Characterization:* Entire passage.

Writing about places: descriptions of favorite (or detested) places, reflections on the natural world—for its own sake or for the writer's; interpretations of places as contexts for social criticism—to call attention to problems, to promote corrective action; interpretations of places as contexts for exploration and adventure; guides for prospective travelers to a particular place, region, country.

"Nobody Sticks Around After a Loss," by Ray Hatcher. *As John dresses he notices through the steel-grated window that the parking lot is emptying fast; nobody sticks around after a loss. Air from the cheap K-mart fan gives John goose pimples. With no one in the locker room except himself, he is struck by the emptiness. He hears the water drip from a leaky shower head, and the meow of an abandoned cat. A stale smell of body odor and moldy clothes fills his sinuses. On the filthy carpet his laundry bag resembles a dead animal run over by a truck, and in the dim light the shoulder pads piled on top of the lockers look like the carcasses of some prehistoric creatures. The locker room door echoes as he slams it. Nobody sticks around after a loss.*

Point of view: sympathetic third-person observer. *Tone:* melancholy. *Scene:* deserted locker room. *Symbolic details:* steel-grated window, cheap fan, dripping shower, abandoned cat....*Figurative language:* laundry bag resembles a dead animal, shoulder pads look like prehistoric carcasses. *Characterization:* defeated athlete.

Writing about science: definitions, explanations or interpretations of things, phenomena, concepts and theories, processes—for a general or a specialized audience; critique of others' research; research or technical reports; case histories; literature reviews; grant proposals.

"Acid Rain," by Kelly Shea. *The "certain substances" added [to rain, dew, mist] are pollutants, namely sulfur and nitrogen oxides, formed from smelting and the burning of coal, oil, and gas. When these fossil fuels are burned, the oxides are evolved. When combined with water in any form, the oxides produce—surprise!—sulfuric and nitric acids. So when the oxides are emitted into the atmosphere, and then precipitation comes down through them, the acids are formed, causing acid rain.*

So, how are lakes and streams affected, when most industrial smelting factories and comparable industries are located in and around cities? How can the Parthenon be endangered when there are obviously no factories in the immediate area? First, don't forget automobiles, crafty culprits contributing to the emission of the dangerous oxides. But the four-wheeled demon...

Persona: breezy, knowledgeable interpreter. *Tone:* vigorous, cheerful. *Figurative language:* automobiles, four-wheeled demons, crafty culprits. *Stylistic features:* rhetorical questions, exclamation — "surprise!"

Writing about controversy: direct arguments; implied arguments (through single case, dramatic vignette, satire); investigative reporting.

"December Seventh is the Ides of March," by Cheryl Watanabe. *After the homes were lost, the businesses destroyed, after the furniture was sold or stolen, after the fathers were taken away and the rights of the land-born children erased you come — to offer money and recognition. Deeds not willing to be forgotten haunt you: Utah or California, horse stalls for hotels, manure for freshener, the death of our sons in Italy whose parents, buried deep in the desert, watered the brush with tears. But your offer comes too late. The children have grown, the night classes paid for, the businesses reestablished, and prominence regained. Your money is not wanted and is not needed. Save your inflated dollars. We have wealth enough to forgive with charity. Just put it in the textbooks, you never put it in the textbooks.*

In California thongs are still Nipper Flippers or Jap Slaps. People imitate Japanese (or is it Chinese?) when I walk by. December seventh is the Ides of March. I'm asked how I can see, is my field of vision narrowed?

Persona: Japanese-American social critic. *Tone:* measured and angry. *Scene:* desert internment camp. *Symbolic details:* horse stalls for hotels, manure for freshener, parents watering the brush with tears. *Figurative language:* December seventh is the Ides of March. *Stylistic features:* epigram (wealth enough to forgive with charity), unusual capitalizations (Nipper Flippers, Jap Slaps), rhetorical questions.

The students in these courses, graduate and undergraduate alike, quickly form a community. In their roles as readers, writers, editors, critics — risktakers all — they become friends, holding the safety net for their colleagues up there on the tightrope. They have as a common culture the shared texts they themselves have created. Even though they write in different voices, with different personae, they truly speak the same language, the language of creative nonfiction. Most students don't want the course to end. Neither do I. So I remind them that advanced writers will continue to advance; the course is only the beginning.

Notes

1. The allusion here and in my title to the strategy of the rhetorical question in Elliot Mishler's "Meaning in Context: Is There Any Other Kind?" is intentional. The answer can only be "no."

2. Holman and Harman 202. That this standard *Handbook to Literature* has no separate entry for or definition of *nonfiction,* even in the most recent (1986) edition implicitly verifies my earlier point, that nonfiction is conventionally excluded from the province of literature. Even its very label is negative, implying not what it is but what it is not.

3. The title page to the first edition (1719) reads, "The Life and Strange Surprizing Adventures of Robinson Crusoe, of York, Mariner: Who lived Eight and Twenty Years, all alone in an un-inhabited Island on the Coast of America, near the Mouth of the Great River of Oroonoque; Having been cast on Shore by Shipwreck, wherein all the Men perished but himself. With An Account how he was at last as strangely deliver'd by Pyrates. Written by Himself." This perfectly mimics the rhetorical conventions and design of the conventional title pages of bona fide eighteenth-and nineteenth-century autobiographies, of which two randomly selected examples will suffice: "Death Valley in '49. Important Chapter of California Pioneer History. The autobiography of a pioneer, detailing his life from a humble home in the Green Mountains to the gold mines of California; and particularly reciting the sufferings of the band of men, women and children who gave 'Death Valley' its name," by William Lewis Manly (1894); and the comparatively restrained, "The Life and Times of Frederick Douglass, Written by Himself. His early life as a slave, his escape from bondage, and his complete history" (1892, revised fourth edition).

4. It is odd that the interrogator, William Zinsser, himself a sophisticated writer of nonfiction, should make this arbitrary, artificial, and basically wrong discrimination between truth and "good writing"; his own experience must tell him that these are not antithetical.

5. Certainly this is the emphasis of much contemporary criticism of autobiography. Georges Gusdorf articulated a number of basic critical premises in "Conditions and Limits of Autobiography," which contends that "Every autobiography is a work of art and at the same time a work of enlightenment; it does not show us the individual seen from outside in his visible actions but the person in his inner privacy, not as he was, not as he is, but as he believes and wishes himself to be and to have been.... In giving his own narrative, the man is forever adding himself to himself. So creation of a literary world begins with the author's confession: the narrative that he makes of his life is already a first work of art, the first deciphering of an affirmation that, at a further stage of stripping down and recomposing, will open out in novels, in tragedies, or in poems" (45). Three (among many) excellent critical works that in various ways reinforce this premise are Paul John Eakin's *Fictions in Autobiography: Studies in the Art of Self-Invention,* Linda H. Peterson's *Victorian Autobiography: The Tradition of Self-Interpretation,* and William L. Andrew's *To Tell a Free Story: The First Century of Afro-American Autobiography, 1760–1865.*

6. In a 1984 survey of 115 advanced composition teachers, Priscilla Tate found 40 different titles of "post-freshman" writing courses, excluding advanced composition, journalism, and creative writing courses.

Works Cited

Andrews, William L. *To Tell a Free Story: The First Century of Afro-American Autobiography, 1760–1865*. Urbana: U of Illinois P, 1986.

Baker, Russell. *Growing Up*. New York: Congdon, 1982.

——. "Life with Mother." *Inventing the Truth*. Ed. William Zinsser. Boston: Houghton, 1987. 33–51.

Bloom, Lynn Z. *Fact and Artifact: Writing Nonfiction*. San Diego: Harcourt, 1985.

Bruss, Elizabeth W. *Autobiographical Acts: The Changing Situation of a Literary Genre*. Baltimore: Johns Hopkins UP, 1976.

Corder, Jim W. "Rhetorical Analysis of Writing." *Teaching Composition: Ten Bibliographical Essays*. Ed. Gary Tate. Fort Worth: Texas Christian UP, 1976. 223–40.

Defoe, Daniel. *Robinson Crusoe*. London: W. Taylor, 1719.

Dicks, Bernice W. "State of the Art in Advanced Expository Writing: One Genus, Many Species." *Journal of Advanced Composition* 3 (1982): 172–91.

Dillard, Annie. "To Fashion a Text." *Inventing the Truth*. Ed. William Zinsser. Boston: Houghton, 1987. 54–76.

——*Pilgrim at Tinker Creek*. 1974. New York: Bantam, 1975.

Dobrin, David N. "Is Technical Writing Particularly Objective?" *College English* 47 (1985): 237–51.

Douglass, Frederick. *Life and Times of Frederick Douglass*. 1892. New York: Collier, 1962.

Eakin, Paul John. *Fictions in Autobiography: Studies in the Art of Self-Invention*. Princeton: Princeton UP, 1985.

Gusdorf, Georges. "Conditions and Limits of Autobiography." Trans. James Olney. *Autobiography: Essays Theoretical and Critical*. Ed. James Olney. Princeton: Princeton UP, 1980. 28–48.

Halloran, S. Michael. "The Birth of Molecular Biology: An Essay in the Rhetorical Criticism of Scientific Discourse." *Rhetoric Review* 3 (1984): 70–83.

Hatlen, Burton. "Why Is *The Education of Henry Adams* 'Literature,' While *The Theory of the Leisure Class* Is Not?" *College English* 40 (1979): 665–76.

Holman, C. Hugh, and William Harmon. *A Handbook to Literature*. 5th ed. New York: Macmillan, 1986.

Manly, William Lewis. *Death Valley in '49*. 1894. Ann Arbor: University Microfilms, 1966.

McCarthy, Mary. *Memories of a Catholic Girlhood*. New York: Harcourt, 1957.

McCord, Phyllis Frus. "Reading Nonfiction in Composition Courses: From Theory to Practice." *College English* 47 (1985): 747–62.

Mishler, Elliott G. "Meaning in Context: Is There Any Other Kind?" *Harvard Educational Review* 49 (1979): 1–19.

Peterson, Linda H. *Victorian Autobiography: The Tradition of Self-Interpretation*. New Haven: Yale UP, 1986.

Rygiel, Dennis. "On the Neglect of Twentieth-Century Nonfiction: A Writing Teacher's View." *College English* 46 (1984): 392–400.

Searle, John R. *Speech Acts: An Essay in the Philosophy of Language*. Cambridge: Cambridge UP, 1969.

Tabachnick, Stephen E. "The Problem of Neglected Literature." *College English* 43 (1981): 32–44.

Tate, Priscilla W. Letter to survey respondents (author included). 16 April 1985.

Thomas, Lewis. "A Fear of Pheromones." *The Lives of a Cell: Notes of a Biology Watcher*. 1974. New York: Bantam, 1975. 17–21.

18

Writing Is More Than Words

Olivia Frey
Mary Ellen Ross

The students in Mary Ellen Ross's Psychology of Counseling are watching the stage and taking notes about what they see. They are not watching a play. Two of their classmates are having a mock counseling session. The "client," Tim, speaking out of his real life experiences, says that his mother might have cancer, and he has been under a lot of stress. It has affected his health, his studies, and his emotional well-being. The "counselor," Linda, is trying hard to listen and understand her client's anxiety.

When Ross interrupts the interaction, Tim reports having felt very scattered—as though he had been jumping from topic to topic. She points out that this confusion parallels the confusion he is experiencing in his own life, and so there is an appropriate congruence between what he is feeling and how he is talking about it.

The students then discuss how effective a listener Linda was: "That paraphrase you used in the beginning was really helpful in letting him know you understood what he was talking about." "I was amazed that you could keep everything in mind that he said and go back to each point in turn." They also respond to Tim as "client": "You seemed to become more comfortable as time went on." "I was impressed that you were willing to talk about your fears for your mother."

As a result of their work in the listening lab, Tim, Linda, and others in Psychology of Counseling are on their way to becoming better writers. But what does an activity like this have to do with writing instruction? It is exactly this that we would like to discuss in our essay. After 15 years of Writing across the Curriculum (WAC) at

St. Olaf, many faculty, like Ross, are beginning to see that everything that happens in the classroom has something to do with writing, even if students are not actually putting words on paper. Everything counts, particularly in an upper-level course where advanced writers tend to "play it safe" (Hairston). As Anne Rosenthal says, "writing to learn in a community is more than acquiring an array of genres" (6). Rosenthal takes her cue from Ken Bruffee, who states that writing in a community is the process of becoming a part of a "social context in which students can experience and practice the kinds of conversation valued by... knowledgeable peers" ("Collaborative Learning" 642). In such a community writing is not just tacked on; it is part of the ongoing disciplinary conversation that students have with each other and with their teacher. In this context the writing, all the words, will be more meaningful, and the writing will be more likely to improve.

It would be difficult to initiate such conversations with students if faculty were not talking this way among themselves. At St. Olaf, therefore, we run two types of WAC workshops during the summer, one cross-disciplinary and the other focusing on one discipline. In the single discipline workshops we have retained the core of the model devised by Toby Fulwiler, such as writing groups, but have also added conversation about and exploration of a discipline. Last summer, psychology faculty participated in the workshop, and this summer, biology faculty plan to participate. Realizing that there are a variety of communities that faculty, and students, are members of, we will continue to encourage faculty to take both kinds of WAC workshops. For some faculty, these discussions about their disciplines—with members of their own departments or of other departments—make explicit certain assumptions and methodological frameworks that have remained unspoken for much of their professional lives. The WAC workshops take the first step in creating that community life, or in the case of some departments revitalizing it, and fostering "the sorts of conversation members of the community value" that Bruffee and Rosenthal deem an essential beginning for a community of discourse.

In the psychology WAC workshop last summer, faculty discussed such matters as who psychologists are and what the discipline is about, why psychologists value one method over another, why psychologists write articles the way that they do. At one point, faculty compared Mark Snyder's "The Many Me's of the Self-Monitor" in *Psychology Today* with his very different essay, "On the Nature of Self-Monitoring," co-authored with Steve Gangstad and published in the *Journal of Personality and Social Psychology*. Faculty considered the different writing styles of each as well as reasons the two were so different. Faculty also thought about themselves as psychologists—why they had become interested in psychology, and in teaching, why they did one type of research or study rather than another.

All had answers or at least observations, and everyone was interested in listening to each other. Theirs was the conversation that we think Bruffee is talking about. These faculty left the workshop not only with more ideas about writing in their classes but with a renewed personal interest in their own discipline. They had reminded themselves of why their work matters to them and why they want students to study psychology. They also left with an awareness of what they had *not* been telling their students—about themselves and about the discipline—that perhaps they could start telling them.

Faculty who take the workshops come away with ideas about how to create a disciplinary community and engage their students in the kinds of conversations that they have had with their colleagues during the summer, in effect, raising to a metacognitive level their students' awareness of the discipline, their role in it, and the writing that they do. When the instructor creates the disciplinary context in this way, students will study the content of the discipline as usual but not limit their conversations to these matters. Students will read their textbooks and listen to lectures, but they will also read what is written and hear what is said "between the lines." Students will study processes as well as products. They will study people, human contexts, and methodology as well as facts, data, theories, and reports. Students are, in effect, "reading" their disciplines as "texts," in the poststructuralist sense of the word.[1] From this perspective, a "text" is not only the words on a page but that which is behind, around, and in front of the words—that which is not words.

Before we talk about why students' writing is likely to improve in the disciplinary community, we would like to provide more detail about what such a community might look like. If we look again at Ross's Psychology of Counseling, we will see one teacher's effort to integrate "social symbolic relationships into...teaching" (Bruffee, "Collaborative Learning" 651).

Psychology of Counseling is a 13-week, upper-level psychology course with an approximate enrollment of 24 students. The course components include characteristics of counseling, counseling theories, active listening lab, and topics in therapy. Students attend listening labs, maintain a journal of their thoughts about the various course components, and complete two projects. One project consists of reading a self-help book of their own choosing, on topics such as developing assertiveness, managing their time, or controlling eating disorders, and devising a plan based on the book to follow throughout the term. The second project is a small-group endeavor in which students research a topic, make a class presentation, and turn in a written document. For instance, a group might develop a peer counseling program and write the counselors' manual.

On the first day of class, Ross talks with her students about the course. Some instructors may not reveal their implicit assumptions, either because they themselves are not conscious of them or because they see such information as unnecessary to learning the course content. But Ross tells her students directly, either in her syllabus or in discussions, the various reasons for studying psychology in general and counseling in particular. She shares with her students her own views about how she thinks learning happens, the roles she envisions for her students, as well as her own personal perceptions of the discipline itself. She tells them that she sees psychology not as a body of facts to be mastered but as a continually evolving field that she and her students can join in constructing. She tells them that counseling is not just a repertoire of techniques that therapists call on when talking to their clients. Ross also invites her students to discuss these matters. The message that she hopes to get across is that they are not there necessarily to get the Truth about psychology. They are all in this together, teacher and students, challenging the boundaries of the discipline as well as their own abilities.

Of course, it would not be enough if Ross were only to say these things. She makes a start at creating community on the first day of class, beginning with her encouragement that they learn each other's names. Students discuss the group process for several class periods. She and her students spend time, next, discussing the roles of community members and specific strategies that help a community work. After Ross introduces the concept of class as community, she encourages discussion of how community might enhance the learning experience and what a class as community might look like. Ross particularly stresses the importance of caring, confidentiality, and trust in building community, concepts that are also crucial in counseling. In this instance, the community inside the class parallels the community that students who become psychologists will work to establish "out there" in the world. In addition to discussing these principles of community, students choose partners for their group projects and are encouraged to meet right away to set up a meeting schedule and to consider ideas for projects, even though the group project deadline is 10 weeks away.

The class as a whole is a community within which smaller communities, like the project groups, form. Ross uses collaborative learning in many ways throughout the semester. For example, she frequently uses small-group discussion time to help ease students into a larger discussion. The small groups provide a "holding environment" (Kegan) both for students trying out new ideas and for those trying out new behaviors such as speaking out in class. Used in these ways, collaborative learning becomes more than simply one pedagogical strategy, it becomes an actual *way of being* in a discipline.

Ross demonstrates that she values community by working hard to listen to, respond to, and respect her students when they talk. In the active listening labs, students talk. They listen to each other talking. They critique each other talking and listening. Ross does model critiquing and comments on what she as a therapist thinks about the content and process of the interaction. But she tries to keep students center stage, literally—they are filmed by video cameras and they watch the films. They talk mostly about talking and listening. They are, in effect, deconstructing and reconstructing the practice of counseling—how and when to talk, how and when to listen, how to notice and respond to a listener's nonverbal cues, and so on. By the second week, Ross hopes that she has conveyed the high value she places on students' ideas. She has not begun the course with an overview of theory (the Truth of Counseling) that students study and are tested on. Instead she makes it possible for students to immediately assume the role of counselor or client or observer of the whole process and to construct their own theories of counseling—what makes good talking or bad, good listening or bad. Ross tries to restore the knower immediately to the known (Polanyi). She works to create an environment in which students can collaborate with her to create the content and structure of the course.

Ross also uses journals to show that she listens to students and values their ideas. For years, WAC instructors have been using journals as a valuable tool for teaching writing in all disciplines—as prods to thinking, as "records of thought," as a way of processing the material (Fulwiler). Ross has discovered that journals can also be valuable as a means of creating community, in this instance by bringing students in as collaborators in making meaning.

Using ideas like those devised by Fulwiler and others, Ross asks students to think "out loud" on paper about some aspect of the material that they cover each day. They can pose questions, raise objection, apply the material to their own lives, relate it to ideas encountered in other sources. They use the journals for all aspects of the course—work in class, listening labs, reading, and projects. Ross also asks students to keep process journal entries on their ideas, plans, schedule, and problems as they work on their term projects. These strategies are standard in most WAC courses, but how might they necessarily help in drawing students into the community as collaborators? The way that Ross responds to what they write affirms students' roles as participants in the disciplinary community. Her responses are inquiries or conversation, not corrections or judgments.

Often teachers' comments in journals are points of information. If a student asks a question we often feel compelled to answer. Our answering and information giving are reflexes that are hard to control, based on the theory that knowledge is an objective reality "out there" that we the authorities have mastered and can enable our students to see. The alternative is to admit that we don't always have the answers. In keeping with the ways that she has conceived the class — the roles of her students and her role as well — Ross acknowledges when she is confused or has learned something from a student's remark. She sometimes asks *real* questions, not phony ones of the type that teachers are wont to ask "to get students to think" (but the students know that the teacher really has the answer, so they don't think; they instead try to figure out the "real" answer in the teacher's head). Ross also reveals the process of her own thinking. In these ways and others, she tries to communicate that she is a partner in thinking.

But being a collaborator does not mean that Ross will never challenge her students. She does challenge them, not as a superior or authorty but as equals in terms of their abilities to know and their rights to a place in the disciplinary community. It is true that she might know more about some things, but it is also true that her students know a lot too, and can come to know what she knows. Many will finally know more. What counts is not how much she or anyone else knows but the process of coming to know together. These are the truths of the disciplinary community that depose the Truth of content.

Ross works throughout the course to affirm her students' abilities to know. During the theory unit, she does not treat her students as receptacles that she fills up with facts and definitions. Actually, by the time her students reach the theory unit, they are fairly confident as knowers and thinkers and would probably resist being treated as blank slates anyway. Nevertheless, Ross works to place the students firmly at the center of these discussions. While students are reading and hearing about theories of counseling they are also testing them. Each student chooses a self-help book, such as *Fat Is a Feminist Issue* or *Adult Children of Alcoholics*, a book that they think might be relevant to some problem they are experiencing. They read the book and follow the plan that they have devised for themselves based on the book's suggestions. They chart their progress weekly in the project section of their journals. If more than one student is working on the same topic, Ross will let them know and encourage them to form support groups. When they are finished, they write up a critique of the book in terms of the theories they have been studying and the book's helpfulness to them. Again the students' approach to theory follows the model that Ross has established in every other facet of the course — the discipline is not a body of facts that the students accept unquestioningly but an evolving process, a body of information that changes, a set of methodologies in evolution that the students can question, challenge, adopt, reject, prod, test.

Ross also tells a lot of stories, a pedagogy that few educators have studied or thought very seriously about, although all teachers tell them and enjoy telling them, and all students seem to enjoy listening to them. Of course, it is the kinds of stories she tells that help create community — stories about her personal life that are appropriate, stories about herself as teacher or counselor. In general she wants to communicate to her students that she is human. She mentions times when she has made mistakes. She pokes fun at herself when it is appropriate, although she is not self-effacing. Ross has also returned to school and tells stories about her own problems with writing papers and studying for tests. She also shares what she has learned at professional conferences. There is no more concrete way to demonstrate to her students that learning is a lifelong process than by sharing stories of her own growth and development. Ross also relates her experiences as a counselor or those of other counselors she has known. Her counseling stories provide another view of counseling, more personal than information her students would get from reading a book by and about people they don't know. In addition, Ross is there, and students can interact with her, a real live counselor, in ways that they would not be able to with the author of a book. Such stories and interactions are one more way to deconstruct (or reconstruct) the discipline and to demonstrate that it is people who make psychology or theories of counseling.

The story may also be a particularly appropriate mode in a context that assumes that knowledge is socially constructed rather than a separate objective truth. While the lecture could be considered the mode of the traditional paradigm of knowledge, the story reflects the new paradigm. A story is the knower in the known. A story is both content and construct. That is, the content is as important as the storyteller, the conditions of storytelling, and the listeners. When Ross first started teaching and lectured fairly regularly, she would spend most of her classroom time behind the podium. But when she told a story, she would step around the podium and sit on a desk, a gesture that symbolizes the way that knowing and learning are redefined in the classroom as disciplinary community.

Judging from what we have seen above of Ross's class, it is undeniable that creating a disciplinary community is hard work. Her desk groans under the weight of journals that students turn in every few weeks. Practical concerns are certainly factors in limiting what students and instructors can do. Nevertheless, we share Bruffee's view that what keeps some teachers from redesigning their classes is not just that it seems like so much more work but that the change would violate intransigent educational biases. The theoretical base of most of our courses, of the college curricular structure as a whole, is, as we have suggested, an epistemology that characterizes knowing as viewing or seeing rather than *constructing* or *making*. Bruffee observes:

> According to the social constructionist view, this visual metaphor, inherent and unavoidable in cognitive thought, accounts for the fact that so much of what we normally say about knowledge, scholarship, research, and college or university instruction is confined within a frustrating circularity oscillating betwen "outer" and "inner" poles of "objectivity" and "subjectivity." This polarity of cognitive language derives from the traditional epistemological notion that the human mind is equipped with two working elements, a mirror and an inner eye. The mirror reflects outer reality. The inner eye contemplates that reflection. Reflection and contemplation together are what, from this cognitive point of view, we typically call thought or knowledge. ("Social Construction" 776)

Creating the disciplinary context according to the social constructionist perspective, on the other hand, returns the knower to the known in ways that we have suggested. The meaning of a discipline is no longer conceived of as an objective reality or truth "out there" that students will "see." A discipline becomes a living, evolving community, the meaning of which the students, their teachers, and other participants join in constructing.

We would now like to turn to an explanation of why students might write better when they are members of such a disciplinary community. Part of the answer can be found if we look at the differences between students who learn according to the old paradigm and students who read the disciplinary text. A student who infers that knowledge is "out there" may have trouble reaching it. Such frustration, in turn, means that students may become less interested and less involved in the learning. In such circumstances, knowing too often becomes reduced to just taking a course or doing an assignment. Ann, a student in Nelson and Hayes's recent research study, "How the Writing Context Shapes College Students' Strategies for Writing from Sources," is typical of the kind of student who doesn't get into her research project. Ann's English teacher has assigned an essay on eighteenth-century British drama. At every stage of writing the paper, from choosing the topic to writing her draft, Ann invests very little in her tasks. Using a process of elimination, she chooses the topic that is best covered in the six history books that she skims. She also doesn't write rough drafts or revise. She sits at her typewriter with her sources around her and writes the first and only draft of her paper.

Ann may have designed the writing task the way that she did because of misperceptions about her discipline and what she inferred about her role in it from the day-to-day routine of her courses. That is, her discipline is a finite, objective body of information that experts in the discipline know and that she is supposed to find out. When she receives a research paper assignment, she interprets it as simply "an exercise in correct expression designed to test her skill in retelling information that her reader already knows" (11). Ann is rewarded for doing just that. She receives an A− on her paper, although the experience has been a miserable one for her:

> I don't know why I can never bring myself to write research papers until the last minute; it's not a difficult thing to do; in fact, it's rather easy. Maybe it's because it's boring. I don't mind reading the stuff, or looking it up either; I just hate writing it down. It's so damn tedious. I can never keep a good train of thought because it's not coming from me or my thoughts; it's coming from some book and all I'm doing is regurgitating information that the teacher already knows. So why bother? I know how to use the Engilsh language (better than most people), I know how to write, I know how to look up information, I'm not interested in any of the topics the teacher gives us, he's read everything there is to read in the library, so why the hell do we have to do this dumb paper when all it is is busy work! (10)

According to Ann, the teacher has "read everything there is to read in the library." For Ann, knowing is reading texts and mastering information, not reading the text of the discipline.

The example of Ann should suggest the link between creating the disciplinary context—where students "read" the disciplinary "text"—and the improvement of writing. An oversimplified but not completely false way of explaining how all of this happens together is to say that when students study the text of the discipline, that is, reconceptualize knowing, and do not simply attempt to master content, the level of thought and discourse naturally rises. But if the level of discourse is raised, will the students naturally follow? Faigley and Hansen in "Learning to Write in the Social Sciences," suggest that students, at least some students, might not. In this study, Kathy still was not writing, or thinking, like a research psychologist by the end of the course, in spite of the fact that the language and content in Psychology 458, Experimental Psychology, were at a very high level, at least as far as we can tell from Faigley and Hansen's description:

> The course was taught largely through discussion of. . .four required experiments. Each experiment dealt with different problems and constructs to be investigated; each had a different design and called for the application of different statistical tests; and each required the student to make justifiable inferences to explain results. Learning to write a report of a psychological experiment was not simply a matter of mastering a four-part organization and the appropriate jargon and style; students also had to learn how to formulate hypotheses, to design ways to verify or reject hypotheses, and to choose and interpret the results of statistical tests. (142)

Although it is one crucial aspect of engaging students in disciplinary conversations, raising the level of discourse in a class, by itself, will not create the disciplinary context nor, in turn, guarantee that students will mature as writers.

It might be valuable for a moment to shift our focus from the class community to the act of writing, particularly to *advanced writing*.[2] If we do this, we will see some interesting parallels between writing and reading the disciplinary text. The student who reads the disciplinary text thinks about knowledge and goes about knowing similarly to an advanced writer thinking about writing and going about writing. First, a student who reads the disciplinary text does not think of knowing the discipline as only mastering a finite body of information. Neither does the advanced writer think of writing as only following the rules or mastering a body of writing skills. Second, a student who reads the disciplinary text attends as much to methodology, context, and processes as to facts or data. Similarly, the advanced writer attends to context — purpose, audience, and the like — and is conscious not only of what she is doing but how she is doing it, that is, process. Third, a student who reads the disciplinary text is not outside looking in or looking at, but firmly at the center of the disciplinary community making meaning. Again, the advanced writer is at the center of the writing, and her process is "knowledge transforming" rather than "knowledge telling" (Scardamalia and Bereiter).

Nevertheless, these connections may not help us to see why creating the disciplinary context will necessarily *make* better writers. It may simply reinforce what we already know, that is, that writing is closely akin to thinking and that thoughtful students will also, probably, be good writers, and vice versa. Of course, nothing is guaranteed to make advanced writers because writing is a complex task, and the factors influencing each stage of it are "numerous and complex" (Nelson and Hayes 18). Nevertheless, we assume with Nelson and Hayes that "teachers play a powerful role in determining how students interpret and respond to assignments" (18). By extension, we assume that while the teacher and classroom context may not guarantee exceptional writing performance, they can be significant factors in influencing a student's writing ability.

How creating the disciplinary context and bringing students into this community might affect writing ability can be seen if we note the features of what Nelson and Hayes term "high-investment writing situations," which contrast strikingly with the features of Ann's writing situations. In their study, high-investment writing situations were those conditions that, in general, encouraged students "to make writing a meaningful activity that promoted learning and student involvement" (19). Students in low-investment situations were those students, like

Ann, who saw writing as primarily busy work and regurgitation of someone else's ideas. Students in high-investment situations, on the other hand, had a personal interest in the writing. Their goal was not simply to reproduce information but to transform it. They wrote with a sense of purpose and audience. For these high-investment students writing was meaningful and satisfying.

Nelson and Hayes delineated four characteristics of a writing situation that they found to encourage high-investment strategies.

1. Providing immediate feedback.

2. Focusing on high level goals. [These include encouraging students to transform knowledge rather than simply tell it or reproduce it. Such a condition would require teachers "to give up their roles as 'examiners' who are looking only for errors in form and content," and, instead, assume the role of collaborator. It would also require that teachers "convince students that they value original thinking."]

3. Providing an audience other than the teacher.

4. Getting writers started early. (19–20)

By creating the disciplinary context as Ross has done, enabling students to be in the discipline, a teacher fosters the conditions requisite for high-investment writing strategies for research papers. In other words, when a teacher structures a research assignment that will elicit high-investment strategies, she is doing the same kinds of things that are involved in creating the disciplinary context.

Consider Ross's class again. Students and faculty who are colleagues in a disciplinary community work together rather than in isolation, and so immediate and constant feedback are inevitable. By joining in the community in this way, too, the instructor is less examiner than collaborator. Such projects under such conditions also mean that students cannot help but think in terms of community or colleagues, that is, audience. In fact, Ross urges her students to consider a variety of audiences—those who will hear their oral presentations and those for whom their projects will be written—and how projects will differ as a response to the various needs of their audiences. These different audiences are real to the students, not an abstract principle of writing. Writers will also get started early, because most of what happens in the course will help students shape their projects. Work in a disciplinary community resists fragmentation of the sort common in a traditional curriculum ("We've just talked about Faulkner's 'The Bear' in class, and this afternoon I'm going to start my research paper on AIDS."). Finally, and most importantly, because of the way that it reconceptualizes knowledge and knowing, the course as disciplinary community will engage the student in making meaning, a stance that inherently requires original thinking and active participation. If the conditions of a writing assignment that Hayes and Nelson outline seem to be successful in encouraging high-investment research paper writing, then it would seem to follow logically that a whole course, like Ross's, that creates such condition would have a similar sort of impact on student writing.

Nelson and Hayes suggest how the disciplinary community might help all writers advance. Such a disciplinary context might also be effective in encouraging the growth of our best writers, who frequently reach a plateau and then stall. Maxine Hairston writes that advanced writers will even resist change that might lead to growth because of fear of failure. According to Hairston, while many advanced students get high grades on their papers, their writing rarely evidences genuine improvement from assignment to assignment. What these writers have actually become good at is manipulating the forms. But these forms have remained merely formulas. Hairston suggests that students put on such rhetorical "masks" because they have been "taught" to do so, just as Ann inferred that writing a research paper meant spitting back information to a teacher who had "read everything." Although, again, there are no guarantees, creating a disciplinary community and disciplinary context will allow the student to approach the community and its discourse in a new, more authentic way.

The disciplinary community may ensure a more authentic approach to its discourse, first, by virtue of the fact that it is a community. Hairston has suggested that the advanced students who merely imitate forms are less interested in communicating than they are in sounding like professionals. But the classroom as community requires communication to sustain it — the members will demand it. If students don rhetorical masks at first, some will eventually throw them off. And if these masks are also "barriers. . .to keep from exposing the vulnerable real self" (Hairston 199), the deep connections that naturally form in a community of knowers will provide the safety and support for students to throw off the mask and write an "authentic voice".

Writing may become more authentic within a disciplinary community, and subsequently improve, in a second way. When students become members of a disciplinary community and become part of the process of questioning and discovery, the discipline itself is demystified. When the discipline is "out there," the language will be obscure. When the discipline is accessible, the language will be too. It sounds like magic. But to paraphrase Donald Murray, magic isn't magic either. The process is more like this. A student's first words in a community will be her own. She will be conversing daily with her peers about the ideas of the discipline, but in her own language. In the community, her teacher and her peers will affirm this use. The student then gains confidence in her own thinking about the discipline and in her own voice saying things about the discipline. This is an essential step in the process of learning to converse using the language of the discipline. Without affirmation at these early stages, we think it unlikely that the student will be able to converse confidently in the discourse of the discipline.

While students are conversing with each other and with their teacher, they will frequently hear and will themselves attempt to use the language unique to that community. Their first attempts will be tentative, much like a child's first steps or first experiments with language. The same sorts of interaction would be needed at this stage between student and teacher as between parent and child — not scolding and correction (i.e., papers marked up with red ink), but guidance and affirmation. If a child is corrected too often, she stops talking. If a student fails too often, she will revert to safe formulas. But with guidance from the teacher, students will work together to decode the language of the discipline, affirming each other's successes and encouraging each other when more precision is needed.

There might be some kind of fleeting satisfaction in being able to say that students' writing in Ross's class, because she works to create the disciplinary community, is better than the writing of any other students at St. Olaf. We can't prove this, not only because we don't have the data, but because, again, the factors that influence student writing are so various. And Ross accepts that her stratagies will not always work. Sometimes, some students, for developmental reasons, are miserable in small groups. Gender or learning style may determine whether or not some students are comfortable working alone or in a group. Nevertheless, Ross believes that her restructured courses work more often for more students than when she taught using traditional lectures and tests. More students get into what they are doing. Ross recalls the time when five of her students stood at her office door to turn in their final project, a manual for peer counselors. The students could barely suppress their excitement.

"We wanted to turn in our written project," Karin said as Christi handed Ross a pamphlet-sized document.

As Ross took the pamphlet from Christi, the whole group seemed to be holding its collective breath.

"This looks professional," she said, "I'm impressed. It looks like a pamphlet I might find in a counseling or doctor's office."

The students breathed again, grinned, and all talked at once.

"We all wanted to be here when we turned it in."

"It's done and I'm so proud of it."

"We were thinking of seeing if the Counseling Center might want copies."

As the rest walked off down the hall, Karin lingered. Ross said to her, waving the pamphlet, "It seems as though it's hard for you to leave this."

Karin looked thoughtful, and then said, "Yea. It's not like turning in just a regular term paper. This was special. It felt important, and it was fun."

Within the environment of the disciplinary community, the documents that students write are "important." Their writing is meaningful, and the documents sound authentic. They *are* authentic, or "professional," as Ross commented to Christi. That is, the voices that we hear when we read some of these documents are of writers who are serious, who know why they are writing, who want to write and share; writers who love their work in psychology and who want to continue when they leave St. Olaf. Creating the disciplinary community does bring at least some part of the discipline to life for all students, helping their writing to improve in the process.

One might respond that, of course, it's easy to create the disciplinary context with a discipline like counseling, because counseling is something that we do. But isn't history something that we do or make? and literary criticism? Not that we *do* these things in the sense of technical training or pre-professional preparation; but *do* in the sense of *make* or *create* or *transform*. When teachers have time, in the summer or on sabbatical, we immediately stop reading and talking about these things—reporting what others have done. We do them ourselves. Imagine doing history or biology, not just during stolen moments during vacations or in the summer but with our students, all year.

Notes

1. Paul Hernadi writes that "speech and writing...closely link discourse to doing and making" (749). Louise Z. Smith makes similar points in her argument that English departments should "house" WAC. Her view is that "the literary/non-literary distinction is collapsing as the secular branch of post-structuralist theory places all texts within 'the world' of history, culture and science." It follows naturally, then, she writes, that "English departments, relatively conversant with modes of textual analysis, can play a valuable role in theoretical dialogues—and their pedagogical ramifications—across the curriculum" (392–93). Social constructionist Clifford Geertz writes of "textual study" of "act[s] or institution[s]." He calls that which is written between the lines in a disciplinary "text" its "semiotic connections." These include "the relationship of [the social text's] parts to one another; the relation of it to others culturally or historically associated with it; the relation of it to those who in some sense construct it; and the relation of it to realities conceived as lying outside of it" (32). Also see Edward M. White.

2. We realize that there is considerable disagreement about exactly what

constitutes advanced writing and when and how to introduce these skills to students. Such disagreement is attested to by the existence of this very volume of essays. Nevertheless, we more or less agree with Michael Carter, in his essay for this volume, when he defines advanced writing in terms of expertise, "the movement from a dependence on rules to guide behavior to a dependence on the 'intuition' founded on experience within a particular domain."At the same time, we would agree with Mike Rose that it is pedagogically dangerous to oversimplify cognition and doom our students to a rigidly linear process of instruction in writing, which the notion of expertise to some extent depends on. We would like to sidestep the whole issue, conveniently, by assuming that so-called advanced writing comprises the sorts of abilities that we hope to foster in all of our students, whether they are in basic or advanced courses. Also see Gould and Heyda and Branscombe and Heath for similar warnings against the "cognitive reductionism" that Rose discusses.

Works Cited

Branscombe, Amanda, and Shirley Brice Heath. "'Intelligent Writing' in an Audience Community: Teacher, Students, and Researcher." *The Acquisition of Written Language: Response and Revision.* Ed. Sarah Warshauer Freedman. Norwood, NJ: Ablex, 1985. 3−32.

Bruffee, Kenneth A. "Collaborative Learning and the 'Conversation of Mankind.'" *College English* 46 (1984): 635−52.

——. "Social Construction, Language, and the Authority of Knowledge: A Bibliographical Essay." *College English* 48 (1986): 773−90.

Faigley, Lester, and Kristine Hansen. "Learning to Write in the Social Sciences." *College Composition and Communication* 36 (1985): 140−49.

Fulwiler, Toby. "The Personal Connection: Journal Writing across the Curriculum." *Language Connections: Writing and Reading across the Curriculum.* Ed. Toby Fulwiler and Art Young. Urbana: NCTE, 1982. 15−31.

Geertz, Clifford. *Local Knowledge.* New York: Basic, 1983.

Gould, Christopher, and John Heyda. "Literacy Education and the Basic Writer: A Survey of College Composition Courses." *Journal of Basic Writing* 5 (1986): 8−27.

Hairston, Maxine. "Working with Advanced Writers." *College Composition and Communication* 35 (1984): 196−208.

Hernadi, Paul. "Doing, Making, Meaning: Toward a Theory of Verbal Practice." *PMLA* 103 (1988): 749−58.

Kegan, R. *The Evolving Self: Problem and Process in Human Development.* Cambridge: Harvard UP, 1982.

Murray, Donald. *A Writer Teaches Writing.* 2nd ed. Boston: Houghton, 1985.

Nelson, Jennie, and John R. Hayes. "How the Writing Context Shapes College Students' Strategies for Writing from Sources." Center for the Study of Writing, August 1988. Technical Report No. 16.

A Variety of Course Structures

Polanyi, Michael. *Personal Knowledge*. Chicago: U of Chicago P, 1958.

Rose, Mike. "Narrowing the Mind and Page: Remedial Writers and Cognitive Reductionism." *College Composition and Communication* 39 (1988): 267–302.

Rosenthal, Anne. "Writing to Learn in a Community: Engaging Students in Scholarly Conversations." Annual Meeting of the Midwest/Modern Language Association. St. Louis, Nov. 1985.

Scardamalia, M., and C. Bereiter. "Knowledge Telling and Knowledge Transforming in Written Composition." *Advances in Applied Psycholinguistics*. Vol.1. Ed. S. Rosenberg. New York: Cambridge UP, in press.

Smith, Louise Z. "Why English Departments Should 'House' Writing Across the Curriculum." *College English* 50 (1988): 390–95.

Snyder, Mark, and Steve Gangestad. "On the Nature of Self-Monitoring: Matters of Assessment, Matters of Validity." *Journal of Personality and Social Psychology* 51 (1986): 125–39.

Snyder, Mark. "The Many Me's of the Self-Monitor." *Psychology Today* March 1980: 33–40, 92.

White, Edward M. "Post-Structural Literary Criticism and the Response to Student Writing." *College Composition and Communication* 35 (1984): 186–95.

Afterword

Needed Scholarship in Advanced Composition

Gary A. Olson

Periodically, we in advanced composition attempt to assess our field, survey and analyze the recent scholarship, and suggest what work needs to be done. Perhaps the two best-known of these assessments are Rita Sturm's "Advanced Composition, 1980: The State of the Art" and Bernice W. Dicks's "State of the Art in Advanced Expository Writing: One Genus, Many Species." Sturm's article, published in 1980, is an "intentionally impressionistic" review of "trends and concerns" in advanced composition and is based on information gathered from three sources: data "listed on about 200 membership applications to the Association of Teachers of Advanced Composition (ATAC); more than 300 syllabi, course descriptions, and letters voluntarily contributed to ATAC's information file; and an uncounted number of personal discussions with colleagues throughout the country" (37). Dicks's essay, published two years later, is a survey of conference presentations and published articles on advanced composition since 1954.

Rather than survey scholarship published since Dicks's article, I'd like to speak as editor of the *Journal of Advanced Composition* — as someone who has the interesting and often frustrating task of reading and evaluating much of the work on advanced composition, not only articles published in JAC but hundreds of submitted manuscripts that, for one reason or another, are never published. From this perspective I'd like to make a few suggestions about scholarship needed in the field.

Many writers define *advanced composition* broadly: all writing above the freshman level, including advanced expository writing, business and technical communication, and writing across the curriculum. However, for the purpose of this discussion, I'll focus on only two of these areas: the kind of general, theoretical essays that are likely to interest advanced composition teachers; and articles concerning advanced expository writing—the course many of us think of when we hear the term *advanced composition.*

While many of us *do* equate advanced composition with advanced expository writing, the consensus ends there. Both Sturm and Dicks point out that the history of advanced composition has been a struggle to define *advanced composition* and even *advanced* itself. For example, Dicks reports that a workshop at the 1963 convention of the Conference on College Composition and Communication attempted to define the course,

> only to report—predictably—that there was no agreement on "what Advanced Composition should be, or is" or the "objectives..., the content, the order of topics, the number or length of essays, the emphasis various factors in composition should get, or what related material to bring in." (174)

I see no indication that these problems of definition and identity are any closer to resolution than they were in 1982, when Dicks was writing. In fact, except for an occasional article, scholars seem to have ignored, or forgotten, or evaded the subject. Even William A. Covino's award-winning essay, "Defining Advanced Composition: Contributions from the History of Rhetoric," does not resolve any of these pressing questions, other than to suggest that advanced writers should avoid certainty in their thinking and writing and seek the problematic and an understanding of multiple perspectives.[1]

Notwithstanding Covino's sensible advice to avoid certainty (and the stagnation that accompanies it), I do believe that *some* consensus about advanced composition would help us feel that we have a common purpose, a shared identity. Such an identity would certainly prove useful when we must convince chairs and deans to implement new courses, lower course enrollment levels, and so on. Yet, despite the ongoing need for such fundamental work, many of the same questions that Sturm and Dicks asked are still unanswered today. What does *advanced* mean? Does it refer to a level of writing proficiency or the placement of a course in an institution's curriculum? That is, what makes advanced composition different from freshman English—the kind of instruction or the kind of student? (Let's not lose sight of the fact that at some institutions *advanced composition* is a kind of re-medial course designed to assist those who did not reach acceptable levels of writing proficiency in freshman English.) What should the course look like? Should it be an intensive immersion in rhetoric and the subtleties of style? Should it be a course in argumentation or critical thinking? Should it prepare students to write academic discourse or the kind of practical writing directly applicable to the workplace? Where does the advanced course fit in the curricular sequence? Should it be a junior-or senior-level course? How is it different from graduate-level writing courses? Should there be prerequisites? Should enrollment be limited?

Sturm's conclusion in 1980 is just as applicable today:

> We need dialogue and research in many areas, but most urgently we need to address the following:
>
> - an updated set of guidelines
> - a sharper delineation of the level of writing implied by the title "advanced"
> - the sequencing of writing courses
> - the reasons for the new student interest in advanced writing
> - the curricula most likely to prepare students for the writing requirements in specific professions
> - the career writing opportunities in specific professions (42–43)

How we address these kinds of issues, though, is important. In the past, researchers have tended to rely on questionnaire surveys and descriptive methodologies.[2] I believe it is time to transcend this data-gathering mode and attempt to establish a firm theoretical rationale for advanced composition. Perhaps one reason we are experiencing such difficulty in defining advanced composition is that we have a course but no clearly articulated theoretical/pedagogical reason for its existence. We should, however, be able to draw on the vast body of general composition theory and research to develop a coherent, reasonable rationale for advanced composition, establishing its purpose and objectives. With such a rationale in hand, it will be much easier to devise effective curricula and pedagogies because we will know where we want to go and why. In 1984, long after writing centers were firmly ensconced in universities and peer tutoring had become an accepted practice, Kenneth Bruffee set out to establish a theoretical rationale for peer tutoring and writing centers; we need someone to do the same for advanced composition.[3]

A coherent theoretical rationale for advanced composition will pave the way for numerous other articles, particularly those exploring pedagogical applications. Certainly, we're all interested in articles in which the author clearly demonstrates how such practices derive from current theory and research and how they can be applied to the advanced composition classroom in general. Once we establish a solid theoretical rationale for advanced composition and then define it and its goals, we will be able to devise reasonable, effective pedagogies for advanced courses.

Undoubtedly, teachers and scholars of advanced composition are also interested in general theoretical articles relevant to rhetoric and composition as a field because such work often has direct bearing on advanced writing instruction. Especially needed are essays on ideology, gender, social constructionism, cultural criticism, liberatory pedagogies, and applications of poststructuralist critical theory to rhetoric and composition. Such topics are of immediate interest because they are among the subjects shaping composition theory today and because there is a great deal that we don't know about them. What role does ideology play in learning to write? What role does ideology play in the profession, in the kind of scholarship we choose to engage in, and in the kind of scholarship that gets published (and doesn't)?

What role does gender play in the advanced composition classroom? Is gender a significant factor in the social dynamics of small groups? If knowledge is socially constructed, what effect does gender have on the knowledge that *is* created? Should composition classes, especially advanced classes, teach students to become "cultural critics"?[4] That is, in teaching students to become critical thinkers, shouldn't we (as Evelyn Ashton-Jones and I suggest in another chapter of this book) go beyond instruction in logic to teach students how to explore the role of *context* in the making of meaning? In fact, is our concept of critical thinking a limited one? Exactly what is *critical literacy,* and what is our role in helping advanced students develop it? Are Paulo Freire's ideas of critical literacy relevant to advanced composition instruction in the 1990s? In what ways? What modifications are necessary? Why?

And what about the proliferation of poststructuralist approaches to critical theory? What applications do these theories have to rhetoric and composition and to advanced writing instruction? Is reader-response criticism really relevant to composition classes? What *are* the reading/writing connections that should be made in an advanced composition class? Why? What does deconstruction have to offer to composition theory or to composition pedagogy?[5] Will deconstructive techniques help students become better thinkers? Better writers?[6]

Certainly, these are only a few of the concerns that interest teachers and scholars of advanced composition. I haven't even mentioned articles that examine the relevance of classical rhetoric or the nature of the essay or the field as a whole. My real purpose here is to encourage readers to investigate, to ask questions, to avoid the type of closure and certainty that Covino warns of. Whether discussing composition theory in general or advanced writing in particular, we will thus be able to join and shape the vital conversation that essays such as those appearing in this collection initiate and that journals such as *College Composition and Communication* and the *Journal of Advanced Composition* sustain from issue to issue. This conversation is important not only for advanced composition but for the present and future of composition studies.

Notes

1. Covino's article won Honorable Mention in the first annual James L. Kinneavy Award for the most outstanding article in the *Journal of Advanced Composition.*

2. The most recent example is a report by Shumaker, et al. appearing in the *Journal of Advanced Composition.*

3. Bruffee's original article, "Peer Tutoring and the 'Conversation of Mankind,'" was published in *Writing Centers: Theory and Administration.* A slightly revised and more well-known, version, "Collaborative Learning and the 'Conversation of Mankind,'" appeared later the same year in *College English.*

4. Bizzell discusses cultural criticism as it applies to scholarship in the field, but what about attempts to introduce such an approach into the classroom?

5. Apparently, deconstruction has much to offers. JAC's interview with Jacques Derrida indicates that deconstruction potentially can enrich both composition theory and pedagogy.

6. Reed Way Dasenbrock's article "Becoming Aware of the Myth of Presence" is a good example of an application of Jacques Derrida's work to composition theory and pedagogy. Dasenbrock's article won the first annual James L. Kinneavy Award for the most outstanding article in the *Journal of Advanced Composition.*

Works Cited

Bizzell, Patricia. "'Cultural Criticism': A Social Approach to Studying Writing." *Rhetoric Review* 7 (1989): 224–30.

Bruffee, Kenneth A. "Collaborative Learning and the 'Conversation of Mankind.'" *College English* 46 (1984): 635–52.

——. "Peer Tutoring and the 'Conversation of Mankind.'" *Writing Centers: Theory and Administration.* Ed. Gary A. Olson. Urbana: NCTE, 1984. 3–15.

Covino, William A. "Defining Advanced Composition: Contributions from the History of Rhetoric." *Journal of Advanced Composition* 8 (1988): 113–22.

Dasenbrock, Reed Way. "Becoming Aware of the Myth of Presence." *Journal of Advanced Compositon* (1988): 1–11.

Derrida, Jacques. "Jacques Derrida on Rhetoric and Composition: A Conversation." By Gary A. Olson. *Journal of Advanced Composition* 10 (1990): 1–21.

Dicks, Bernice W. "State of the Art in Advanced Expository Writing: One

Genus, Many Species." *Journal of Advance Composition* 3 (1982): 172–91.

Shumaker, Ronald C., Larry Dennis, and Lois Green. "Advanced Exposition: A Survey of Patterns and Problems." *Journal of Advanced Composition* 10 (1990): 136–44.

Sturm, Rita. "Advanced Composition, 1980: The State of the Art." *Journal of Advanced Composition* 1 (1980): 37–43.

Bibliography of Articles
Concerning Advanced Composition

Katherine H. Adams
John L. Adams

As many authors in this collection have noted, less research has been done on advanced composition than on other parts of the writing curriculum, and several of the best essays are available only as ERIC documents. This annotated bibliography is not exhaustive, but it does contain the research—including surveys and definitions and practical advice on specific course structures—that we have found most helpful in shaping our advanced classes.

Beck, James P. "'Advanced Composition' and Occasion-Sensitivity." *Journal of Advanced Composition* 2 (1981): 79–88.

Beck claims that because of its importance in real world writing, occasion sensitivity should be emphasized in advanced composition classes. The essay provides assignments requiring students to analyze and write for some audience other than their teachers.

Bisson, Lillian M. "From Composition to Career: Sequential Assignments for Professional Writing." Conference on College Composition and Communication. Dallas, March 1981. ERIC, 1981. ED 202026.

Bisson notes that when many students move from personal writing to research, what they have learned about good prose seems to disappear. They write prepackaged sentences, approach assignments aimlessly, and frequently turn in essays with no clear thesis. She then describes an excellent way to help writers bridge the gap between writer-based and reader-based prose: a four-part writing cycle consisting of (1) freewriting on the topic, (2) a long paragraph on the subject stemming exclusively from personal experience, (3) a short essay incorporating outside data for a general audience, and (4) a structured report for a specialized audience using sources from a particular field along with the more general sources previously used. Throughout the article, Bisson includes many specific suggestions for making self-discovery a part of career-related assignments.

Bloom, Lynn Z. "Diving into the Mainstream: Configurations of Advanced Composition." Conference on College Composition and Communication. New York, March 1984. ERIC, 1984. ED 243114.

Referring to Bernice Dicks's survey about advanced composition (article annotated here), Bloom notes the vast range of subject matter taught in advanced classes. She then notes that most advanced composition teachers implicitly agree that their students (1) will be competent writers and revisers at the end of the course, (2) will be conscious stylists, (3) will know the norms of discourse in their disciplines, and (4) will treat writing as a serious, meaningful activity and "treat their audiences with respect."

Christensen Francis. "The Course in Advanced Composition for Teachers." *College Composition and Communication* 24 (1973): 163–70.

Christensen notes the obvious importance of courses in composition for teachers, discusses "Guidelines for the Preparation of Teachers of English" (in College Composition and Communication *and* College English, *October 1967), and then describes what he considers minimal composition training for English teachers: a course in grammar and one in composition that includes instruction in both rhetoric and factual and imaginative writing.*

Clark, Wilma. "Writing for Publication in an Advanced Course for Undergraduates." *Journal of Advanced Composition* 3 (1982): 24–36.

Students in Clark's advanced class submitted essays to an editor of the Milwaukee Journal *Sunday supplement, who later visited the class to discuss each work. The students revised well for style but encountered problems with global revision, especially rewriting to reach a particular audience. Clack explains how students in such a course must learn to continue developing an essay while delaying closure.*

Covino, William L. "Defining Advanced Composition: Contributions from the History of Rhetoric." *Journal of Advanced Composition* 8 (1988): 113–22.

Covino contends that advanced composition pedagogy usually mirrors the ideas of Peter Ramus, Francis Bacon, Hugh Blair, and others who associated intellectual maturity with consistency, certainty, and resolution. He offers that advanced classes should focus on persistent questioning and uncertainty, qualities that Plato, Aristotle, and Cicero considered the mark of an advanced rhetor.

Dicks, Bernice W. "State of the Art in Advanced Expository Writing: One Genus, Many Species." *Journal of Advanced Composition* 3 (1982): 172–91.

An excellent source for those interested in the variety of texts, content, pedagogy, and teacher training methods for advanced composition classes, Dicks's article summarizes reports from various CCCC workshops, articles on the subject in College English *and* College Composition and Communication, *and results from her 1979 questionnaire. Her bibliography is one of the best for locating additional advanced composition materials.*

Fulkerson, Richard. "Some Theoretical Speculations on the Advanced Composition Curriculum." *Journal of Advanced Composition* 1 (1980): 9–12.

Using a model similar to M. H. Abrams's four-part structure for literary studies, Fulkerson claims that we judge all writing primarily from one of these perspectives: expressive, rhetorical, formalist, or mimetic. For applications of the model, he suggests that advanced composition teachers might (1) design a course on each theory of discourse, (2) divide one course into the four parts, and/or (3) become more aware of their preferences in evaluating prose.

Gebhardt, Richard. "The Subject Is Writing." *Journal of Advanced Composition* 1 (1980): 13–17.

This article recommends writing itself as the subject of advanced composition students' essays. Gebhardt provides a useful list of books, articles, and assignments for teaching such a course to future writing teachers or professional writers.

Griffin, C. W. "Writing-across-the-Curriculum Programs: Theory and Practice, a Selected Bibliography." *Journal of Advanced Composition* 4 (1983): 161–72.

Griffin provides an annotated bibliography for theories behind writing-across-the-curriculum programs and implementation of those theories at various colleges and universities.

"Guidelines and Directions for College Courses in Advanced Composition." *College Composition and Communication* 28 (1967): 266–68.

Participants from CCCC workshops in 1966 and 1967 report on advanced composition's definition, variety and focus, emphasis, content, instructor qualifications, and modes of instruction. Among other interesting assertions, they contend that "the primary content of any advanced writing course is the writing itself" and that advanced composition courses "must be staffed with at least the same care used to staff advanced courses in literature."

Hagaman, John. "Encouraging Thoughtful Revision in a Kinneavy-Framed Advanced Composition Course." Annual Meeting of the New York College English Association Conference. Saratoga Springs, NY, October 1980. ERIC, 1980. ED 196040.

Hagaman describes his course based on Kinneavy's ideas in A Theory of Discourse. *With each assignment, a peer group provides descriptive and evaluative information about various writing features by using instructor-designed continuum scales. Hagaman includes sample scales for expressive, referential, and persuasive discourse.*

Hairston, Maxine. "Working with Advanced Writers." *College Composition and Communication* 35 (1984): 196–208.

In this important analysis, Hairston lists frequent writing problems of advanced writers and discusses possible reasons for them, showing how teachers often encourage students to write wordy, inflated, and lifeless prose. Then, using Maslow's self-actualization theories, she recommends workshop methods and grading techniques that can help students break away from no-risk formulas.

Hammond, Eugene. "Freshman Composition—Junior Composition: Does Coordination Mean Sub-ordination?" *College Composition and Communication* 35 (1984): 217–21.

Discussing overlap between freshman and advanced courses, Hammond argues that freshman teachers should not hold back information because it will be covered in a junior course. He cites students' need for writing practice to explain how freshman and advanced courses can have similar goals and assignments without the risk of needless repetition.

Hogan, Michael P. "Advanced Composition: A Survey." *Journal of Advanced Composition* 1 (1980): 21–29.

Examining teachers' views on advanced composition guidelines set forth at CCCC workshops in 1966 and 1967, Hogan provides revealing data about the variety of theory and pedagogy in advanced courses in 1979.

Jenseth, Richard. "Assignment Sequencing in Advanced Composition." *The ATAC Newsletter* 1 (1989): 10–11.

Drawing on William Coles and Walker Gibson's work on assignment sequencing for freshman composition, Jenseth describes the more complex and challenging sequences appropriate to the advanced course.

Laban, Lawrence F. "Maximizing Student Alternatives: A Variable-Credit Advanced Composition Course." Conference on College Composition and Communication. Kansas City, MO, March 1977. ERIC 1977. ED 147848.

Laban describes a variable credit course designed to efficiently help non-English majors with specific writing tasks.

Larson, Richard. "A Special Course in Advanced Composition for Prospective Teachers." *The Journal of Teacher Education* 20 (1969): 168–74.

Larson argues for a special advanced composition course primarily for teachers and discusses features, such as an emphasis on rhetorical theory, that the course should include.

Moore, Leslie, and Linda Peterson. "Convention as Transition: Linking the Advanced Composition Course to the College Curriculum." *Journal of Advanced Composition* 4 (1983): 173–87.

Moore and Peterson contend that English teachers, frequently concerned with the conventions of various literary forms, can help students in other disciplines learn about and use the conventions in various fields. Emphasizing three relationships important in most conventions—writer and reader, writer and writers, and writer and field of discourse—the authors explain how they taught a freshman writing-across-the-curriculum course dealing with the written discourse of five other disciplines. Their explanation includes worthwhile suggestions about involving colleagues from other departments in such classes.

Olson, Gary A. "Incorporating Sentence Combining into the Advanced Composition Class." *Journal of Advanced Composition* 2 (1981): 119–26.

Arguing against the assumption that sentence combining helps only lower-level writers, Olson explains how his advanced students use combining and then discusses their improvement.

Pelz, Karen. "James Britton and the Pedagogy of Advanced Composition." *Journal of Advanced Composition* 3 (1982): 1–9.

For advanced composition classes, Pelz recommends more expressive writing—exploratory writing that is close to the self. She then suggests helpful pedagogy and lists appropriate assignments from Ken Macrorie, Gene Krupa, and others.

Ronald, Kate. "The Politics of Teaching Professional Writing." *Journal of Advanced Composition* 7 (1987): 23–30.

Concerned that students in professional writing classes may learn only how to follow formats, Ronald argues that they will know more about the roles, rhetoric, and values of their professions if they use what James Britton calls the "spectator's stance" to analyze and write about works in their fields.

Shumaker, Arthur W. "How Can a Major in Composition Be Established?" *Journal of Advanced Composition* 2 (1981): 139–46.

Shumaker explains in detail the composition major at Depauw University, lists some advantages and disadvantages of such a program, and provides suggestions for establishing a major at other schools.

Singley, Carol J., and Kathryn B. Stockton. "Merging Discovery and Control: New Approaches to Persuasion and Argumentation." Penn State Conference on Rhetoric and Composition. University Park, PA, 1984. ERIC, 1984. ED 264554.

The authors describe an advanced composition course at Brown in which students begin the course writing assignments that are related to the control-end of the continuum (i.e., advertisements) and proceed toward essays related more closely to discovery (i.e., philosophical writings). The course appears to be a viable model for those who feel that discovery in argumentation should be more than merely searching for techniques to manipulate the audience effectively.

Stewart, Donald C. "An Advanced Composition Course that Works." *College Composition and Communication* 25 (1974): 197–200.

This advanced composition class offers the wide range of students four different options for the types of papers to write. The author also notes books and essays on composition that all of his students read and discuss.

Stewart, Donald C. "Practical Work for Advanced Composition Students." *College Composition and Communication* 31 (1980): 81–83.

Stewart explains how his advanced composition students grade essays from his freshman writers. He claims that both groups benefit from having a real audience and that the advanced students, mostly education majors, sharpen their evaluative skills.

Snyder, Carol. "Analyzing Classifications: Foucault for Advanced Writers." *College Composition and Communication* 35 (1984): 209–16.

Snyder shows how classifications shape thought, criticizes the standard restate-the-distinctions classification assignment, and provides an invention method enabling students to explore and question classifications in their fields of study.

Winterowd, W. Ross. "Transferable and Local Writing Skills." *Journal of Advanced Composition* 1 (1980): 1–3.

The author discusses the difference between local skills (those related to a given genre or special form) and transferable skills (the basics of any writing, such as organizational ability and syntactic fluency). He describes Stephen D. Krashen's distinction between acquisition and learning, claims that most transferable skills are learned, and then explains obvious implications for teaching advanced composition.

Contributors

John L. Adams is an instructor of English at Loyola University/New Orleans. His publications include articles in *The Journal of Teaching Writing, The Writing Instructor,* and *Rhetoric Society Quarterly,* and an advanced composition textbook, *The Accomplished Writer* (Prentice, 1988).

Katherine H. Adams is director of the writing-across-the-curriculum program and associate professor of English at Loyola University/New Orleans. Her publications include an advanced composition textbook, *The Accomplished Writer* (Prentice, 1988), and articles in such journals as *College Composition and Communication, Rhetoric Society Quarterly,* and *Rhetoric Review.* She is currently writing *A History of Professional Writing Instruction: One Hundred Years of Confusion and Growth* for SMU Press. She was the founder and first director of the Smoky Mountain Writing Project.

Charles M. Anderson is assistant professor of English at the University of Arkansas at Little Rock where he teaches writing and rhetoric. He is co-director of the Little Rock Writing Project and teaches courses on literature and medicine at the University of Arkansas Campus for the Medical Sciences. He has presented numerous papers at national conventions, published essays and reviews in books and journals, and published a monograph with Southern Illinois University Press on the early essays of surgeon-writer Richard Selzer, entitled *Richard Selzer and the Rhetoric of Surgery* (1989).

Evelyn Ashton-Jones, an assistant professor at the University of Idaho, is associate editor of the *Journal of Advanced Composition* and treasurer of the Association of Teachers of Advanced Composition. Her publications have appeared in *Writing Center Journal, Writing Program Administration,* and *Teaching English in the Two-Year College.* She is co-editor of *Advanced Placement English: Theory, Politics, and Pedagogy,* a collection of essays published by Boynton/Cook (1989).

Lynn Z. Bloom, professor of English and Aetna Chair of Writing at the University of Connecticut, has taught advanced composition to graduates and undergraduates for 25 years. *Fact and Artifact: Writing Nonfiction* (Harcourt,

1985) and its complement, *The Lexington Reader* (Heath, 1986), epitomize Bloom's views on the theory and practice of advanced nonfiction writing. Many of her other nonfiction writings are on biography and autobiography, including *Doctor Spock: Biography of a Conservative Radical* (Bobbs, 1972), editions of two women's World War II diaries (Natalie Crouter's *Forbidden Diary* (Franklin, 1980) and Margaret Sam's *Forbidden Family* (U of Wisconsin P, 1989), and numerous articles.

Janet Carr is an instructor of English at Northeastern University in Boston. She is assistant coordinator of the Middler Year Writing Requirement, a program of advanced composition for third-year students. She has led workshops and given papers at numerous professional conferences. She is currently engaged in research on catalysts for change in teaching composition.

Michael Carter is an assistant professor of English at North Carolina State University. He has published articles on rhetorical history and composition theory in several journals, including *College English, Rhetoric Review*, and *Rhetoric Society Quarterly*.

Richard M. Coe has taught in Canada, and the United States. He has published numerous articles on rhetoric, literacy, composition, drama, popular culture, and literary critical method, including the prize-winning essay, "Rhetoric 2001." His *Toward a Grammar of Passages* (Southern Illinois UP, 1988) introduces an instrument for studying formal structures based on the New Rhetorical conception of form as both a constraining and a generative social factor in the writing process. A thoroughly revised edition of his innovative textbook was just published by Prentice-Hall under the new title *Process, Form, and Substance: A Rhetoric for Advanced Writers* (1990). Coe, who also chairs the Canadian Council of Teachers of English Commission on Public Doublespeak, is an associate professor at Simon Fraser University, where he won a teaching excellence award in 1984.

William A. Covino teaches in the language, literacy, and rhetoric graduate program at the University of Illinois at Chicago. Along with a number of essays on rhetoric and composition, he has written *The Art of Wondering: A Revisionist Return to the History of Rhetoric* (Boynton/Cook, 1988) and *Forms of Wondering: A Dialogue on Writing, for Writers* (Boynton/Cook, 1990).

Timothy R. Donovan is an associate professor of English at Northeastern University in Boston. He is coordinator of the Middler Year Writing Requirement and is also director of the Institute on Writing and Teaching at Martha's Vineyard. He has published numerous articles on composition pedagogy, teacher training, and writing program administration, and he is co-editor of *Perspectives on Research and Scholarship in Composition* (MLA, 1985) and *Eight Approaches to Teaching Composition* (NCTE, 1980).

Jeanne Fahnestock is associate professor in the Department of English Language and Literature at the University of Maryland where she also serves as director of the Junior Composition Program. She is primarily interested in argument theory, both in large-scale schemes of structure and invention and in the sentence-level interdependence of claims. She has coauthored two texts with Marie Secor, *A Rhetoric of Argument* (McGraw, 1990), and *Readings in Argument* (Random, 1985), published articles in *College Composition and Communication* on argument theory and coherence and had work on stasis theory appear in publications of the Speech Communication Association and The Rhetoric Society of America.

Olivia Frey and **Mary Ellen Ross** are both on the faculty of St. Olaf College in Northfield, Minnesota. Olivia is an associate professor of English and director of the writing program. Mary Ellen is an assistant professor of psychology and is a psychotherapist in private practice. Their current project is a study of the role of stories in healing.

Mary Fuller is an associate professor of English at Miami University in Oxford, Ohio. She has published *Literature: Options for Reading and Writing* (Harper, 1989) now in its second edition. She has also published research on response to student writing, gender and language, and teacher training. She is past director of the writing program at Miami University and co-director of the Ohio Writing Project. She teaches graduate courses in discourse theory and rhetorical theory, and undergraduate courses in gender and language, beginning writing, and advanced composition.

Toby Fulwiler is professor of English and director of the writing program at the University of Vermont where he teaches courses in composition and American literature. His recent books include *College Writing* (Scott, 1988) and *Teaching with Writing* (Boynton/Cook, 1987). In addition he has edited *The Journal Book* (Boynton/Cook, 1987), and co-edited *Reading, Writing, and the Study of Literature* (Random, 1989). He is currently writing an advanced composition textbook, *The Writer's Voice,* for Harcourt.

John T. Gage is the director of the composition program at the University of Oregon and author of *The Shape of Reason* (Macmillan, 1987) and *In the Arresting Eye: The Rhetoric of Imagism* (LSU Press, 1981), in addition to many articles about classical and modern rhetoric, composition, and poetry.

Tori Haring-Smith is an associate professor in the departments of English and theatre at Brown University where she directs the writing program and the writing-across-the-curriculum program. Her publications include books on A. A. Milne, the stage history of *The Taming of the Shrew*, and a guide to writing programs. She is currently working on two projects: a textbook, *Writing Together*, which approaches writing through collaborative learning, and a book on active and inductive learning strategies. In 1984 she founded the National Conference on Peer Tutoring in Writing, and she directs the consult-evaluator program for the National Council of Writing Program Administrators. Each year she speaks at numerous conferences and travels to about 25 colleges and universities to conduct faculty workshops on writing across the curriculum, critical thinking, and collaborative learning. In addition to this work, she is an active director in the Brown University theatre program and the mother of a four-year-old son.

Michael Keene, associate professor of English at the University of Tennessee, Knoxville, holds a PhD from the University of Texas. His publications include

Writing Scientific Papers and Reports (Wm. C. Brown, 1981), *Effective Professional Writing* (Heath, 1987), chapters in collections published by MLA, Greenwood Press, and ATTW, and articles in numerous journals.

Gary A. Olson teaches in the graduate program in rhetoric and composition at the University of South Florida where he also edits the *Journal of Advanced Composition*. Besides publishing articles in such journals as *College English, College Composition and Communication,* and *Liberal Education,* Olson has edited and co-authored several books and textbooks, including *Writing Centers: Theory and Administration* (NCTE, 1984). His most recent book, *Advanced Placement English: Theory, Politics, and Pedagogy* (co-edited with Elizabeth Metzger and Evelyn Ashton-Jones) has just been published by Boynton/Cook (1989).

Elizabeth Penfield has taught freshman composition and advanced writing for most of her 22 years in the classroom. After directing the freshman writing program at the University of New Orleans for seven years, she became English department chair and now serves as associate dean for the College of Liberal Arts. She also founded and directed the UNO/Greater New Orleans Writing Project, an affiliate of the National Writing Project. Her publications include textbooks such as *Short Takes* (Scott, Foresman, 1990) (1987) and *The Writer's Roles* (Scott, Foresman, 1985), and numerous articles.

Ray Wallace, an assistant professor of English at the University of Tennessee, Knoxville, holds a Doctor of Arts from Illinois State University in rhetoric/composition and TESOL. He has published his research in *TESOL Quarterly, The Writing Center Journal, The Computer-Assisted Composition Journal, Focuses, TESL Reporter,* and other writing and ESL-related journals. He has taught in Illinois, Hawaii, and Tennessee.

Sam Watson is professor of English at the University of North Carolina, Charlotte, where he also coordinates cross-campus faculty development programs in writing. His research interests range from epistemology (especially the thought of Michael Polanyi) to classroom practices and serious teacher-reflections on their practices. He is director of the Southeastern Region, National Writing Project (SWEP) and has edited *Writing in Trust: A Tapestry of Teachers' Voices,* a book of classroom reflections written by practicing teachers, K-university.

Richard E. Young received his PhD in English Language and Literature from the University of Michigan in 1964. From 1964 to 1969 he was a research associate at Michigan in the Center for Research on Language and Language Behavior, working on tagmemic rhetoric, especially on discourse structures larger than the sentence and rhetorical invention. From 1971 to 1976 he was chairman of the Department of Humanities. From 1978 to 1983 he was head of the Department of English at Carnegie Mellon University, during which time he oversaw the development of its graduate programs in rhetoric. At present he is professor of English literature and rhetoric at Carnegie Mellon and director of the language across the curriculum program.